# BRAND LEADERSHIP

# BRAND LEADERSHIP

David A. Aaker

Erich Joachimsthaler

POCKET
BOOKS

LONDON • SYDNEY • NEW YORK • TORONTO

First published in Great Britain in 2000 by Simon & Schuster UK Ltd
This edition first published in 2009 by Pocket Books
An imprint of Simon & Schuster UK Ltd
A CBS COMPANY

1 3 5 7 9 10 8 6 4 2

Simon & Schuster UK Ltd
1st Floor
222 Gray's Inn Road
London
WC1X 8HB

www.simonandschuster.co.uk

Simon & Schuster Australia
Sydney

A CIP catalogue copy for this book is available
from the British Library.

ISBN: 978-1-84739-835-2

Printed by CPI Cox &Wyman, Reading, Berkshire RG1 8EX

## PERMISSIONS

The authors gratefully acknowledge permission from the following sources to reprint material in
their control:
adidas DFB-adidas Cup streetball challenge photograph.
Andersen Consulting for use of the shark advertisement.
Britvic Soft Drinks for the Tango advertisement. Copyright © Britvic Soft Drinks 1999.
FlowTex Technologie GmbH & Co. KG for reproducing text and visuals from the FlowTex
collateral material.
General Electric for the use of the GE logo.
Häagen-Dazs for the Häagen-Dazs Café storefront photograph.
Kimberly-Clark for the K-C World Wide Web site page entitled "Girlthing" with accompanying
text. © 1996–1999 Kimberly-Clark.
Leo Burnett London for permission to reproduce photographs from the McDonald's in Sweden
advertisement.
L.L. Bean for the L.L. Bean 1999 catalogue cover.
Maggi GmbH for 100 Years Maggi Liquid Seasonings advertisment.
Marriott for the use of Courtyard by Marriott, Fairfield Inn by Marriott, Marriott Residence Inns,
and Marriott Hotels • Resorts • Suites logos.
MasterCard for the MasterCard and World Championship Soccer advertisement.
Maxfli Golf, a division of Dunlop-Slazenger, for two Maxfli golf ball packaging photographs.
McDonald's and McDonald's Sweden for the use of the McDonald's Swedish ad campaign.
Nike for the use of the "McEnroe's favorite 4-letter word" phrase, the "Just do it" advertisement,
and photographs of the Nike-painted building and the NikeTown storefront.
Polo Ralph Lauren Corporation for the use of the Polo Ralph Lauren logos.
Procter & Gamble for the 1930s Camay advertisement and the McElroy memo, and copyright
permission for the Pantene Pro-V advertisement.
The Advertising Archives for permission to use the Pantene Pro-V advertisement
Virgin Management Ltd. for the Richard Branson photograph.

# CONTENTS

# PREFACE

When brand equity became the hot topic of the late 1980s, it may have seemed like another management fad that would last only a few years. Instead, however, one industry after another has discovered that brand awareness, perceived quality, customer loyalty, and strong brand associations and personality are necessary to compete in the marketplace. Some organizations, such as hospitals, oil field suppliers, and software firms, are discovering brands for the first time. Others, such as banks, packaged-goods marketers, and automobile manufacturers, are realizing that they need to revitalize their brands and their brand management system to keep pace with the ever-changing competitive scene.

Powerful forces are fueling this continuing interest in brands. Overcapacity, vicious price competition, the proliferation of similar products, and powerful retailers are only some of the factors that make brand building imperative; in fact, the alternative is not only unpleasant but unhealthy for most managers' careers. This book shows how brand leadership can be achieved in the face of these forces.

This is the third book in a trilogy about creating and managing brands. The first book, *Managing Brand Equity*, reviewed the evidence that brands do create value, discussed exactly how that value is created, and defined and structured the concept of brand equity. It also covered the role of names and symbols and explained the good, the bad, and the ugly aspects of brand extensions.

The second book, *Building Strong Brands*, helped managers develop brand strategy in three ways. First, it introduced the construct of brand identity or vision to guide the brand-building process. Second, it analyzed how to make multiple brands work together as part of a system that creates synergy, clarity, and leverage across brands. Third, it discussed how brand equity should be measured, especially across products and countries.

This third book develops four themes that raise brand management to the level of leadership. First, it extends the concept of brand identity to include a brand essence statement, the use of multiple identities to appeal to different markets, and the elaboration of effective brand identities. Elaborating a brand identity can help communicate the identity clearly to those involved in its implementation, which often includes a company's partners as well as its employees.

Second, it addresses the problem of brand architecture—how brands should relate to each other, how far they should be stretched, and what roles they should play within the total brand system. The brand architecture concept is defined, as are its principal accompanying components and tools. This book pays particular attention to the brand relationship spectrum, detailing how subbrands and endorsed brands can become powerful tools that increase the leverage of strong brands.

Third, it explores how to move beyond advertising to build brands effectively and efficiently. Brilliant execution that breaks out of the clutter is one key. The ability to access and manage alternative media is another. A host of best-practice examples illustrate these points, including lessons from Adidas and Nike. Two vehicles that have been underanalyzed, sponsorships and the Internet, are considered in detail. The consumer sweet spot, the driving idea, the consumer relationship model, and the business relationship model are all introduced as tools to help brand managers create home-run brand-building programs.

Fourth, it considers the organizational challenge of managing brands in a global context. Multiple businesses and products carrying the brand name and the need to compete in diverse markets (often involving a host of countries) make brand management more complex, and more critical as well. The challenge lies in creating an organization and process to build strong brands while also realizing the economies and leverage that are available.

This book is based in part on a large field study of brand strategies.

We conducted more than three hundred case studies in Europe, the United States, and elsewhere, with an emphasis on contexts where brands must deal with cross-country realities. The focus of each case study was to identify and evaluate the brand strategy and its implementation. Many of these studies are rich with insight and have warranted a detailed description, while the rest are drawn on to illustrate specific concepts and methods. The book has also benefited from numerous consulting engagements in which we have had a chance to test models and ideas.

There are many who contributed to this book. At the risk of overlooking some, we start by noting respected colleagues who have shared insights about brands through the years, not only adding to our own store of knowledge but also making this adventure in branding more interesting: Jennifer Aaker of Stanford University, Roberto Alvarez of ESADE and the Haas School of Business, Arnene Linquito of AT&T, Rob Holloway and Larry Ruff of Levi Strauss, Nancy Carlson of Mobil, Andy Smith of bigwords.com, Anthony Simon and Johnny Lucas of Best Foods, Kambiz Safinya and Paul Campbell of Schlumberger, Sandeep Sander of Sander & Company, Gert Burmann of Volkswagen, Michael Hogan of Frito-Lay, Jerry Lee and Katy Choi of Brand & Company, Susan White and Charles Castano of Compaq, Peter Sealey (now associated with CKS/USWeb and the Haas School of Business), Duane Knapp of Brand Strategies, Peter Georgescu and Stuart Agres of Young and Rubicam, Alexander Biel of Alexander Biel Associates, and Russ Winer, Rashi Glazer, Paul Farris, Mark Parry, Robert Spekman, Joe Pons, Paddy Miller, Stein Jacobsen, Michael Rukstad, Guillermo d'Andrea, and other colleagues at the Haas School, the Darden School, Harvard, IAE, and IESE. We would also like to thank Scott Galloway, Connie Hallquist, Sterling Lanier, and others at Prophet Brand Strategy, as well as James McNamara, Hubert Weber, and Steve Salee of The Brand Leadership Company, all of whom contributed ideas and support to the project. Dana Pillsbury of The Brand Leadership Company was of special help throughout, and Monica Marchlewski was exceptional at getting the exhibits sorted out.

Special thanks go to Scott Talgo and Lisa Craig of the St. James Group and to Kevin O'Donnell and Jason Stavers of Prophet Brand Strategy, who made significant contributions to the Web and the brand architecture chapters and who are stimulating and insightful students of brands. We also thank John Quelch, Dean of the London School of Business, who generously allowed us to use material from his excellent case on MasterCard's World Cup sponsorship. Special thanks are also due Kevin Keller of Dartmouth and Bob Jacobson of the University of Washington, who helped the first-named author to tackle some fascinating brand questions in a scientific manner and made the process a joy.

We had help on the manuscript from some outstanding students, Terra Terwilliger, James Cook, Joao Adao, Penny Crossland, Marc Sachon (now at Stanford School of Engineering), Madhur Metha (now at Chase), Brian Hare (now at Translink), Eva Krauss (now at Ogilvy & Mather), Edward Hickman (now at Technical Solutions Group), Nancy Spector, and especially Julie Templeton (now at Clorox) and Michael Dennis (now with MBA Enterprise Corps), who won the award for improving the manuscript the most. A host of Haas students helped clean and refine the manuscript in the final stages of production, and we are in their debt. We also benefited from the work of a superb copy editor, Chris Kelly, and from the editing and general assistance of Carol Chapman, who was once again an indispensable help and a joy to work with. At The Free Press, Celia Knight kept things moving along, Anne-Marie Sheedy cheerfully helped in many ways, and we have been blessed with a world-class editor and friend, Bob Wallace, who offered encouragement, guidance, and editorial insight. This is the third branding book that he has brought to life. Finally, we want to thank our families, who provided support for yet another writing project.

# PART I

---

# INTRODUCTION

# 1

# Brand Leadership— The New Imperative

It's a new brand world.

—Tom Peters

A brand strategy must follow the business strategy.

—Dennis Carter, Intel

## BRAND MANAGEMENT—THE CLASSIC MODEL

In May 1931, Neil McElroy, who later rose to be a successful CEO of Procter & Gamble (P&G) and still later became the U.S. secretary of defense, was a junior marketing manager responsible for the advertising for Camay soap. Ivory ("99.44% pure" since 1879) was then the king at P&G, while the company's other brands were treated in an ad hoc manner. McElroy observed that the Camay marketing effort was diffuse and uncoordinated (see the 1930 Camay ad in Figure 1–1), with no budget commitment or management focus. As a result, Camay drifted and languished. Frustrated, McElroy wrote a now-classic memo proposing a brand-focused management system.

The McElroy memo (excerpted in Figure 1–2) detailed the solution—a brand management team that would be responsible for creating a brand's marketing program and coordinating it with sales and

FIGURE 1–1

*Camay ad, June 1930*

manufacturing. This memo, which built on the ideas and activities of several people inside and outside P&G, has had a profound effect on how firms around the world manage their brands.

The system McElroy proposed was geared to solve "sales problems" by analyzing sales and profits for each market area in order to

FIGURE 1–2

---

# EXCERPT FROM THE 1931 NEIL McELROY P&G "BRAND MANAGEMENT" MEMO

This May 1931 memo, written in part to defend the hiring of two new people, describes a brand management team consisting of a "brand man," an "assistant brand man," and several "field check-up" employees. The following excerpt describes the duties and responsibilities of the "brand man" (with occasional clarifications added in brackets).

**BRAND MAN**

(1) Study carefully shipments of his brands by units.

(2) Where brand development is heavy and where it is progressing, examine carefully the combination of effort that seems to be clicking and try to apply this same treatment to other territories that are comparable.

(3) Where brand development is light

(a) Study the past advertising and promotional history of the brand; study the territory personally at first hand—both dealers and consumers—in order to find out the trouble.

(b) After uncovering our weakness, develop a plan that can be applied to this local sore spot. It is necessary, of course, not simply to work out the plan but also to be sure that the amount of money proposed can be expected to produce results at a reasonable cost per case.

(c) Outline this plan in detail to the Division Manager under whose jurisdiction the weak territory is, obtain his authority and support for the corrective action.

(d) Prepare sales helps and all other necessary material for carrying out the plan. Pass it on to the districts. Work with the salesmen while they are getting started. Follow through to the very finish to be sure that there is no let-down in sales operation of the plan.

(e) Keep whatever records are necessary, and make whatever field studies are necessary to determine whether the plan has produced the expected results.

(4) Take full responsibility, not simply for criticizing individual pieces

FIGURE 1–2 (*continued*)

of printed word copy, but also for the general printed word plans for his brands.

(5) Take full responsibility for all other advertising expenditures on his brands [such as in-store displays and promotions].

(6) Experiment with and recommend wrapper [packaging] revisions.

(7) See each District Manager a number of times a year to discuss with him any possible faults in our promotion plans for that territory.

identify problem markets. The brand manager conducted research to understand the causes of the problem, developed response programs to turn it around, and then used a planning system to help ensure that the programs were implemented on time. The responses used not only advertising but also other marketing tools, such as pricing, promotions, in-store displays, salesforce incentives, and packaging changes or product refinements.

In part, the classic brand management system was successful at P&G and elsewhere because it was typically staffed by exceptional planners, doers, and motivators. The process of managing a complex system—often involving R&D, manufacturing, and logistics in addition to advertising, promotion, and distribution-channel issues—required management skills and a get-it-done ethic. Successful brand managers also needed to have exceptional coordination and motivational skills because the brand manager typically had no direct line authority over the people (both inside and outside the company) involved in implementing branding programs.

Although it was not specifically discussed in his memo, the premise that each brand would vigorously compete with the firm's other brands (both for market share and within the company for resources) was an important aspect of McElroy's conceptualization of brand management. Contemporary accounts of McElroy's thoughts suggest the source for this idea was General Motors, which had distinct brands like Chevrolet, Buick, and Oldsmobile competing against one another. The brand manager's goal was to see the brand win, even if winning came at the expense of other brands within the firm.

The classic brand management system usually limited its scope to a relevant market in a single country. When a brand was multinational, the brand management system usually was replicated in each country, with local managers in charge.

Finally, in the original P&G model, the brand manager tended to be tactical and reactive, observing competitor and channel activity as well as sales and margin trends. When problems were detected, the goal of the response programs was to "move the needle" as soon as possible, with the process largely driven by sales and margins. Strategy was often delegated to an agency or simply ignored.

## BRAND LEADERSHIP— THE NEW IMPERATIVE

The classic brand management system has worked well for many decades for P&G and a host of imitators. It manages the brand and makes things happen by harnessing the work of many. However, it can fall short in dealing with emerging market complexities, competitive pressures, channel dynamics, global forces, and business environments with multiple brands, aggressive brand extensions, and complex subbrand structures.

As a result, a new model is gradually replacing the classic brand management system at P&G and many other firms. The emerging paradigm, which we term the *brand leadership model*, is very different. As Figure 1–3 summarizes, it emphasizes strategy as well as tactics, its scope is broader, and it is driven by brand identity as well as sales.

### FROM TACTICAL TO STRATEGIC MANAGEMENT

The manager in the brand leadership model is strategic and visionary rather than tactical and reactive. He or she takes control of the brand strategically, setting forth what it should stand for in the eyes of the customer and relevant others and communicating that identity consistently, efficiently, and effectively.

To fill this role, the brand manager must be involved in creating the business strategy as well as implementing it. The brand strategy should be influenced by the business strategy and should reflect the same strategic vision and corporate culture. In addition, the brand identity should not promise what the strategy cannot or will not

FIGURE 1–3

*Brand Leadership—The Evolving Paradigm*

| | THE CLASSIC BRAND MANAGEMENT MODEL | THE BRAND LEADERSHIP MODEL |
|---|---|---|
| **From Tactical to Strategic Management** | | |
| Perspective | Tactical and reactive | Strategic and visionary |
| Brand manager status | Less experienced, shorter time horizon | Higher in the organization, longer time horizon |
| Conceptual model | Brand image | Brand equity |
| Focus | Short-term financials | Brand equity measures |
| **From a Limited to Broad Focus** | | |
| Product-market scope | Single products and markets | Multiple products and markets |
| Brand structures | Simple | Complex brand architectures |
| Number of brands | Focus on single brands | Category focus—multiple brands |
| Country scope | Single country | Global perspective |
| Brand manager's communication role | Coordinator of limited options | Team leader of multiple communication options |
| Communication focus | External/customer | Internal as well as external |
| **From Sales to Brand Identity as Driver of Strategy** | | |
| Driver of strategy | Sales and share | Brand identity |

deliver. There is nothing more wasteful and damaging than developing a brand identity or vision based on a strategic imperative that will not get funded. An empty brand promise is worse than no promise at all.

### Higher in the organization

In the classic brand management system, the brand manager was too often a relatively inexperienced person who rarely stayed in the job more than two to three years. The strategic perspective calls for the brand manager to be higher in the organization, with a longer-term job horizon; in the brand leadership model, he or she is often the top marketing professional in the organization. For organizations where there is marketing talent at the top, the brand manager can be and often is the CEO.

*Focus on brand equity as the conceptual model*

The emerging model can be captured in part by juxtaposing brand image and brand equity. Brand image is tactical—an element that drives short-term results and can be comfortably left to advertising and promotion specialists. Brand equity, in contrast, is strategic—an asset that can be the basis of competitive advantage and long-term profitability and thus needs to be monitored closely by the top management of an organization. The goal of brand leadership is to build brand equities rather than simply manage brand images.

*Brand equity measures*

The brand leadership model encourages the development of brand equity measures to supplement short-term sales and profit figures. These measures, commonly tracked over time, should reflect major brand equity dimensions such as awareness, loyalty, perceived quality, and associations. Identifying brand identity elements that differentiate and drive customer-brand relationships is a first step toward creating a set of brand equity measures.

### FROM A LIMITED TO A BROAD FOCUS

In the classic P&G model, the scope of the brand manager was limited to not only a single brand but also one product and one market. In addition, the communication effort tended to be more focused (with fewer options available), and internal brand communication was usually ignored. In the brand leadership model, the challenges and contexts are very different, and the task has been expanded.

*Multiple products and markets*

In the brand leadership model, because a brand can cover multiple products and markets, determining the brand's product and market scope becomes a key management issue.

*Product scope* involves the management of brand extensions and licensing programs. To which products should the brand be attached? Which products exceed the brand's current and target domains? Some brands, such as Sony, gain visibility and energy from being extended widely; customers know there will always be something new and exciting under the Sony brand. Other brands are very protective of a strong set of associations. Kingsford Charcoal, for instance, has stuck to charcoal and products directly related to charcoal cooking.

*Market scope* refers to the stretch of the brand across markets. This stretch can be horizontal (as with 3M in the consumer and industrial markets) or vertical (3M participating in both value and premium markets). Some brands, such as IBM, Coke, and Pringles, use the same identity across a broad set of markets. Other situations, though, require multiple brand identities or multiple brands. For example, the GE brand needs different associations in the context of jet engines than it does in the context of appliances.

The challenge in managing a brand's product and market scope is to allow enough flexibility to succeed in diverse product markets while still capturing cross-market and cross-product synergies. A rigid, lockstep brand strategy across product markets risks handicapping a brand facing vigorous, less-fettered competitors. On the other hand, brand anarchy will create inefficient and ineffective marketing efforts. A variety of approaches, detailed in Chapters 2 and 4, can address these challenges.

### Complex brand architectures

Whereas the classic brand manager rarely dealt with extensions and subbrands, a brand leadership manager requires the flexibility of complex brand architectures. The need to stretch brands and fully leverage their strength has led to the introduction of endorsed brands (such as Post-its by 3M, Hamburger Helper by Betty Crocker, and Courtyard by Marriott) and subbrands (such as Campbell's Chunky, Wells Fargo Express, and Hewlett-Packard's LaserJet) to represent different product markets, and sometimes an organizational brand as well. Chapters 4 and 5 examine brand architecture structures, concepts, and tools.

### Category focus

The classic P&G brand management system encouraged the existence of competing brands within categories—such as Pantene,

Head & Shoulders, Pert, and Vidal Sassoon in hair care—because different market segments were covered and competition within the organization was thought to be healthy. Two forces, however, have convinced many firms to consider managing product categories (that is, groupings of brands) instead of a portfolio of individual brands.

First, because retailers of consumer products have harnessed information technology and databases to manage categories as their unit of analysis, they expect their suppliers to also bring a category perspective to the table. In fact, some multicontinent retailers are demanding one single, worldwide contact person for a category, believing that a country representative cannot see enough of the big picture to help the retailer capture the synergies across countries.

Second, in the face of an increasingly cluttered market, sister brands within a category find it difficult to remain distinct, with market confusion, cannibalization, and inefficient communication as the all-too-common results. Witness the confused positioning overlap that now exists in the General Motors family of brands. When categories of brands are managed, clarity and efficiency are easier to attain. In addition, important resource-allocation decisions involving communication budgets and product innovations can be made more dispassionately and strategically, because the profit-generating brand no longer automatically controls the resources.

Under the new model, the brand manager's focus expands from a single brand to a product category. The goal is to make the brands within a category or business unit work together to provide the most collective impact and the strongest synergies. Thus, printer brands at HP, cereal brands at General Mills, or hair care brands at P&G need to be managed as a team to maximize operational efficiency and marketing effectiveness.

Category or business unit brand management can improve profitability and strategic health by addressing some cross-brand issues. What brand identities and positions will result in the most coherent and least redundant brand system? Is there a broader vision driven by consumer and channel needs that can provide a breakthrough opportunity? Are there sourcing and logistical opportunities within the set of brands involved in the category? How can R&D successes be best used across the brands in the category?

*Global perspective*

Multinational brand management in the classic model meant an autonomous brand manager in each country. As the task of competing successfully in the global marketplace has changed, this perspective has increasingly shown itself to be inadequate. As a result, more firms are experimenting with organizational structures that support cohesive global business strategies which involve sourcing, manufacturing, and R&D as well as branding.

The brand leadership paradigm has a global perspective. Thus a key goal is to manage the brand across markets and countries in order to gain synergies, efficiencies, and strategic coherence. This perspective adds another level of complexity—Which elements of the brand strategy are to be common globally and which are to be adapted to local markets? Implementing the strategy involves coordination across more people and organizations. Moreover, developing the capability to gain insights and build best practices throughout the world can be difficult. The wide range of organizational structures and systems used to manage brands over countries will be discussed in Chapter 10.

*Communication team leader*

The classic brand manager often just acted as the coordinator and scheduler of tactical communication programs. Further, the programs were simpler to manage because mass media could be employed. Peter Sealey, an adjunct professor at UC Berkeley, has noted that in 1965 a P&G product manager could reach 80 percent of eighteen- to forty-nine-year-old women with three 60-second commercials. Today, that manager would require ninety-seven prime-time commercials to achieve the same result. Media and market fragmentation has made the communication task very different.

In the brand leadership model, the brand manager needs to be a strategist and communications team leader directing the use of a wide assortment of vehicles, including sponsorships, the Web, direct marketing, publicity, and promotions. This array of options raises two challenges: how to break out of the box to access effective media options, and how to coordinate messages across media that are managed by different organizations and individuals (each with separate perspectives and goals). Addressing both challenges involves generating effective brand identities and creating organizations that are suited to brand management in a complex environment.

Furthermore, rather than delegating strategy, the brand manager must be the owner of the strategy—guiding the total communication effort in order to achieve the strategic objectives of the brand. Like an orchestra conductor, the brand manager needs to stimulate brilliance while keeping the communication components disciplined and playing from the same sheet of music.

In Part IV of this book, a variety of case studies will show how communication strategies using a broad scope of media can be coordinated to generate synergy and efficiency as well as impact. In particular, Chapters 7 and 8 will provide a close look at two increasingly important vehicles—sponsorship and the Web.

### Internal as well as external communication

Communication in the new paradigm is likely to have an internal focus as well as the usual external focus on influencing the customer. Unless the brand strategy can communicate with and inspire the brand partners both inside and outside the organization, it will not be effective. Brand strategy should be owned by all the brand partners. Chapter 3 will present a variety of ways that a brand can be leveraged to crystallize and communicate organizational values and cultures.

### FROM SALES TO BRAND IDENTITY AS THE DRIVER OF STRATEGY

In the brand leadership model, strategy is guided not only by short-term performance measures such as sales and profits but also by the brand identity, which clearly specifies what the brand aspires to stand for. With the identity in place, the execution can be managed so that it is on target and effective.

The development of a brand identity relies on a thorough understanding of the firm's customers, competitors, and business strategy. Customers ultimately drive brand value, and a brand strategy thus needs to be based on a powerful, disciplined segmentation strategy, as well as an in-depth knowledge of customer motivations. Competitor analysis is another key because the brand identity needs to have points of differentiation that are sustainable over time. Finally, the brand identity, as already noted, needs to reflect the business strategy and the firm's willingness to invest in the programs needed for the brand to live up to its promise to customers. Brand identity development and elaboration are examined in Chapters 2 and 3.

## BRAND BUILDING PAYS OFF

Because the classic brand management model focused on short-term sales, investments in brands were easy to justify. They either delivered sales and profits or they did not. In contrast, the brand leadership paradigm focuses on building assets that will result in long-term profitability, which is often difficult or impossible to demonstrate. Brand building may require consistent reinforcement over years, and only a small portion of the payoff may occur immediately—in fact, the building process may depress profits in the short run. Further, brand building is often done in the context of competitive and market clutter that creates measurement problems.

The brand leadership model is based on the premise that brand building not only creates assets but is necessary for the success (and often the survival) of the enterprise. The firm's highest executives must believe that building brands will result in a competitive advantage that will pay off financially.

The challenge of justifying investments to build brand assets is similar to justifying investments in any other intangible asset. Although the three most important assets in nearly every organization are people, information technology, and brands, none of these appear on the balance sheet. Quantitative measures of their effect on the organization are virtually impossible to obtain; as a result, only very crude estimates of value are available. The rationale for investment in any intangible, therefore, must rest in part on a conceptual model of the business that is often not easy to generate or defend. Without such a model, though, movement toward brand leadership is inhibited.

Later in this chapter, we will review studies showing that brand building has resulted in significant asset growth and that investments in brands affect stock return. First, however, we will contrast brand building with its strategic alternative, price competition—because that is where the logic starts.

### AN ALTERNATIVE TO PRICE COMPETITION

Few managers would describe their business context without mentioning excess capacity and vicious price competition. Except, perhaps, for the operators of the Panama Canal, not many companies are blessed with the absence of real competitors. The following scenario

## PICKING STOCKS

Suppose that you will be given 0.1 percent of the stock of one of the following companies. Which firm's stock would you prefer, given the following information about their sales, profits, and assets (as of January 1998)?

|  | SALES | ASSETS | PROFITS |
|---|---|---|---|
| General Motors | $166B | $229B | $7B |
| Coca-Cola | 19B | 17B | 4B |

On the basis of this data, most people would pick General Motors and turn their back on Coca-Cola. Yet in January 1998, Coke had a market value more than four times that of GM, in part because the value of the Coke brand equity was over twice the value of the entire GM firm.

is all too familiar: Pressure on prices is caused by new entrants, over-capacity, sliding sales, or retail power. Price declines, rebates, and/or promotions ensue. Competitors, especially the third- or fourth-ranked brands, respond defensively. Consumers begin to focus more on price than on quality and differentiated features. Brands start resembling commodities, and firms begin to treat them as such. Profits erode.

It does not take a strategic visionary to see that any slide toward commodity status should be resisted. The only alternative is to build brands.

The price premium paid for Morton salt (few products are more of a commodity than salt), Charles Schwab (discount brokerage services), or Saturn (subcompacts from General Motors) show that a slide into commodity status is not inevitable. In each instance, a strong brand has been able to resist pressures to compete on price alone. Another case in point is Victoria's Secret, which saw sales increase and profits skyrocket when they stopped their policy of running forty to fifty price promotions each week.

The importance of price as a driving attribute can be overestimated. Surveys show that few customers base their purchase decisions solely on price. Even customers of Boeing aircraft, with reams of quantitatively supported proposals in front of them, will, in the final analysis, turn to a subjective appraisal based on their affinity with and trust in the Boeing brand. One of Charles Schultz's *Peanuts* cartoons makes this point in ironic fashion. Lucy, behind what looks like a lemonade stand, has reduced the price of her psychiatric services from $5 to $1 to 25 cents. She obviously thinks that such services are bought only on price—a funny premise in a cartoon, but not how things work in real life. Tom Peters said it well: "In an increasingly crowded marketplace, fools will compete on price. Winners will find a way to create lasting value in the customer's mind."

## THE VALUE OF THE BRAND

The value of a brand cannot be measured precisely, but it can be estimated roughly (for example, within plus or minus 30 percent). Because of the wide margin of error, such estimates cannot be used to evaluate marketing programs, but they can show that brand assets have been created. These estimates can also provide a frame of reference when developing brand-building programs and budgets. For example, if a brand is worth $500 million, a budget of $5 million for brand building might be challenged as being too low. Similarly, if $400 million of the brand's value was in Europe and $100 million was in the United States, a decision to split the brand-building budget evenly might be questioned.

Estimating the value of a brand involves straightforward logic. First, the earnings stream of each major product market carrying the brand is identified. (For Hewlett-Packard, one product market might be the business computer market in the United States.) The earnings are then divided into those attributable (1) to the brand, (2) to fixed assets like plants and equipment, and (3) to other intangibles like people, systems, processes, or patents. The earnings attributable to the brand are capitalized, providing a value for the brand in that product market. Aggregating the various product market values provides an overall value for the brand.

The earnings attributable to fixed assets are relatively easy to estimate; they are simply a fair return (for example, 8 percent) on the value of the fixed assets. The balance of the earnings has to be divided into brand-driven earnings and earnings attributable to other intangibles. This division is made subjectively based on the judgments of knowledgeable people in the organization. One key deter-

## WHAT IS BRAND EQUITY?

The goal of the brand leadership paradigm is to create strong brands—but what is a strong brand, anyway? In *Managing Brand Equity*, brand equity was defined as the brand assets (or liabilities) linked to a brand's name and symbol that add to (or subtract from) a product or service. These assets can be grouped into four dimensions: brand awareness, perceived quality, brand associations, and brand loyalty.

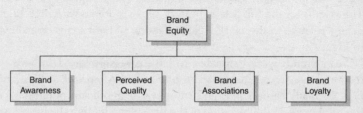

These four dimensions guide brand development, management, and measurement.

- *Brand awareness* is an often undervalued asset; however, awareness has been shown to affect perceptions and even taste. People like the familiar and are prepared to ascribe all sorts of good attitudes to items that are familiar to them. The Intel Inside campaign has dramatically transferred awareness into perceptions of technological superiority and market acceptance.
- *Perceived quality* is a special type of association, partly because it influences brand associations in many contexts and partly because it has been empirically shown to affect profitability (as measured by both ROI and stock return).
- *Brand associations* can be anything that connects the customer to the brand. It can include user imagery, product attributes, use situations, organizational associations, brand personality, and symbols. Much of brand management involves determining what associations to develop and then creating programs that will link the associations to the brand.
- *Brand loyalty* is at the heart of any brand's value. The concept is to strengthen the size and intensity of each loyalty segment. A brand with a small but intensely loyal customer base can have significant equity.

minant in making these judgments is the strength of the other intangibles. (For airlines, for example, the value of controlling airport gates is a significant driver of earnings.) Another key determinant is the strength of the brand in terms of its relative awareness, perceived quality, customer loyalty, and associations.

Interbrand is a firm that generates brand values using the above logic but with its own refinements. In its June 1999 study of brands with a significant market presence outside their home countries, the values of the largest global brands involved eye-opening numbers. The results for the top fifteen brands, plus six others with high brand values relative to the market capitalization of their firms, are shown in Figure 1–4.

Sixty brands were estimated to have a value over $1 billion; the leaders were Coca-Cola at $83.8 billion and Microsoft at $56.7 billion. In many cases, the brand value was a significant percentage of the total market capitalization of the firm (even though the brand was not on all its products). Of the top fifteen brands, only General Electric had a brand value under 19 percent of the firm's market value. In contrast, nine of the top sixty brands had values that exceeded 50 percent of the whole firm's value, and BMW, Nike, Apple, and Ikea had brand–firm value ratios over 75 percent.

Among the top sixty global brands, there were some interesting patterns. All of the top ten (and nearly two-thirds of the total) were U.S. brands, a finding that reflects the size of the U.S. home market and the early global initiatives of American firms. Nearly one-fourth of the group (including four of the top ten) were in the computer or telecommunications industry; this supports the premise that brands are critical in the high-tech world despite arguments that "rational" customers buy largely on the specifications of product attributes rather than brands.

The Interbrand study rather dramatically illustrates that creating strong brands does pay off and that brands have created meaningful value. It is an important statement about the wisdom and feasibility of creating brand assets.

## THE IMPACT OF BRAND BUILDING ON STOCK RETURN

Although the Interbrand study shows that brands have created value, it does not demonstrate that specific brand-building efforts result in

FIGURE 1–4
*Value of Global Brands as Measured by Interbrand*

| RANK ORDER | BRAND | BRAND VALUE $ BILLIONS | MARKET CAPITALIZATION $ BILLIONS | BRAND VALUE AS PERCENT OF MARKET CAPITALIZATION |
|---|---|---|---|---|
| 1 | Coca-Cola | $83.8 | $142.2 | 59% |
| 2 | Microsoft | 56.7 | 271.9 | 21 |
| 3 | IBM | 43.8 | 158.4 | 28 |
| 4 | GE | 33.5 | 328.0 | 10 |
| 5 | Ford | 32.2 | 57.4 | 58 |
| 6 | Disney | 32.3 | 52.6 | 58 |
| 7 | Intel | 30.0 | 144.1 | 21 |
| 8 | McDonald's | 26.2 | 40.9 | 64 |
| 9 | AT&T | 24.2 | 102.5 | 24 |
| 10 | Marlboro | 21.0 | 112.4 | 19 |
| 11 | Nokia | 20.7 | 46.9 | 44 |
| 12 | Mercedes | 17.8 | 48.3 | 37 |
| 13 | Nescafé | 17.6 | 77.5 | 23 |
| 14 | Hewlett-Packard | 17.1 | 54.9 | 31 |
| 15 | Gillette | 15.9 | 42.9 | 37 |
| 16 | Kodak | 14.8 | 24.8 | 60 |
| 22 | BMW | 11.3 | 16.7 | 77 |
| 28 | Nike | 8.2 | 10.6 | 77 |
| 36 | Apple | 4.3 | 5.6 | 77 |
| 43 | Ikea | 3.5 | 4.7 | 75 |
| 54 | Ralph Lauren | 1.6 | 2.5 | 66 |

Source: Raymond Perrier, "Interbrand's World's Most Valuable Brands," report of a June 1999 study sponsored by Interbrand and Citigroup, 1999.

enhanced profits or stock returns. For example, Coca-Cola's brand value may be based on its century-old heritage and customer loyalty rather than any recent brand-building effort. What evidence is there that brand building directly affects profits or stock return?

Everyone can recite anecdotes of how brands like Coke, Nike,

Gap, Sony, and Dell have created and leveraged brand strength. The book *Managing Brand Equity* presented four case studies that illustrate both destroying and creating brand value. The failure to support customers at WordStar (at one time the leader in word-processing software) and the loss of perceived quality at Schlitz (once a close second among U.S. beer brands) were both priced out as $1 billion brand disasters; the Datsun to Nissan name change was only somewhat less of a brand equity blunder. The creation and management of the Weight Watchers brand during the 1980s, however, was a $1 billion brand success story.

Two studies, both by Robert Jacobson (from the University of Washington) and David Aaker have gone beyond anecdotes to find causal links between brand equity and stock return. The first study is based on the EquiTrend database from Total Research, and the second is based on the Techtel database of high-technology brands.[1]

### The EquiTrend Study

Since 1989, EquiTrend has provided an annual brand power rating for 133 U.S. brands in 39 categories, based on a telephone survey of 2,000 respondents. Since 1992, the survey has increased its frequency and the number of brands covered. The key brand equity measure is perceived quality, which has been found by Total Research to be highly associated with brand-liking, trust, pride, and willingness to recommend. It is essentially the average quality rating among those who had an opinion about the brand.

The extent to which the EquiTrend brand equity measure influenced stock return was explored using data from thirty-three brands representing publicly traded firms for which the corporate brand drove a substantial amount of sales and profits. The brands were American Airlines (AMR), American Express, AT&T, Avon, Bic, Chrysler, Citicorp, Coke, Compaq, Exxon, Kodak, Ford, GTE, Goodyear, Hershey, Hilton, IBM, Kellogg, MCI, Marriott, Mattel, McDonald's, Merrill Lynch, Pepsi, Polaroid, Reebok, Rubbermaid, Sears, Texaco, United Airlines, VF, Volvo, and Wendy's. In addition to brand equity, two additional causal variables were included in the model: advertising expenditures and return on investment (ROI).

Consistent with a wide body of empirical research in finance, a strong relationship between ROI and stock return was found.

Remarkably, the relationship between brand equity and stock return was nearly as strong. Figure 1-5 shows graphically how similar the impact of brand equity and ROI is. Firms experiencing the largest gains in brand equity saw their stock return average 30 percent; conversely, those firms with the largest losses in brand equity saw stock return average a negative 10 percent. And the brand equity impact was distinct from that of ROI—the correlation between the two was small. In contrast, there was no impact of advertising on stock return except that which was captured by brand equity.

The relationship of brand equity to stock return may be in part caused by the fact that brand equity supports a price premium which contributes to profitability. An analysis of the larger EquiTrend database has shown that brand equity is associated with a premium price. Thus, premium-priced brands like Kodak, Mercedes, Levi Strauss, and Hallmark have substantial perceived quality advantages over competitors such as Fuji Film, Buick Automobiles, Lee's Jeans, and American Greeting Cards. This relationship is undoubtedly based upon a two-way causal flow—a strong brand commands a price premium, and a price premium is an important quality cue. When a high level of perceived quality has been (or can be) created, raising the price not only provides margin dollars but also aids perceptions.

FIGURE 1-5
*The EquiTrend Study*

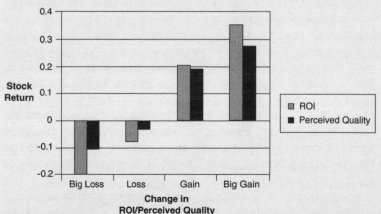

### The Techtel Study of High-Technology Brands

How relevant is brand equity in high-technology markets? Industry executives and others often argue that because high-tech products have different characteristics than frequently purchased consumer goods and services, brand building is less critical—instead, the keys to success are product innovation, manufacturing capability, and distribution. The implication is that high-tech companies should avoid transferring investment resources from these key activities to so-called softer activities like brand building. Since investments to create awareness, organizational associations, brand personality, or brand symbols are regarded as frivolous, brand communication is relegated to product details.

These arguments revolve around the belief that the buyers and the buying process are more rational in the high-tech realm than in other markets. The organizational setting is thought to stimulate more rational thought and less emotion, and the personal/professional risk involved in acquiring such complex products is thought to motivate buyers to process—if not seek out—relevant information. (This is in sharp contrast to many consumer goods categories, where the products are trivial enough that consumers have little or no motivation to process information.) Because the products also tend to have short life cycles—sometimes measured in months—and each new version has a significant amount of news associated with it, communicating this new information as it appears is seen as the primary imperative.

Nevertheless, brand-building initiatives have been at least partially credited with the market success of a growing list of high-technology brands. The Intel Inside campaign contributed a visible price premium, positive associations, and sales growth to the Intel brands. Dozens of high-technology firms, including large firms such as Oracle and Cisco, have sought to duplicate this success. Branding specialist Lou Gerstner shifted huge amounts of resources behind the IBM brand, and the company's subsequent turnaround has been attributed in part to this decision. Gateway and Dell created brands that made a difference, and even Microsoft has launched a major brand program for the first time. These anecdotes, though, still fall short of real evidence that brand building pays off in the high-technology area.

The Techtel study was conducted to empirically explore the relationship between high-technology brand building and stock return.

Since 1988, Techtel has undertaken quarterly surveys of the personal and network computing markets. Respondents are asked whether they have a positive, negative, or no opinion of a company. Using this data, brand equity can be measured by the difference between the percentage of respondents with a positive opinion and those with a negative opinion. Nine brands from publicly traded firms (Apple, Borland, Compaq, Dell, Hewlett-Packard, IBM, Microsoft, Novell, and Oracle) populate the database.

The results have been very similar to those shown in Figure 1–5. Again, ROI is found to have a significant influence on stock return. And again, brand equity is found to have nearly as strong an influence as ROI, with the relative impact of brand equity about 70 percent of that of ROI. Showing that brand equity pays off in the high-tech context, where many argue that brands are of minor import, is impressive. The conclusion is clear: Brand equity, on average, drives stock return.

## CHANGES IN BRAND EQUITY

The question, however, still remains: What caused brand equity to change? Was it simply new product announcements and innovations, or is there more to brand equity in the high-tech context than product attributes? To explore this issue, we examined all of the major changes in brand equity by consulting industry experts, company executives, and trade magazines. We found evidence that brand equity was influenced by the following factors:

- Major new products. Although thousands of new products did not have a visible impact on brand equity, the positive impact of such products as the ThinkPad on IBM, the initial Newton introduction on Apple, and Windows 3.1 on Microsoft is clear.
- Product problems. While the introduction of Newton helped Apple, the subsequent disappointment also had an adverse effect on Apple's brand equity. Intel's mismanagement of a defect in the Pentium chip affected its equity.
- Change in top management. The arrival of Lou Gerstner at IBM and the reinvolvement of Steve Jobs with Apple both were associated with brand equity improvements. These visible CEOs articulated major changes in business strategy that clearly influenced their brands.

FIGURE 1–6
*Brand Equity: The Rise of Windows 95 versus The Fall of Apple Computer By Quarters 1994–1997*

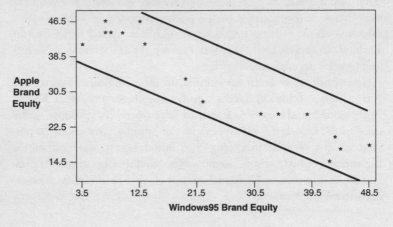

- Competitor actions. A sharp brand equity downturn experienced by Hewlett-Packard was in part due to some hard-hitting advertising from a competitor, Canon. The impact of Windows 95 on Apple's brand equity was dramatic (as shown in Figure 1–6), and it was mirrored by the increase in equity for Windows 95, as the latter succeeded in neutralizing Apple's ownership of the user-friendly interface. That result was, in fact, a strategic and tactical goal of Microsoft.
- Legal actions. Microsoft, after enjoying a stable brand equity level over a long time period, suffered a sharp decline because of the antitrust case brought against it.

One of the problems with empirical tracking is that, in general, brand equity does not change much over time. Because the samples involved are small enough to generate a substantial error factor, it takes a fairly large shock to see an impact. In this study of high-tech brands, it is interesting that the causes of the larger changes in equity can be identified. The findings suggest that the brand name needs to be managed and protected in a broad sense; it is not enough to manage the advertising. In fact, while advertising campaigns surely have an impact over time, they only created a major change in brand equity when they were paired with one of the three dramatic new products (ThinkPad, Newton, and Windows 3.1).

## BRAND LEADERSHIP TASKS

So, building brands pays off, and the brand leadership model is a perspective that will be needed to build strong brands in the next decade. What is involved in achieving brand leadership? Ultimately there are four challenges that need to be addressed, as summarized in Figure 1–7. The first is to create a brand-building organization. The second is to develop a comprehensive brand architecture that provides strategic direction. The third is to develop a brand strategy for the key brands that includes a motivating brand identity, as well as a position that differentiates the brand and resonates with customers. The fourth is to develop efficient and effective brand-building programs together with a system to track the results.

FIGURE 1–7
*Brand Leadership Tasks*

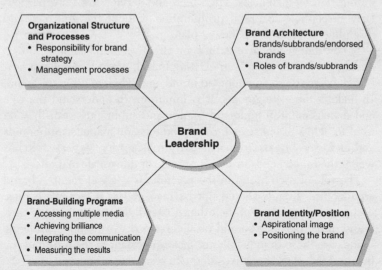

## THE ORGANIZATIONAL CHALLENGE

The first challenge, as noted above, is to create an organizational structure and process that will lead to strong brands. Someone (or some group) needs to be in charge, so brands are not at the mercy of ad hoc decisions made by those with no long-term vested interest in the brand. When the brand has multiple products, markets, and/or countries, each with its own manager, the organizational process needs to provide a common set of inputs, outputs, and vocabulary that all will use. The communication system should allow for the sharing of insights, experience, and brand-building initiatives. In short, the organization must establish a brand-nurturing structure and culture.

## THE BRAND ARCHITECTURE CHALLENGE

Brand architecture involves identifying the brand and subbrands that are to be supported, their respective roles, and, critically, their relationships to each other. An effective, well-conceived architecture will lead to clarity in customer offerings, real synergies in the brands and their communication programs, and an ability to leverage brand assets. It is destructive and wasteful to have a host of brands drifting among a confused set of offerings, surrounded by monumental communication inefficiencies. High-tech and service firms are particularly susceptible to brand proliferation without the guidance and discipline of any brand policy or plan.

A key dimension in creating an effective brand architecture is deciding when to stretch an existing brand, when to employ a new brand, when to use an endorsed brand, and when to use a subbrand. In making these judgments, it is important to understand the role and management of endorsed brands and subbrands—can they be used to help a brand stretch over products and markets? Subbrands and endorsed brands are particularly relevant for vertical stretches where the brand needs to access upscale or downscale markets.

The role of each brand in the portfolio is a key element of brand architecture. Brands should not be managed as if they were silos, each one independent of the other. Instead, the relative role of each brand in the portfolio should be determined. For example, strategic brands are those brands that are most important to the future of the firm and that should receive adequate resources to succeed.

## THE BRAND IDENTITY AND POSITION CHALLENGE

Each actively managed brand needs a brand identity—a vision of how that brand should be perceived by its target audience. The brand identity is the heart of the brand leadership model, because it is the vehicle that guides and inspires the brand-building program. If the brand identity is confused or ambiguous, there is little chance that effective brand building will occur.

The brand position can help prioritize and focus the brand identity by setting forth the communication objectives: What message will best differentiate the brand and appeal to the target segments?

## THE BRAND-BUILDING PROGRAM CHALLENGE

Communication and other brand-building programs are needed to realize the brand identity. In fact, brand-building programs not only implement the brand identity but also help define it. An advertising execution or sponsorship can bring clarity and focus to a brand identity that otherwise might appear sterile and ambiguous. Having execution elements on the table can make strategies more vivid and less ambiguous and can provide some confidence that the strategies are achievable.

The key to most strong brands is brilliant execution that bursts out of the clutter, provides a boost to the brand, and creates a cumulative impact over time. The difference between good and brilliant cannot be overstated. The problem, of course, is that there is a lot of good around and little brilliance. The challenge is to be noticed, to be remembered, to change perceptions, to reinforce attitudes, and to create deep customer relationships. Good execution rarely moves the needle unless inordinate amounts of resources are expended.

Brilliant execution requires the right communication tools. These tools are often more than just advertising—in fact, sometimes advertising plays a small role or even no role. One key is to access alternative media. The strong brands of tomorrow are going to understand and use interactive media, direct response, promotions, and other devices that provide relationship-building experiences. Another key is to learn to manage the resulting communication program so that it is synergetic and consistently on strategy.

Successful management involves measurement. Without measurement, budgets become arbitrary and programs cannot be evaluated. The key to effective measurement is to have indicators that tap all dimensions of brand equity: brand awareness, perceived quality, customer loyalty, and associations that include brand personality as well as organizational and attribute associations. Relying on short-term financial indicators alone is a recipe for brand erosion rather than brand building.

## THE PLAN OF THIS BOOK

The concept of brand identity and the analyses that support it are extensively discussed in *Building Strong Brands*. Experience in working with and implementing the brand identity model, however, has made it clear that aspects of the model and its use could productively be elaborated. Thus, in Chapter 2, a brief overview of brand identity and positioning is presented, after which eight observations provide suggestions to those who will implement these concepts. In Chapter 3, we present a variety of ways that the brand identity and position can be elaborated in order to guide communication and other brand-enhancing programs more effectively.

Brand architecture issues are discussed in Chapters 4 and 5. Chapter 4 presents the brand relationship spectrum as a way to understand and use subbrands and endorsed brands. Chapter 5 defines brand architecture and describes an audit system that will guide those who need to improve their brand architecture.

Brand building beyond advertising is the focus of Chapters 6, 7, 8, and 9. Chapter 6 provides a case study of the novel brand-building approaches used by Adidas and Nike. Using sponsorships to build brands is covered in Chapter 7, and brand building on the Web is discussed in Chapter 8. Chapter 9 provides several case studies of out-of-the-box brand building, as well as some general guidelines.

Finally, Chapter 10 draws on a study of how thirty-five global firms structure their organizations to create strong brands. It also develops a model of four organizational structures that are used by successful global firms.

**QUESTIONS FOR DISCUSSION**

1. Look at the dimensions in Figure 1–3. For each dimension, position your organization on a seven-point scale between classic brand management and the brand leadership paradigm. Compare your actual position on each dimension with where you should be, given your competitive and market context.
2. Examine forces influencing brand management in your industry, such as competitive pressures, channel dynamics, global realities, and market factors. How will your brand strategy have to change to win in the emerging environment?
3. Comment on the studies showing how brand equity affects financial returns.

# PART II

## BRAND IDENTITY

# 2

# Brand Identity—
# The Cornerstone of
# Brand Strategy

A brand is the face of a business strategy.
—Scott Galloway, Prophet Brand Strategy

You cannot win the hearts of customers unless you have a heart yourself.
—Charlotte Beers, J. Walter Thompson

## THE STORY OF VIRGIN ATLANTIC AIRWAYS

In 1970, Richard Branson and a few friends founded Virgin Records as a small mail-order company in London, England; a modest retail store on Oxford Street followed in 1971. The partners chose the name Virgin because of their youthfulness and lack of business experience. Within thirteen years, however, the company grew into a chain of record shops and the largest independent label in the United Kingdom, with artists as diverse and important as Phil Collins, the Sex Pistols, Mike Oldfield, Boy George, and the Rolling Stones. The 1990s saw the retail business grow to include more than a hundred Virgin "megastores" sprinkled around the world. Many, such as the Times Square store, made a significant brand statement with their signage, size, and interior design.

In February 1984, a young lawyer approached Richard Branson with a proposal to start a new airline. Virgin's board of directors considered the idea absurd, but Branson thought that his experience in the entertainment industry could add significant value to an airline business. Because he personally found air travel boring and unpleasant, his idea was to make flying fun, with an attractive value proposition: "To provide all classes of traveler with the highest quality of travel at the lowest cost." Branson got his way, and within three months the first Virgin Atlantic airplane took off from London's Gatwick Airport.

Defying the odds (and vigorous attempts by British Airways to crush it), Virgin has prospered. By 1997 it had served thirty million customers, exceeded $3.5 billion in annual sales, and become the second airline (in passengers) in most of its markets and routes. Even though Virgin Atlantic is only about as big as Alaska Airlines, it enjoys the same consumer awareness and reputation as large international carriers. For example, a 1994 survey showed that over 90 percent of all British consumers had heard of Virgin Atlantic. Focus groups consistently show that Virgin is a trusted brand with innovative products and high standards of service.

## THE VIRGIN BRAND IDENTITY

Virgin's success is due to a host of factors, including Richard Branson's instincts in choosing new business ventures, his strategic vision, the quality and entrepreneurial drive of the management teams and venture partners that run Virgin's businesses, and good luck. But the Virgin brand is the glue that holds this ever-expanding empire together. Four clearly defined values and associations describe the Virgin core brand identity: service quality, innovation, fun, and value for money. Virgin Atlantic Airways is a particularly good illustration of these values.

### Service Quality

There are thousands of moments of truth in the airline business when the customer experiences service quality firsthand. In this context Virgin Atlantic has performed extraordinarily well, as evidenced by the multiple quality awards it has received. For example, in 1997, Virgin was named the best transatlantic carrier for the seventh consecutive year, with the best business class for the ninth consecutive year. Other accolades range from best in-flight entertainment to best business class wine selection to best ground/check-in staff. Virgin measures well against such outstanding service-oriented airlines as British Airways, Ansett Airlines, and Singapore Airlines.

### Innovation

Virgin's philosophy on innovation is simple: be first and dazzle customers. Virgin pioneered sleeper seats in 1986 (British Airways followed nine years later with the cradle seat), in-flight massages, child safety seats, individual video screens for business-class passengers, and new service classes positioned above the normal coach and business-class offerings of other airlines. In short, Virgin has pushed innovation like no other airline. Three percent of revenues are allocated to new service quality innovations—nearly double the spending of the average U.S. carrier.

### Fun and entertainment

Virgin's airport lounges provide putting greens, masseurs, beauty therapists, and facilities to shower, take a Jacuzzi, and nap. On some routes, the airline offers first-class passengers a new tailor-made suit waiting at their destinations. Customers even have the option of checking in at the airport via a convenient, McDonald's-style drive-through window. The goal is to create memorable, fun, entertaining experiences. These are not run-of-the-mill improvements on standard services, such as offering a special vegetarian menu or a cup of Starbucks coffee.

### Value for money

Virgin Atlantic Upper Class is a service priced at the business-class level but equivalent to many other airlines' first class service. Similarly, Mid Class offers business-class service at full-fare economy prices, and most Virgin Economy tickets are available at a discount. While this lower price point may offer a clear consumer advantage, however, Virgin does not emphasize its price position. Cheapness *per se* is not the message at Virgin.

While the four core identity dimensions are the primary drivers of the Virgin brand, the Virgin brand identity also includes three extended identity dimensions: its underdog business model, its brand personality, and its symbols.

### The underdog

Virgin's business model is straightforward. The company typically enters markets and industries populated by established players (such as British Airways, Coca-Cola, Levi Strauss, British Rail, and Smirnoff) that are portrayed as being somewhat complacent, bureaucratic, and unresponsive to customer needs. In contrast, Virgin is perceived as the underdog who cares, innovates, and delivers an attractive alternative to what customers have been buying. When British Airways attempted to prevent Virgin from gaining routes, Virgin painted British Airways as a bully standing in the way of an earnest youngster whose alternative promised better value and service. Virgin, personified by Branson, is the modern-day Robin Hood, the friend of the little guy.

### The Virgin personality

The Virgin brand has a strong, perhaps edgy, personality largely reflecting its flamboyant service innovations and the values and actions of Branson, its founder. Virgin as a person would be perceived as someone who

- Flaunts the rules
- Has a sense of humor that is outrageous at times
- Is an underdog, willing to attack the establishment
- Is competent, always does a high-quality job, and has high standards

Interestingly, this personality spans several unrelated characteristics: fun-loving, innovative, and competent. Many brands would like to do the same but feel that they must choose among such personality extremes. The key is not only the personality of Branson himself but also the fact that Virgin has delivered on each facet of this personality.

### Virgin symbols

The ultimate Virgin symbol is, of course, Branson himself (shown in Figure 2–1). He represents much of what Virgin stands for. There are other symbols as well, however, including the Virgin blimp, the Virgin Island (accessible to Virgin Atlantic customers as an ultimate frequent flyer reward), and the Virgin logo. Written in script and at

FIGURE 2–1
*Richard Branson*

an angle, the logo provides a contrast to the brands that display their
names in more conventional fonts and are portrayed symmetrically.
The script (reminiscent of Intel Inside) provides a sense that Branson
might have written it, and the rakish angle is a bit of a statement that
Virgin is not just another big corporation.

### Stretching the Virgin Brand

Virgin is a remarkable example of how a brand can be successfully
stretched far beyond what would be considered reasonable by any
standard. The Virgin brand has been extended from record stores to
airlines to colas to condoms to dozens of other categories. The Virgin
Group comprises some 100 companies in 22 countries and includes a
discount airline (Virgin Express), financial services (Virgin Direct), a
cosmetics retail chain and direct sales operation (Virgin Vie), several
media companies (Virgin Radio, Virgin TV), a rail service (Virgin Rail),
soft drinks and other beverages (Virgin Cola, Virgin Energy, Virgin
Vodka), a line of casual clothing (Virgin Clothing, Virgin Jeans), a new
record label (V2 Records), and even a bridal store (Virgin Bride).

In fact, the decision to extend Virgin, a brand then associated with rock music and youth, to an airline could have become a legendary blunder had it failed. However, because the airline was successful and was able to deliver value with quality, flare, and innovation, the master brand developed associations that were not restricted to a single type of product. The elements of the Virgin brand identity—quality, innovation, fun/entertainment, value, the underdog image, a strong brand personality, and Branson—work for a large set of products and services. It has become a lifestyle brand with an attitude whose powerful relationship with customers is not based solely on functional benefits.

One reason that the brand works over all the extensions is that two of Virgin's subbrands, Virgin Atlantic Airways and the Virgin Megastores, act as anchors for the group. Because each is a "silver bullet" (a subbrand that drives the image of a parent brand), these two brands receive the majority of Virgin's resources and management attention.

There are difficulties and risks in stretching a brand, but also significant benefits, as Sony, Honda, GE, and other brands with extended product portfolios have demonstrated. First, multiple offerings can gain a brand more visibility and awareness. Second, the extensions can potentially add and reinforce key associations (such as quality, innovation, fun, and value in the case of Virgin). Third, with a strong flexible parent brand, a new name does not have to be established when new products or services are introduced—for example, the Virgin brand can be used with a descriptor to create Virgin Cola or Virgin Rail.

### COMMUNICATING THE BRAND—THE ROLE OF PUBLICITY

The Virgin brand has been driven in part by pure visibility, largely based on publicity personally generated by Branson. Realizing that Virgin Atlantic could not compete with British Airways in advertising expenditures, Branson used publicity stunts to create awareness and develop associations. When the first Virgin Atlantic Airways flight took off in 1984 with friends, celebrities, and reporters on board, Branson appeared in the cockpit wearing a leather World War I flight helmet. The onboard video (a prerecorded tape) showed Branson and two famous cricket players as the pilots greeting the passengers from the cockpit.[1]

Branson's publicity efforts have not by any means been limited to

Virgin Atlantic. For the launching of Virgin Bride, a company that arranges weddings, he showed up in a wedding dress. At the opening of Virgin's first U.S. megastore in New York's Times Square, in 1996, Branson (a balloonist who holds several world records) was lowered on a huge silver ball from 100 feet above the store. These and other stunts have turned into windfalls of free publicity for the Virgin brand. Although some of the stunts are outrageous, they do not cross the line; Virgin excites, surprises, even shocks, but does not offend. For example, Virgin would not push the envelope as far as Benetton did with its advertisements that featured dramatic scenes concerning condom use, hunger, and racial problems.

Branson has fully mastered his role. By employing British humor and the popular love of flaunting the system, he has endeared himself to consumers. By never deviating from the core brand values of quality, innovation, fun, and value for money, he has gained their loyalty and confidence. Evidence of this high level of trust in Branson and Virgin abound. When BBC radio asked 1,200 people who they thought would be the most qualified to rewrite the Ten Commandments, Branson came in fourth, after Mother Teresa, the pope, and the archbishop of Canterbury. When a British daily newspaper took a poll on who would be the most qualified to become the next mayor of London, Branson won by a landslide.

The challenge for a brand that is built on a track record of success and exceptional innovation like Virgin's is formidable—the next daring expansion could turn into a disastrous example of overreaching. Virgin's Waterloo could be its Virgin Rail business. With nearly thirty million annual trips, the rail business is highly visible, and the ability to deliver high service levels is not entirely in Virgin's control because the company must depend on railway operations and even other rail companies. During its first year, Virgin Rail had significant and visible problems with punctuality and service. In retrospect, such a risky venture might have been better off under another brand to offer some measure of protection to the Virgin brand.

The critical issue for Virgin, then, will be to manage the brand as its consumers (and Branson) age and as it mushrooms into an ever-broader range of businesses. Can Virgin preserve its core identity across all of its product categories and maintain its energetic personality over time? A clear brand identity will be the key to meeting that challenge.

# THE BRAND IDENTITY PLANNING MODEL

A strong brand should have a rich, clear brand identity—a set of associations the brand strategist seeks to create or maintain. In contrast to brand image (the brand's current associations), a brand identity is aspirational and may imply that the image needs to be changed or augmented. In a fundamental sense, the brand identity represents what the organization wants the brand to stand for.

Those involved with the brand (that is, the brand team and their partners)—should be able to articulate the brand identity and should care about it. If either element is lacking, a brand is unlikely to achieve its potential and will be vulnerable to market forces emphasizing undifferentiated products and price competition. Too many brands drift aimlessly and appear to stand for nothing in particular. They always seem to be shouting price, on sale, attached to some deal, or engaging in promiscuous channel expansion—symptoms of a lack of integrity.

Brand identity, as noted in Chapter 1, is one of the four pillars (along with brand architecture, brand-building programs, and organizational structure and processes) of creating strong brands. The brand identity construct was developed in detail in *Building Strong Brands*. We will review and extend that conceptualization here to include the brand essence, a compact summary of what the brand stands for. In addition, eight practical tips on developing and using brand identities are drawn from our experience of applying the concept to many firms and brands.

The brand identity planning process, summarized in Figure 2–2, provides a tool to understand, develop, and use the brand identity construct. In addition to the brand identity itself, it includes two other components, the strategic brand analysis and the brand identity implementation system, which are discussed next.

## STRATEGIC BRAND ANALYSIS

To be effective, a brand identity needs to resonate with customers, differentiate the brand from competitors, and represent what the organization can and will do over time. Thus the strategic brand analysis helps the manager to understand the customer, the competitors, and the brand itself (including the organization behind the brand).

The *customer analysis* must get beyond what customers say to what lies underneath what they do. Creative qualitative research is often useful toward this end. Another challenge is to develop a segmentation scheme that can drive strategy. To do this, the manager must discover which segmentation variables have real leverage and understand the size and dynamics of each segment.

The *competitor analysis* examines current and potential competitors to make sure that the strategy will differentiate the brand and that communication programs will break away from the clutter in a meaningful way. Studying competitor strengths and strategies as well as positions can also provide insight into the brand-building task.

The *self analysis* identifies whether the brand has the resources, the capability, and the will to deliver. The analysis needs to uncover not only the brand's heritage and current image but also the strengths, limitations, strategies, and values of the organization that is creating the brand. Ultimately, a successful brand strategy needs to capture the soul of the brand, and this soul resides in the organization.

## BRAND IDENTITY IMPLEMENTATION SYSTEM

A brand identity is implemented through the development and measurement of brand-building programs. As Figure 2–2 suggests, there are four components to implementation: brand identity elaboration, brand position, brand-building programs, and tracking.

*Brand identity elaboration* is a set of tools designed to add richness, texture, and clarity to the brand identity. Without this elaboration, elements of the brand identity (such as leadership, friendship, trust, and relationship) may be too ambiguous to guide decisions about what actions will support the brand and what will not. Chapter 3 will explore brand identity elaboration and discuss some techniques, such as strategic imperatives, role models, and the development and use of visual metaphors. Chapters 2 and 3 together are designed to help brand stewards develop and use the brand identity construct.

With a clear and elaborated identity, the implementation task turns to *brand position*—the part of the brand identity and value proposition that is to be actively communicated to the target audience. Thus the brand position, which should demonstrate an advantage over competitor brands, represents current communication objectives. Some elements of the brand identity may not be part of the brand position because, although important, they do not differentiate. Or the brand may not be ready to deliver on a promise, or the audience may not be ready to accept the message. As the delivery of more aspirational elements of the brand identity becomes feasible and believable, the brand position can become more ambitious.

With the brand position and brand identity in place, *brand-building programs* can be developed. A common misconception is that building brands is nothing more than advertising. In fact, advertising sometimes plays only a minor role in the process. Brands can be built through a variety of media, including promotions, publicity, packaging, direct marketing, flagship stores, the Web, and sponsorships. Communication involves all points of contact between the brand and the audience, including product design, new products, and distribution strategy.

One challenge that can not be wholly delegated to an advertising agency is deciding which of the many media options will most effectively build your brand. Another is creating brilliant communication strategies and executions that break out of the clutter and make a difference. Part IV of this book addresses these challenges.

The final step in implementation is *tracking* the brand-building program. *Building Strong Brands* presented ten brand equity dimensions as a framework to structure the tracking problem. The Brand Equity Ten include two sets of brand loyalty measures (price premium and customer satisfaction), two sets of perceived quality/leadership measures (perceived quality and leadership/popularity), three sets of association measures (perceived value, brand personality, and organizational associations), one set of awareness measures, and two sets of market behavior measures (market share and market price/distribution coverage). These measures provide a tracking system that will work across brands and products, as well as a point of departure for those who need an instrument tailored to a specific brand and context.

Strategic analysis, brand identity development, and brand identity implementation are treated as sequential in the Brand Identity Planning Model. In practice, however, there is overlap and backtracking, and it is difficult to separate strategy from execution. In large measure, the execution defines the strategy and demonstrates its feasibility, so one may have to venture into execution in order to know whether a strategy is optimal.

## BRAND IDENTITY—A REVIEW

Brand identity is a set of brand associations that the brand strategist aspires to create or maintain. These associations imply a promise to customers from the organization members. Because a brand identity is used to drive all the brand-building efforts, it should have depth and richness; it is not an advertising tagline or even a positioning statement.

When realized, the brand identity should help establish a relationship between the brand and the customer by generating a value proposition potentially involving functional, emotional, or self-expressive benefits or by providing credibility for endorsed brands (such as Betty Crocker's Hamburger Helper). The endorser's role is to help create credibility for the endorsed brand (Hamburger Helper) rather than directly provide a value proposition.

Figure 2–2 provides an overview of brand identity and its related constructs. Note that there are twelve categories of brand identity elements organized around four perspectives—the *brand as product* (product scope, product attributes, quality/value, use experience, users, country of origin), *organization* (organizational attributes, local versus global), *person* (brand personality, customer/brand relationships), and *symbol* (visual imagery/metaphors and brand heritage). Although each category has relevance for some brands, virtually no brand has associations in all twelve categories.

Note also that the brand identity structure includes a *core identity*, an *extended identity*, and a *brand essence*. Typically, the brand identity will require from six to twelve dimensions in order to adequately describe the brand's aspiration. Because such a large set is unwieldy, it is helpful to provide focus by identifying the core identity (the most important elements of the brand identity). All dimensions of the core identity should reflect the strategy and values of the organization, and at least one association should differentiate the brand and resonate with customers. The core identity is most likely to remain constant as the brand travels to new markets and products—if customers perceive the brand according to the core identity, the battle is won.

The core identity creates a focus both for the customer and the

FIGURE 2–2
*Brand Identity Planning Model*

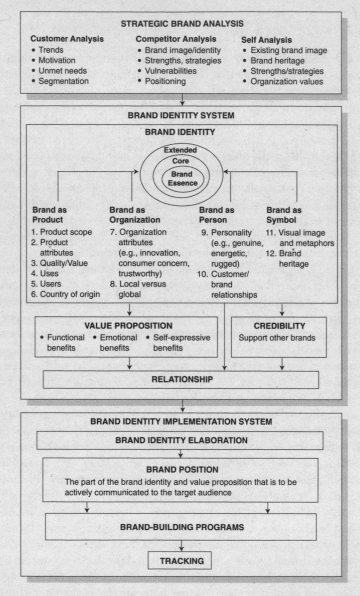

STRATEGIC BRAND ANALYSIS

**Customer Analysis**
- Trends
- Motivation
- Unmet needs
- Segmentation

**Competitor Analysis**
- Brand image/identity
- Strengths, strategies
- Vulnerabilities
- Positioning

**Self Analysis**
- Existing brand image
- Brand heritage
- Strengths/strategies
- Organization values

**BRAND IDENTITY SYSTEM**

**BRAND IDENTITY**

Extended
Core
Brand
Essence

**Brand as Product**
1. Product scope
2. Product attributes
3. Quality/Value
4. Uses
5. Users
6. Country of origin

**Brand as Organization**
7. Organization attributes (e.g., innovation, consumer concern, trustworthy)
8. Local versus global

**Brand as Person**
9. Personality (e.g., genuine, energetic, rugged)
10. Customer/ brand relationships

**Brand as Symbol**
11. Visual image and metaphors
12. Brand heritage

**VALUE PROPOSITION**
- Functional benefits
- Emotional benefits
- Self-expressive benefits

**CREDIBILITY**
Support other brands

**RELATIONSHIP**

**BRAND IDENTITY IMPLEMENTATION SYSTEM**

**BRAND IDENTITY ELABORATION**

**BRAND POSITION**
The part of the brand identity and value proposition that is to be actively communicated to the target audience

**BRAND-BUILDING PROGRAMS**

**TRACKING**

organization; for example, for Mobil it is leadership, partnership, and trust, and for Saturn it is world-class cars and treating customers with respect as friends. These core identities are easier to communicate both inside and outside the organization than the full, extended identity.

The extended identity includes all of the brand identity elements that are not in the core, organized into meaningful groupings. Often the core identity is a terse description of the brand, and this terseness can generate ambiguity; as a result, brand implementation decisions benefit from the texture and completeness provided by the extended identity. Moreover, there are useful elements of the extended identity (such as the brand personality and a specification of what the brand is not) that do not usually fit comfortably into the core identity.

Figure 2–3 shows the brand identity for Virgin. The core identity contains four concepts—quality, innovation, fun/entertainment, and value. The extended identity adds the underdog position, brand personality, and symbols.

## THE BRAND ESSENCE

The core identity usually has two to four dimensions that compactly summarize the brand vision. It often is useful, however, to provide even more focus by creating a brand essence: a single thought that captures the soul of the brand. In some cases, it is not feasible or worthwhile to develop a brand essence, but in others it can be a powerful tool.

A good brand essence statement does not merely string a set of core identity phrases together into a sentence, since this would provide little value beyond the core identity. Instead, it provides a slightly different perspective while still capturing much of what the brand stands for. The brand essence can be viewed as the glue that holds the core identity elements together, or as the hub of a wheel linked to all of the core identity elements.

The brand essence should have several characteristics: It should resonate with customers and drive the value proposition. It should be ownable, providing differentiation from competitors that will persist through time. And it should be compelling enough to energize and inspire the employees and partners of the organization. (Even an understated essence such as "It simply works better" or "Take a dif-

FIGURE 2–3
*Virgin Brand Identity*

*Brand essence*
- **Iconoclasm**

*Core identity*
- **Service quality**
  Consistent best-of-category quality delivered with humor and flair.
- **Innovation**
  First with truly innovative, value-added features and services.
- **Fun and entertainment**
  A fun and entertaining company.
- **Value for money**
  Provide value in all its offerings, never just the high-priced option.

*Extended identity*
- **Underdog**
  Fighting the established bureaucratic firm with new creative offerings.
- **Personality**
    - Flaunts the rules.
    - Sense of humor, even outrageous.
    - Underdog, willing to attack the establishment.
    - Competent, always does a good job, high standards.
- **Virgin symbols**
    - Branson and his perceived lifestyle.
    - Virgin blimp.
    - Virgin script logo.

*Value proposition*
- **Functional benefits**
    - A value offering with quality, plus innovative extras delivered with flair and humor.
- **Emotional benefits**
    - Pride in linking to the underdog with an attitude.
    - Fun, good times.
- **Self-expressive benefits**
    - Willingness to go against the establishment, to be a bit outrageous.

*Relationship*
- **Customers are fun companions.**

ferent road," however, can be inspirational to those who take it seriously and recognize its challenge.)

Strong brand essence statements usually have multiple interpretations that make them more effective. For Nike the brand essence might be "Excelling," which could encompass such diverse components of the Nike identity as technology, top athletes, aggressive personalities, the track shoe heritage, and subbrands like Air Jordan, as well as customers who strive to excel. For American Express, "Do more" expresses the thrust of the organization that walks the extra mile, a product set that offers more than competitors, and a customer base that is not satisfied with a conventional lifestyle but engages in more and different activities.

### BRAND ESSENCE VERSUS TAGLINE

The brand essence is distinct from a tagline. When searching for a brand essence, it is counterproductive to evaluate candidates on whether they would make a good tagline. A brand essence represents the identity, and one of its key functions is to communicate and energize those inside the organization. In sharp contrast, the tagline represents the brand position (or communication goals), and its function is to communicate with the external audience. A brand essence should be timeless or at least expected to be relevant for a long time period, while a tagline may have a limited life. Further, a brand essence is likely to be relevant across markets and products, whereas a tagline is more likely to have a confined arena. Though it might seem efficient to have a brand essence statement that also functions as a tagline, insisting that statement candidates meet both criteria is diverting at best (and counterproductive at worst).

The IBM brand essence, ("Magic you can trust") captures the aspirational aspect of their products and service, combined with the trust generated by the company's heritage, size, and competence. Because of its varied markets, however, IBM uses several taglines: "Solutions for a small planet" is relevant for a customer seeking solutions and inspiring to those with a global vision, while "E-Business" positions IBM as the dominant choice for those seeking help with e-commerce. Sony's brand essence ("Digital dream kids") captures the core identity of Sony well but is not being used as a tagline, while "My Sony" is far removed from the essence but works as a tagline for a specific part of the Sony business. Hellmann's (Best Foods) Mayonnaise uses the essence statement "Simple goodness with a dash of indulgence," which is richer than the tagline "Bring out the best."

Among the host of taglines that would not be appropriate for a brand essence statement are the following:

Do you Yahoo?

Moving at the speed of business (UPS)

Did somebody say McDonald's?

Like a rock (Chevy Trucks)

On the road of life there are passengers and drivers: Drivers wanted (Volkswagen)

#### WHAT THE BRAND IS VERSUS WHAT THE BRAND DOES

A host of decisions need to be made about the brand essence: Should it focus on owned associations (Volvo—the practical, safe car) or should it be aspirational (Volvo—the stylish car)? Should it be understated (Compaq—it simply works better) or based on a dream (Compaq—enriches your life)? A key choice, however, is whether the essence will focus on what the brand *is* or on what it *does* for customers. Does it draw on a rational appeal that emphasizes functional benefits (Mercedes delivers quality and reliability), or does it stimulate feelings that connect to the brand (Mercedes is success)?

A brand essence that draws on a meaningful functional benefit will attempt to own the relevant product attribute. Such an association can provide a significant sustainable advantage, but it can also be limiting in that it tends to put a box around the brand. For this reason, one common brand strategy is to evolve a brand from a product-oriented essence to a more general one. A brand essence that is based on emotional and self-expressive benefits provides a higher-order basis for relationships. It also can be less vulnerable to product-related changes and more easily applied to new contexts.

#### What the brand is—functional benefits

VW: "German engineering"

BMW: "The ultimate driving machine"

Abbey National Bank: "A special kind of security"

Xerox: "The digital document company"

3M: "Innovation"

Banana Republic: "Casual luxury"

Compaq: "Better answers"

Lexus: "Without compromise"

**What the brand does—emotional and self-expressive benefits**

American Express: "Do more"

Pepsi: "The Pepsi generation"

HP: "Expanding possibilities"

Apple: "The power to be your best" (or "Think different")

Sony: "Digital dream kids"

Schlumberger: "The passion of excellence"

Nike: "Excelling"

Microsoft: "Help people realize their potential" (or "Where do you want to go today?")

### THE VALUE PROPOSITION AND THE CUSTOMER-BRAND RELATIONSHIP

The brand identity system includes the value proposition, which is created by the brand identity. In addition to functional benefits, the value proposition can include emotional and self-expressive benefits.

An *emotional benefit* relates to the ability of the brand to make the buyer or user of a brand feel something during the purchase process or use experience. The strongest identities often include emotional benefits, such as the way a customer feels safe in a Volvo, important when shopping at Nordstrom, warm when buying or reading a Hallmark card, or strong and rugged when wearing Levi's.

Emotional benefits add richness and depth to owning and using the brand. Without the memories that Sun-Maid Raisins evoke, the brand would border on commodity status. The familiar red package links many users to the happy days of helping Mom in the kitchen (or an idealized childhood for some who wish that they had such experiences). The result can be a different use experience—one with feelings—and a stronger brand.

A *self-expressive benefit* exists when the brand provides a vehicle by which a person can proclaim a particular self image. Of course, we all have multiple roles—one person may be a wife, mother, writer, tennis player, music buff, and hiker. Each role will have an associated self-concept that the person may want to express; the purchase and use of brands is one way to fulfill that self-expressive need. A person might express a self-concept of being adventurous and daring by owning Rossignol powder skis, hip by buying clothes from the Gap, sophisticated by wearing Ralph Lauren fashions, successful and in control by driving a Lincoln, frugal and unpretentious by shopping at Kmart, competent by using Microsoft Office, or nurturing by preparing Quaker Oats hot cereal for children in the morning.

Finally, the brand identity system also includes a *relationship construct*. One goal of a brand should be to create a relationship with its customer, one that may resemble a personal relationship. Thus a brand could be a friend (Saturn), a mentor (Microsoft), an advisor (Morgan Stanley), an enabler (Schwab), a mother (Betty Crocker), a lively buddy (Bud Light) or a son (Good News from Gillette). The Saturn brand/customer relationship based on treating customers intelligently as a friend, for example, is not captured well by functional or emotional benefits, although they are also present.

## ON DEVELOPING A BRAND IDENTITY SYSTEM— AVOIDING COMMON MISTAKES

Drawing on first-hand experience in developing and helping others develop brand identities, we have identified eight guidelines that are summarized in Figure 2–4 and detailed below. As you read, focus on the suggestions most relevant to the context that applies to your brand.

### 1. Avoid a Limited Brand Perspective

One common brand management mistake is to view the brand too narrowly. Some people succumb to the "tagline trap," the belief that the brand identity should be captured in a three-word phrase. But even the brand essence statement should not be the only (or even the dominant) part of the brand identity, because a brand is more complex than a simple phrase can represent. For example, 3M is not just innovation; it stands for a large set of associations, including quality, adhesives and adhesive products, video and audio tape, and a Midwestern personality.

FIGURE 2–4
*Creating Effective Brand Identity Systems*

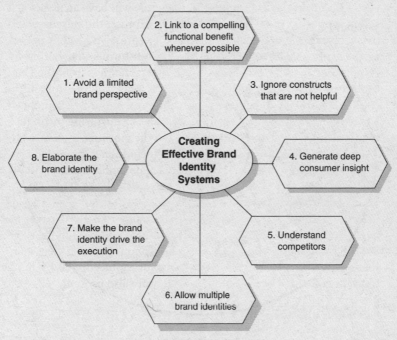

An even more common problem is the product-attribute fixation trap which occurs when the brand is viewed as simply a set of attributes delivering functional benefits. Companies in the high-tech and industrial marketing world are particularly susceptible to the assumption that customers process only factual information about brands and base their choices solely on the attributes most important to them. In fact, it is usually more accurate and helpful to conceive of a brand as what is left over after the impact of attributes has been subtracted.

Figure 2–5 summarizes the distinction between a product and a brand. The product includes characteristics such as product scope (Crest makes dental hygiene products), product attributes (*Vogue* has fashion news), quality/value (Kraft delivers a quality product), uses (Subaru cars are made for driving in the snow), and functional benefits (Wal-Mart provides extra value). A brand includes these product characteristics and much more:

FIGURE 2–5
*A Brand Is More Than a Product*

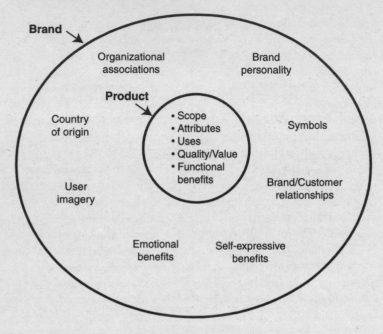

- User imagery (those who wear Armani clothes)
- Country of origin (Audi has German craftsmanship)
- Organizational associations (3M is an innovative company)
- Brand personality (Bath and Body Works is a retail brand with energy and vitality)
- Symbols (the stagecoach represents Wells Fargo Bank)
- Brand/customer relationships (Gateway is a friend)

In addition to functional benefits, a brand potentially delivers

- Self-expressive benefits (a Hobart user expresses a self-image of being the best)
- Emotional benefits (Saturn users feel pride in driving an American-made car)

All of these elements of a brand are potentially useful, but three deserve comment: organizational associations, brand personality, and symbols.

*Organizational associations* tend to be most relevant for service, high-tech, and durable-goods brands, where the organization behind the brand has a visible link with the customer. Firms that develop a reputation of being innovative, socially responsive, a leader, strong, or concerned about the customer can resist competitors with a temporary product or value advantage. These organizational associations are powerful because they tend to be intangible and thus difficult to compete against. It is usually easy to outspec a competitor who is positioned on attributes, but more difficult to compete against the associations of a company such as Hewlett-Packard or GE, which are based on the programs, values, heritage, and people of the organization.

Organizational associations need to reflect the business strategy. One global brand had the following identity elements: global leadership, industry standards of excellence for quality and services, service commitment in all markets around the world, and the lowest price position. The business strategy, however, was not in place to support a low-price position; it is hard to deliver global leadership, excellence in quality, and a global service commitment and still be a value supplier. Strategy and branding are about making choices and trade-offs.

*Brand personality* can help provide needed differentiation even in a parity market, thereby delivering real equity in several ways. First, a personality can make the brand interesting and memorable. Think about it—the worst comment that can be made about a person is that he or she has no personality. It is better to be a jerk. A brand without a personality has trouble gaining awareness and developing a relationship with customers. Second, brand personality stimulates consideration of constructs such as energy and youthfulness, which can be useful to many brands. Third, a brand personality can help suggest brand-customer relationships such as friend, party companion, or advisor. With the personality metaphor in place, relationship development becomes clearer and more motivating.

One litmus test of a brand strategy development is whether brand personality was considered and appears in the identity statement. If the answer is no the brand is probably being conceived too narrowly.

A *symbol* can be elevated to the level of brand strategy rather than being delegated to tactical communications. A strong symbol can provide cohesion and structure to an identity, making it much easier to gain recognition and recall. Symbols can be anything that represents the brand: a tagline ("Nobody doesn't like Sara Lee"), a character (the Pillsbury doughboy), a visual metaphor (the Prudential rock), a logo (Nike's swoosh), a color (Kodak yellow), a gesture (Allstate's "good hands"), a musical note (Hellmann's Mayonnaise), a package (the blue cylinder for Morton salt), or a program (the Ronald McDonald House charities). In any case, the symbol plays a key role in creating and maintaining brand equity and should be a part of the extended identity or, occasionally, the core identity. Consider the strategic role of the Wells Fargo stagecoach in the brand's awareness level and associations of reliability and innovation.

An extended identity can help a brand break out of the box and avoid the product-attribute fixation and advertising tagline traps. There are several advantages to developing a rich extended brand identity:

• First, a richer brand identity is a more accurate reflection of the brand. Just as a person cannot be described in one or two words, neither can a brand. Three-word taglines or an identity limited to attributes will simply not be accurate.

• Second, the point of the brand identity is to provide real guidance to decision makers about what a brand stands for. When it is more complete, there is less ambiguity about what should and should not be done. If the brand identity is excessively terse, omitting key constructs, then communication elements inconsistent with the brand will more likely emerge.

• Third, because the brand identity is aspirational, it should involve the whole organization by capturing values and culture. Leadership and concern for the customer, for example, may not be in the brand essence but still could be vital in guiding the brand strategy.

• Fourth, the extended identity provides a home for constructs that help the brand move beyond attributes. In particular, brand personality and symbols normally fail to make the cut when a terse brand position is developed, yet both are often extremely helpful strategically as well as tactically.

## 2. Link the Brand to a Compelling Functional Benefit Whenever Possible

The product-attribute fixation trap is very real, and it is useful (even critical) to broaden the brand to include personality, organizational associations, symbols, and emotional and self-expressive benefits. This does not mean, however, that attributes—particularly new and differentiating ones—and functional benefits should be ignored on the basis that a "real" brand does not focus on attributes. Every brand should seek to own a functional benefit that is relevant to the customer, as BMW does for driving performance, Volvo does for safety, and the Gap does for fashionable, casual clothing. Owning a superior position on a key attribute can be powerful.

A functional benefit advantage over the competition can be enhanced or even created by the artful management of other associations that reinforce it. In fact, the goal should be to create a personality and provide emotional and self-expressive benefits that are drawn from and support the ownership of an attribute and functional benefit.

Association-rich symbols that establish personalities are excellent devices to create and reinforce attribute and functional-benefit associations. Among the many symbols that support functional benefits are the following:

- The Michelin man (tires with power and energy)
- The Energizer bunny (batteries that just keep on going)
- The Pillsbury doughboy (fresh and light foods)

In fact, it is easier to use a symbol to communicate an attribute than to use factual information. Consider the power of the lonesome Maytag repairman to efficiently and effectively communicate dependability. In the absence of the repairman as a symbol, it would be difficult for Maytag to own dependability as an attribute.

A strong visual metaphor can explain a complex functional benefit in a vivid and memorable way. Andersen Consulting's philosophy was that it made a difference by looking at an organization holistically, whereas many of its competitors were specialists who generated marginal improvements by looking at specific problems (which often were only symptoms of a larger problem). Its ad agency, Young & Rubicam, created a series of visual metaphors that brilliantly illus-

**FIGURE 2–6**
*The Andersen Consulting Visual Statement*

What shape is your business in?

Andersen
Consulting

trated the point and provided the basis of a global advertising campaign that started in 1995. One showed some air spoilers attached to a turtle, a dramatic example of myopic thinking. Another, shown in Figure 2–6, showed a school of fish who, by working together, created the image of a large shark. These visual metaphors were not only powerful but also culture and language independent; they carried the message everywhere.

A laboratory study conducted by Stuart Agres of Young & Rubicam shows the value of combining emotional benefits with functional benefits.[2] The study, involving shampoo, found that emotional benefits (you will look and feel terrific) were less effective than functional benefits (your hair will be thick and full of body), but that the combination of the two was significantly superior to either by itself. A follow-up study found that the 47 TV commercials that included both an emotional and functional benefit had a substantially higher effectiveness score (using a standardized commercial laboratory testing procedure) than 121 commercials that had only one benefit. The message is to augment rather than replace functional-benefit–based identities.

### 3. Use Constructs That Fit and Help—Ignore the Others

In addition to the twelve dimensions organized under the brand as product, organization, person, and symbol, the brand identity model contains three types of benefits and a relationship between the customer and brand, making a total of sixteen potential identity-related dimensions. All of these dimensions can be helpful in some contexts, but none of them are so useful that they need to appear in all contexts. Too often there is a compulsion to use all constructs. The result can be a brand identity that is forced, containing elements that are trivial, irrelevant, and sometimes ridiculous.

All these dimensions *do not* have to appear in a given brand identity. A brand identity is not a tax form that requires an entry on every line, nor is it a questionnaire in which every question must be answered to get a perfect score. Rather, each dimension should be evaluated by the following standards to see if it will be helpful.

- Does it capture an element important to the brand and its ability to provide customer value or support customer relationships?
- Does it help differentiate the brand from its competition?
- Does it resonate with the customer?
- Docs it cncrgizc cmployees?
- Is it believable?

A dimension can qualify if it rates extremely high on only one question; it need not qualify on all five. The dimensions that do not contribute much along any of the five areas, however, should not be included. The bottom line is whether it helps and feels right as part of the brand identity.

Which dimensions to use will depend on the context. In services, high technology, and durable goods, organizational associations are usually helpful, but in consumer packaged goods they are less likely to be relevant. A self-expressive benefit is likely to be more relevant in brands that score very high on one of the five major personality dimensions (sincerity, excitement, competence, sophistication, and ruggedness); personality is also likely to be more important when there is little product differentiation. Symbols are most important when they are strong and create a visual metaphor. If a symbol is weak, symbolism may not be a driver for the brand. (Some strong brands have no defining symbols that need to be actively managed.)

#### 4. GENERATE DEEP CUSTOMER INSIGHT

The development of a brand identity is supported by a set of three analyses—a customer analysis, a competitor analysis, and a self-analysis. Any organization that shortchanges these analyses does so at its peril.

One common mistake is to fail to get underneath customers' relationship with the brand. Although quantitative research regarding attribute importance is often worthwhile, it rarely provides the solid insights that lead to strong brand identities and too often leads to the product-attribute fixation trap. Similarly, focus group research may help you avoid gross mistakes, but it is usually too superficial to discover the basis for a real brand-customer relationship. Fortunately, there are approaches that can generate fresh, relevant insights. The following are a few suggestions:[3]

- Consider in-depth individual interviews close to the purchase and use context. Procter & Gamble researchers, for example, sometimes spend a whole day at people's homes in order to get deeper insights into their use of products. They have asked respondents to wear a microphone and discuss their problems and reactions as they go about their normal activities. Levi's follows shoppers around stores with a tape recorder. Comments on items perused and purchased are very illuminating in part because they are spontaneous and represent an active experience.
- Problem research can be insightful. What are the problems associated with specific use experiences? Are any of those problems meaningful and widespread enough to provide the basis of a brand strategy? A study with a representative sample of customers can quantify how worthwhile a particular solution would be to customers and how large the involved segment would be. Problem research in dog food, for example, led to the development of products tailored to the age and size of dogs.
- Archetype research uses a radical technique pioneered by a medical anthropologist named Dr. Rapaille. Participants are asked to lie down in a setting with low lights and soothing music, then consider the questions of interest. The idea is that their cognitive defenses will be lowered, and emotional connections will be more likely to emerge. Applied to Folgers, participants were asked to drift back to their childhoods and recall how coffee was involved in their life.

The insight that the aroma connected with feelings of home led Folgers to a successful position around the tagline "The best part of Wakin' Up . . . is Folgers in your cup!"

- Another insight generator is to get at emotions associated with the use experience. Research in use experiences have found that there are twenty emotions that customers tend to have: anger, discontent, worry, sadness, fear, shame, guilt, envy, loneliness, romantic love, love, peacefulness, relief, contentment, eagerness, optimism, joy, excitement, surprise, and pride.[4] Scales based on these emotions can be used to probe customers or to provide some quantitative support to emotional research.

- With laddering research, customers provide a profile of the relevant emotional and self-expressive benefits associated with buying and using a brand. The process begins by asking about the reason for a purchase decision or brand preference; the answer will usually involve an attribute. The next step is to ask why that attribute is important. A succession of "why" questions leads to some basic emotional and self-expressive benefits. For example, airline travelers might be asked why an attribute such as "wide bodies" is preferred. If the response is "physical comfort," the consumer is then asked why this is desired. The answer could be "to get more done," from which another "why" question might yield an emotional benefit: "to feel better about myself." Similarly, the "ground service" attribute might lead to a series of answers like "to save time," "to reduce tension," "to feel in control," and "to feel secure."

- Look to the loyal customer for brand insights. The hard-core customer will likely have a relationship with the brand that is worth understanding, because it represents the potential that the brand is capable of achieving. The challenge is to reinforce that relationship and expand the loyal base.

### 5. Understand Competitors

Another natural mistake is to neglect one's competitors. It seems natural for us to focus on what we, as a brand and company, are good at and what the customer wants. The problem is that there are usually vigorous competitors and potential competitors to consider. One key to providing a differentiated brand is understanding their approaches,

which usually starts with an analysis of their current and past positioning strategies.

- One helpful exercise is to collect representative ads for each competitor (plus some historical ads, if their strategy has changed) and
  obtain an estimate of their communication budget. Cluster the ads
  into sets. For example, insurance company communication generally clusters into three generic types:
  - Strength (Prudential, Fortus, Traveler's, Northwestern Mutual)
  - Caring/being there for you (Allstate, State Farm, Cigna Group)
  - Looking to the future/helping you plan ahead (UNUM, Mass
    Mutual, Equitable)
- There may also be outliers, such as Transamerica (the pyramid
  symbol) and MetLife (the Peanuts characters). An understanding of
  how the competition is positioned and their relative budgets will
  provide strategic guidance and a reality check. Is it realistic, after
  all, to believe that a message similar to that of a larger advertiser
  will break out of the clutter?
- Another exercise is to look at a competitor's annual report over the
  last four or so years. A brand identity statement can often be
  inferred from the information provided, especially for a corporate
  brand (such as Sony). Further, the future strategy and commitment
  of the organization behind the brand is often discussed in the
  annual report.
- Investigating competitor brand images can also be valuable. What
  do customers think of other brands? Do they like or dislike them?
  What are their personalities? Their organizational associations?
  Their symbols? Quantitative image research can provide a bench-
  mark, but the insight gained from creative, in-depth qualitative
  research using a metaphor creation exercise (such as, if the brand
  were an animal, what animal would it be?) is almost always useful.

It is important to expand the radar screen to include all of your real
competitors—those that will capture your customers both today and
in the future. A computer firm addressing the home market, for
example, may be tempted to look at Dell, Compaq, Gateway, IBM,
Apple, and Packard Bell as the main competitors. Looming over the
home market, however, are Sony, Kodak, Microsoft, TCI, and
Nintendo, all of whom are preparing for battle to control the digital

interface and internet access that are at the heart of the new digital home business. Any brand identity or future vision must take these competitors into account.

### 6. ALLOW MULTIPLE BRAND IDENTITIES

It is extremely desirable to have a single brand identity that works across products and markets. Coca-Cola has long used a core identity across segments and countries. British Airways expected its "World's Favorite Airline" tagline and the supporting identity to work across markets around the globe. The Pantene shampoo brand uses the same identity, position, and tagline ("hair so healthy it shines"), supported by the visual image of great hair, in every country. When a single brand identity can be applied in all contexts, the communication task—both internally and externally—will be not only easier and less costly but also more likely to be effective and solidly linked to the organizational culture and business strategy.

A common identity should be the goal and the baseline strategy. Resist those who claim that their context, whether it is a country or product line, is different and requires a special identity rather than just a different execution (such as a different interpretation of a lifestyle, or a different way of representing an emotional benefit). Departures from the base brand identity should be as few as possible and convincingly justified by theory and data.

Of course, the overriding goal is to create strong brands in all contexts. If multiple identities are needed to create the strongest brands, then such identities should be considered. For example, Hewlett-Packard needs separate identities to adapt the overall HP brand to fit engineers who buy workstations, business professionals who buy minicomputers and laser printers, and consumers who buy subnotebook computers. Therefore, a single identity may be inadequate.

Sometimes, however, a single identity can be stretched over very different contexts. One approach is to use the same identity but emphasize different elements in each market. For example, in one market a brand personality may be in the forefront, while in another an organizational association will be more prominent. Another approach is to have the same identity but to interpret it differently in different markets. Thus a bank's relationship core identity might be presented with a more personal touch for the home market and a more professional touch for the business market, but the spirit and supporting culture would not change.

When multiple identities are needed, the goal should be to have a common set of associations, some of which will be in the core identity. The identity in each market would then be embellished, but in a way that is consistent with the common elements. The nonoverlapping associations should also avoid being inconsistent.

A brand identity might work in a new context if it is augmented. A major oil company needed to augment its identity for some South American settings to include accuracy at the pump, as some local competitors would cheat customers by not providing the gallons indicated. A specific application such as the Sony Walkman might augment the Sony identity of digital technology and entertainment to include some functional benefits appropriate to that product setting.

There can be cases in which even the core identity needs to change across markets, where interpretation and augmentation will not be enough. For example, Levi's is a prestige brand in Europe and the Far East, representing the best of the U.S. imports and supporting an extremely high price. In the United States, in contrast, the identity reflects more functional benefits and the authentic jean heritage. Citibank similarly needs to distinguish between the Far East, where it is a prestige brand, and the United States, where functional benefits play a larger role.

When multiple brand identities are potentially viable, two procedures can be employed. The top-down procedure is to create an identity for the total organization and then adapt that identity to different markets. The advantage is a common identity from which individual markets are unlikely to stray too far.

The bottom-up procedure establishes product- or market-defined organizational units, which are free to create the identity that best meets their needs. These different identities can then be reconciled, perhaps by teams representing the different organizational units. When doing this, Harley-Davidson found that a wide variety of teams created virtually the same identity; the result was one identity that had a lot of buy-in throughout the organization. In a computer company, four different product groups generated their own identities. In the reconciliation meeting, however, three of the four decided that an overall brand identity would work well for them, and the fourth needed only a minor augmentation. Again, the buy-in was strong because the result was generated by the decision makers rather than from above.

## 7. MAKE THE BRAND IDENTITY DRIVE THE EXECUTION

Given a brand identity as the basis of a brand strategy, the next step is to implement that strategy. A disconnect between the brand identity and the implementation, though, can sometimes occur because of an organizational problem. An advertising agency, for example, may develop a brand position that is not driven by the brand identity. Or the communications group may have only a dotted-line connection to the operating people charged with executing the business strategy.

One way to alleviate such problems is to ensure that there is buy-in throughout the organization. The examples in the previous section illustrated how you can create buy-in by having the people and organizations charged with implementation join the brand identity development process. Another solution is to ensure that the brand identity is communicated well; the elaborated identity can play a key role in this task. It is tragic when the brand has not been properly communicated to key people in agencies or companies running sponsorships, and they actually reinvent it.

Another helpful procedure is developing and refining the brand identity in the context of execution. It has been said that strategy *is* execution, and beginning some rough conceptualization of the execution while the brand identity is being created is one way to guarantee cohesion. This may involve expressing the brand identity visually and identifying one or more alternative executional thrusts.

## 8. ELABORATE THE BRAND IDENTITY

The brand identity is often ambiguous, especially when it is reduced to a few words or phrases. It therefore cannot effectively play its role of communicating what the brand stands for, inspiring employees and partners, and guiding decision making. In this case, elaborating the brand identity can be helpful and even necessary. The next chapter will discuss a variety of ways to elaborate the brand identity.

**QUESTIONS FOR DISCUSSION**

1. Develop alternative brand essence statements for Virgin Airlines.
2. Evaluate the brand essence statements listed in the text. What criteria are appropriate? Which seem to be the best? Identify some taglines that are particularly good brand essence statements. Why?
3. Does your brand have a strong position on a functional benefit? How is that being exploited? Has your brand moved beyond product attributes and functional benefits? How?
4. What customer insight is motivating your brand strategy?
5. Use ads or visuals or strategy statements to portray the positions of competitors. How is your brand differentiated from them?
6. Should your brand have multiple identities? Why? How?
7. Is your execution consistent with your strategy? Give a good example of on-strategy and off-strategy execution for your brand and a competitor.

# 3

# Clarifying and Elaborating the Brand Identity

Any CEO who cannot clearly articulate the intangible assets of his brand and understand its connection to customers is in trouble.
—Charlotte Beers, J. Walter Thompson

Stories constitute the single most powerful weapon in the leader's literary arsenal.
—Howard Gardner, Harvard professor and author of *Leading Minds*

The core identities for Saturn and also Gateway Computers include a relationship dimension—the brand is a friend to its customers. But what kind of friend is it? A party friend? A friend who is "there for you"? A traveling companion? A friend you go to baseball games with? A business friend? And how is this friendship different from partnership (Chevron) or relationship (Chase)? What role models, visual images, metaphors, and symbols mean friendship?

A core identity is often summarized by a small set of words or phrases such as Saturn's world-class car and treating customers as a friend or Mobil's leadership, partnership, and trust. Concepts such as quality, innovation, excitement, energy, rich taste, user friendliness, and relationship (as well as friendship, leadership, partnership, and trust) are key elements of the core identity of prominent brands. Unfortunately, though, these terms—whose terseness makes them easy to communicate and remember—can also be ambiguous and thus fail to provide the needed guidance and inspiration.

An extended identity can help resolve this ambiguity, albeit sometimes indirectly. When the personality for a brand based on friendship is detailed, for example, the type of friend emerges. Because
some ambiguity may remain, however, it can be useful to explicitly
elaborate on the words and phrases that represent the core identity.
Elaboration can also be used to clarify elements of the extended
identity (for example, brand personality dimensions like a sense of
humor or being reliable).

An explicit elaboration of the brand identity has three goals. First,
it should reduce ambiguity by adding interpretation and detail to the
elements of the brand identity, thereby making it easier to define
decisions and programs that will strengthen the brand. Second, it
should enhance decision makers' ability to assess the capacity of
identity dimensions to resonate with customers and differentiate the
brand. Third, elaboration can provide ideas and concepts that are
useful in developing on-target, effective brand-building efforts.

## DEFINING LEADERSHIP

Leadership is part of the core identity for many brands, especially
corporate brands, and with good reason. It can inspire employees
and partners by setting a high brand aspiration level; the goal of
being out in front makes the brand-building task exciting and worthwhile. For many customers, a leadership brand provides reassurance,
while for others it implies quality and/or innovation that translates
into solid functional benefits. Buying and using a true leadership
brand also delivers self-expressive benefits—a feeling of importance
and the satisfaction of having good judgment.

Leadership also provides an umbrella that captures a variety of
perspectives and activities. Such a broad meaning can be helpful, but
it can also become so all-encompassing that it ends up providing no
direction—too many communication approaches fit, and too few (or
even none) are excluded.

Consider some possible interpretations of leadership (examples in
parentheses):

- A *competent* leader with superior management skills (Citigroup)
- An *authoritative* leader who gets things done by edict (Microsoft)

- A *supportive* leader who encourages with positive reinforcement (Nordstrom)
- A *coach* who provides the tools and techniques to accomplish tasks (Schwab)
- A *"break the rules"* leader who introduces unusual and sometimes outrageous programs and actions (Virgin)
- An *innovative,* cutting-edge leader who pushes the technology boundaries (3M)
- A *successful* leader with a large market share (Coca-Cola)
- A *quality* leader who sets standards for excellence (Lexus)
- An *inspiring* leader who articulates values and mission (Levi Strauss)

The richness of the leadership brand concept is further illustrated by a study of twenty-three product categories, led by the advertising agency DMB&B under the direction of Joe Plummer. In the study, respondents were asked what was the leader brand in the category and why that brand was selected. The strategies of the resulting brands were then examined.

One finding was that leader brands are not perceived that way because they have high market shares (although some are high-share brands), but because of the trust and perceived quality they deliver. Another finding was that there are four different styles of leadership brands:

*Power brands* own a central category benefit and make continual improvements to maintain that leadership—for example, Gillette (the closest shave), Crest (healthiest teeth), Federal Express (fast, reliable delivery), and Volvo (safety).

*Explorer brands* tap people's desire to grow and learn, to achieve their potential—for example, Microsoft ("Where do you want to go today?"), Nike ("Just do it"), Body Shop (expresses social consciousness).

*Icon brands* symbolize some aspect of a country's national image and history that customers share emotionally—for example, Disney (childhood magic), Coca-Cola (universal friendship), Marlboro (freedom of the American West), and McDonald's (kids, family values).

*Identity brands* build a connection through user imagery, helping people express who they are—for example, Levi's (urban, hip), BMW (successful, upscale, a connoisseur), Birkenstock (nature-oriented values and lifestyle).

In the same study, when respondents were asked to name emerging leaders, they identified two distinct types:

*In-your-face brands* take on the leaders directly by adapting their strategy but doing it better or cheaper. These brands are differentiated in part by being aggressive and energetic—for example, MCI (save money over AT&T with innovative programs) and Pepsi (the Pepsi Challenge, "Generation Next").

*Different-paradigm brands* basically ignore the leader, who is considered irrelevant to the "new paradigm"—for example, Schwab (securities transactions without brokers), Southwest Airlines (no-frills city-to-city air travel delivered with value and a fun personality), and Amazon (the Internet bookstore).

There are many more perspectives on leadership than the handful we have just detailed. The challenge for any brand is to refine and clarify the concept so that it becomes more useful in providing direction. Even when different business units need to have varying perspectives on the same concept, it is still helpful to make the conceptualizations clear. This chapter is directed to that task.

## DEFINING BRAND PERSONALITY— THE L.L. BEAN STORY

L.L. Bean was founded in 1912 by Leon Leonwood Bean, an outdoorsman who lived in Freeport, Maine. The company's first product was a boot with waterproof rubber bottoms and lightweight leather tops, which represented a major advance over the heavy leather boots of the time. When the first 100 pairs sold through the mail had a stitching problem, Bean refunded the customers' money and started over—a decision that led to the legendary L.L. Bean "Guarantee of 100% Satisfaction" and heritage of quality and honesty. The signature boots were followed by a variety of products for those participating in hunting, fishing, and camping activities. Bean himself was active in proposing and testing products into the 1960s.

The L.L. Bean business, now with more than $1 billion in annual revenue, has always been based on catalog sales. The small retail presence on Main Street in Freeport that was developed in 1917 to service drop-by customers, however, has grown into a flagship, brand-statement store. Open twenty-four hours a day (to better serve early-morning hunters and fishermen), it has become a Maine tourist attraction, with more than 3.5 million visitors each year. Although L.L. Bean remains focused on camping, hunting, and fishing, the company has expanded its scope over the years to include casual and sports apparel and other products that are compatible with an outdoor lifestyle. Its core identity includes high-quality functional products, helpful service, and customers and employees who enjoy the outdoors.

Similarly, L.L. Bean wants to update its visual imagery from old-fashioned fishermen and campers with crude, antique equipment to a broader celebration of the outdoors and the passion of the back-country experience. The catalog cover in Figure 3–1 illustrates this goal.

FIGURE 3–1
*L.L. Bean—Celebrating the Outdoors*

The brand personality profile, developed to support L.L. Bean's brand-building activities, included these dimensions: friendly, honest, helpful, for the whole family, practical and economical, sense of humor, a guide, and having a healthy lifestyle. As these terms proved too abstract to provide the true essence of the L.L. Bean brand, over time they were elaborated as follows:

**Friendly**—L.L. Bean is easy to approach because it cares about its customers. It is comfortable and familiar, without pretension.

**Honest**—L.L. Bean is straightforward and open; it would never mislead consumers. The company always presents itself and its products in a factual, no-nonsense manner.

**Helpful**—L.L. Bean's customer service is legendary. Treating its customers well is central to the way it does business, and has been since L.L. founded the company. Employees will do anything they can to help customers, whether it is helping to choose the most appropriate L.L. Bean product for a particular activity or providing answers to questions about the outdoors.

**For the whole family**—While the company's somewhat male image comes from its hunting and fishing heritage and from its founder, L.L. Bean now offers products and services for the entire outdoor-oriented family.

**Practical and economical**—L.L. Bean focuses on the kinds of products and attributes that enhance functionality. Its products are designed in a spirit of Yankee ingenuity, are priced fairly, and perform with an honest, no-nonsense style.

**Sense of humor**—L.L. Bean has always had an appropriate perspective on the role it plays in its customers' lives. It never takes itself too seriously and maintains a classic Yankee sense of humor.

**A guide**—L.L. Bean embodies many of the characteristics that one associates with someone who has expertise and knows the lay of the land.

**Healthy lifestyle**—L.L. Bean customers and employees have an abiding belief in the enduring benefits of outdoor activities and exercise. They consider their time spent in the outdoors to be a major contributor to their physical and mental fitness and therefore to their overall quality of life.

These elaborated personality dimensions clarify what the brand stands for and provide substantial guidance to brand-building programs. For example, the elaborated friendliness dimension might suggest comfortable, familiar merchandise displayed unpretentiously in the catalog and stores. Straightforward honesty also suggests presenting products in a factual, no-nonsense manner. The practical and economical dimension is translated into products and attributes designed to enhance functionality. Finally, the brand as a guide provides a metaphor that suggests expertise, a cornerstone of the Bean heritage.

The elaborated personality also suggests how the L.L. Bean image may need to be expanded. The brand is perceived to be very male, but the personality profile suggests that it includes the whole family. Further, Bean's no-nonsense image should not be allowed to imply that the brand takes itself too seriously. Finally, the brand's New England heritage should not suggest an elderly, old-fashioned country bumpkin but a contemporary person with a passion for the outdoors.

## IDENTITY ELABORATION EXERCISES

To recap, the brand identity, particularly the core identity and the brand essence, will often be represented with single words or compact phrases. Elaboration can make the identity less ambiguous and thus more useful as a guide to brand-building programs.

In the following pages, several brand identity elaboration exercises are described. These exercises can be performed by groups of representative employees or partners who know what the brand stands for and are involved in implementing the vision.

The four categories of exercises are summarized in Figure 3–2. The *audit of identity-supporting programs* reviews the substance behind the brand identity aspirations. *Identity role models* are actions and programs that communicate the brand. The development of *visual metaphors* provides another way to make the identity more vivid. And *brand identity prioritization* determines which dimension should be the focus of positioning and the brand-building efforts.

Ultimately, some kind of communication device, which can be labeled the Identity Elaboration Presentation, will emerge. It can take the form of a book, a video, a visual collage, and/or a handbook. Some efforts to create such instruments are discussed at the end of this chapter.

FIGURE 3–2
*Brand Identity Elaboration*

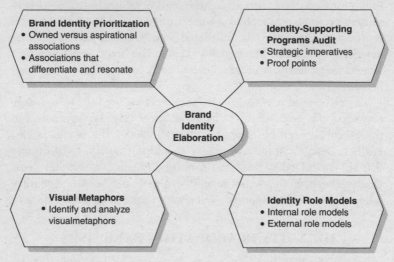

## IDENTITY-SUPPORTING PROGRAM AUDIT

The identity needs to be true to the firm and have substance behind it; it should not be simply an exercise in branding and advertising. Effectively communicating a clear, differentiated brand vision that resonates with customers is not enough. The organization needs to be willing to support the identity with substantial investment in real programs. Identifying the substance and programs supporting the brand provides an elaboration of the brand identity that can be both vivid and tangible.

Two types of programs and investments can support the brand: planned and existing. The first involves strategic imperatives, future programs that must be developed in order to deliver on the brand identity. Proof points that catalog existing programs, initiatives, and assets which support the brand identity describe the second.

### STRATEGIC IMPERATIVES—LINKING BRAND IDENTITY TO BUSINESS STRATEGY

A brand identity statement implies a promise to customers and a commitment by the organization. A strategic imperative is an investment in an asset or program that is essential if the promise to customers is to be delivered.[1] What organizational capabilities and assets are implied by the brand identity? What investments are needed in order to deliver the promise to customers? Some illustrations are provided below.

## A Regional Bank Brand

Core identity includes

Personal and professional relationship with each customer

Strategic imperatives include

Customer database. Equip each customer contact person with access to all of the customer's accounts so that the management of one customer relationship is integrated with all of the others.

Customer service. Develop and implement a program to improve the interpersonal skills of customer contact people. Include a measurement system.

## A New Premium Audio Equipment Subbrand

Core identity includes

The highest quality

Technological leader

Strategic imperatives include

In-house manufacturer rather than external sourcing to control quality

Expanded R&D program on digital technology

## A Value Subbrand for a Household Cleaning Product

Core identity includes

The value brand with competitive quality

Strategic imperatives include

Becoming the low-cost manufacturer

Development of an organizational unit that has a cost culture

The strategic imperatives represent action steps that are needed to deliver substance behind the brand identity. These action steps are thus clearly a part of the brand-building effort—in fact, efforts to revitalize or reposition a brand sometimes are best delayed so that they may be synchronized with the strategic initiatives. In any case, brand building must be more than a dream, or a communication and packaging program; it needs an investment program with a timetable and budget.

Perhaps as important, the strategic imperatives represent a reality check where the investments needed become visible and the feasibility of the brand strategy is assessed. Are the investment resources available? Is the commitment from the organization really there? Is the organization capable of the initiatives that are required? If the answer to any of these questions is no, the organization is unable or unwilling to deliver behind the brand promise. The promise will then become an empty advertising slogan that at best will be a waste of resources, and at worst create a brand liability instead of an asset.

In the previous examples, if the regional bank is not willing to invest the tens of millions necessary to create the database needed to allow appropriate customer interaction, then the relationship bank concept will need to be rethought. If the audio components firm is not willing to design and manufacture its products, a high-end brand may be doomed. If the household cleaning product manufacturer is not willing to create a subunit with a real cost culture, then entering the value market will be a recipe for failure.

Ed Resic, the chief marketing officer at The Limited, once noted that you cannot beat the leader by matching its brand with a parity product. You have to beat it decisively with real substance, which usually involves investment guided by strategic imperatives. A new brand name, position, or personality, or an increase in visibility, will rarely be enough by itself. Where there is substance, however, a strong brand can make the difference between a winner and loser.

The strategic imperative concept suggests that the brand identity should drive the business strategy. This may seem like a bit of a stretch, but it is sometimes an accurate description of the process. The best-case scenario, of course, is when the strategic imperatives involve initiatives that are already under way; then, there is a clear compatibility between the brand strategy and the existing business strategy. If the business strategy is not clearly developed, however, a serious brand identity development effort is often the catalyst for a sharper focus. The strategic imperatives play a key role because they usually introduce some hard choices and lead to the consideration of key options and core issues facing the organization.

When an organization has a well-articulated business strategy supported by a strong culture, the brand identity and strategy are often relatively easy to develop. When the organizational business strategy and culture are fuzzy, though, the brand identity creation effort can be agonizingly difficult. The brand identity in these situations can serve not only to stimulate but also to articulate a major part of the business strategy and the culture.

## PROOF POINTS

While strategic imperatives are organizational initiatives requiring significant investment, proof points are already attached to the dimensions of the brand identity. Proof points are programs, initiatives, and assets already in place that provide substance to the core identity and help communicate what it means. While strategic imperatives are usually few in number and often costly and risky, proof points can be numerous and operational. A brand identity strategy based solely on what is going to happen in the future is at risk for two reasons: the imperatives may not get funded or executed properly, and, even if they are, customer perceptions may not change. Thus, proof points are a necessary foundation.

For example, a core identity dimension for Nordstrom might be customer concern. Proof points would be any assets, skills, programs, or initiatives that support the customer concern thrust, including the following:

- A current reputation for customer service
- A current return policy that is well-known and has credibility
- A compensation program geared to rewarding customer service
- The quality of the current staff and hiring program
- An empowerment policy permitting innovative responses to customer concerns

L.L. Bean has an identity dimension of being geared toward outdoor enthusiasts. Proof points in this case include the brand's heritage and the assets, policies, and programs directed at making L.L. Bean differentiated on that dimension:

- A flagship store that stays open twenty-four hours a day for the convenience of outdoor-oriented customers
- The expertise and professionalism of the customer contact staff, which allow them to offer value-added advice on outdoor activities

When a large firm such as GE, Hewlett-Packard, or Sony has multiple businesses attached to a brand, it can determine whether a core identity element (for example, leadership) will fit in all sectors by discussing proof points with people from the different product groups or different geographic sectors. If all groups can provide proof points showing that leadership is credible as an identity element, then the organization can be more confident in using it as a basis for positioning.

# IDENTITY ROLE MODEL IDENTIFICATION

Communicating a brand identity with lists of bulleted points ultimately can be ambiguous and uninteresting, because such lists fail to capture the emotion of the brand and its vision. Identifying role models can provide the meaning and emotion to help motivate and guide the brand-building effort. We will consider two types—internal role models (that is, those from within the organization) and external role models.

### INTERNAL ROLE MODELS

Internal role models are stories, programs, events, or people that perfectly represent the brand identity—they hit the bull's-eye. Out of five proof points supporting an identity, there might be one program that really reflects the identity best. For example, Nordstorm's return policy may be the most vivid demonstration of its customer focus. An event such as the company-sponsored party in Spring Hill, Tennessee, for all Saturn owners says a lot about the firm's relationship with its customers and how Saturn is indeed a different kind of company.

Stories can communicate the identity and add elements of aspiration and emotion as well. Some of these actions can be legends that are part of the brand heritage—the story of an engineer flying to Alaska to replace a defective seat, for example, reflects Saturn's respect for customers. Or the story of how the 3M Post-it Notes concept began with a 3M engineer who needed a bookmark that would not flutter to the floor while he sang in the choir reflects the innovation that is part of the company's core identity. And the story of how Johnson & Johnson responded to the Tylenol poison scare by pulling its products from stores and redesigning the package clearly indicates how highly the firm values its reputation for trust and safety.

Stories and other internal role models can be powerful communication devices. Psychologists tell us that three times more information can be communicated in story form than by using bulleted lists. Stories potentially can be rich and unambiguous, qualities usually absent in a bulleted list; even so, managers mostly communicate using lists. The emotion attached to stories is important, because those implementing the brand must know *and* care about what it stands for. In fact, stories not only represent the brand but also influence the culture. As Richard Stone, the head of the StoryWork Institute, noted, "To change an organization, you have to change its stories."[2]

Sometimes, particularly when a change in brand image is needed, new role models must be found. In part to identify such role models, Mobil ran a contest that asked its employees to name the programs and activities that best represented its core identity elements of leadership, partnership, and trust. The winner had access to the infield at a major car race for which Mobil was one of the sponsors. The contest received more than three hundred entries and got the entire organization involved in the brand identity. A useful by-product was a set of internal role models that could help elaborate the brand identity and give it depth and emotion.

### Personalize the brand

People, such as a founder or a strong, visible CEO with a clear brand vision, can be powerful role models. Williams-Sonoma pioneers Chuck Williams and Howard Lester have a clear, well-articulated view of what their company should stand for—culinary expertise, serious cooks, best-of-category offerings, style reflecting taste and flair, and innovation in cooking, serving, and entertaining. Williams-Sonoma believes in function first, with no gimmicks. Personalizing the brand identity gives employees and partners both clarity and emotional commitment: Would Chuck or Howard carry that piece, or display it that way? Such a question usually settles the matter.

The impact of the founders can be made more vivid if their picture is a brand symbol, as in the cases of Charles Schwab (broker), Norton Software (now Symantec), and the Smith Brothers (cough drops). When the name and picture are on the door, so to speak, the founder not only is there in spirit but actually appears to be watching over what is being done. Some founders, like Bill Gates of Microsoft and Richard Branson of Virgin, are not formally included in the brand's symbol, but their faces are so familiar (not only to employees but also to others) that the result is similar.

At Williams-Sonoma the founders' touch is still visible; however, L.L. Bean is now a legend rather than a physical presence. Nevertheless, the L.L. Bean brand identity is still rooted in the founder's values and concepts: practical, innovative outdoor wear, guaranteed 100 percent satisfaction, quality, and honesty. Wrapping the L.L. Bean brand identity around the founder gives it credibility as well as clarity.

Bath and Body Works, a Limited company, did not have a founder like Chuck Williams or L.L. Bean strongly associated with the brand, so it created a typical user: Kate, a thirty-two-year-old woman with two kids who lives in a rural area and does handwork (a part of the Bath and Body Works core identity is "handmade and heartfelt"). A graduate of Miami University of Ohio, she has a healthy lifestyle and wholesome midwestern values. The litmus test at Bath and Body Works is whether Kate would like it. At another Limited company, Victoria's Secret, the original founder is represented by a symbolic stand-in named Vickie; the question "Would Vickie do that?" carries a lot of weight. Such personification of the brand strategy makes it easier to implement the strategy with discipline. Everyone is not only more likely to know what to do (and not do) but also more likely to believe and care because of the founder or symbol's charisma.

There are many ways to personalize the brand. When the University of California football program had one player who represented everything they wanted to stand for, they used him as a role model to guide the recruiting plan in the future. A brand can also be personified by a visible spokesperson who becomes closely connected to the brand over the years. Examples include the Maytag repairman, Bill Cosby for Jell-O, Michael Jordan for Nike, and Peter Lynch for Fidelity. Alternatively, employees can represent a brand, as Saturn illustrates by featuring assembly workers in its ads to demonstrate their commitment to building a world-class car and treating customers with respect.

Identification of internal role models starts with what is visible. The candidates will usually be well-known, especially to the veterans in the organization. Difficulty identifying role models, in fact, might be a signal that there is inadequate empowerment throughout the organization.

## EXTERNAL ROLE MODELS

Although internal role models can be extremely powerful because they are already in the context of the brand, they are limited to what has been done within the organization. Casting the net wider to dozens or even hundreds of organizations usually results in role models with more impact and imagination.

Other strong, well-positioned brands from diverse industries can be role models and, as such, can be a powerful metaphor for your brand. The search for an external brand role model can be broad: What brand do you admire? Which comes closest to how you would like to be perceived?

Thus a bank that aspires to be a trusted adviser, offering a broad array of financial services in a friendly but competent style, might look to Home Depot as a role model. Home Depot carries a wide variety of merchandise, has an approachable and friendly image, and gives customers knowledgeable and unpretentious help. Another bank aspiring to communicate to customers its team-based approach to delivering an array of financial services might look to Y&R, which delivers communication services using multifunctional teams organized around clients' needs.

When Tony Blair became the prime minister of the United Kingdom, he conceptualized the "New Britain" as a brand whose identity included elements such as openness, Europe and technology, multiculturalism, and female power.[3] Blair's staff also looked for brands that most represented the New Britain. The identities of top brands on the scale (Häagen-Dazs, Twinings herbal tea, Hooch, New Covent Garden Soup, Linda McCartney Meals, Shape yogurt, and Phileas Fogg) not only clarified the New Britain brand but also provided directions for cross-promotional brand building.

A sports utility vehicle brand that aspires to be chosen by outdoor enthusiasts might productively look to brands like L.L. Bean or REI for brand-building ideas. A perfume that aspires to be sophisticated might look to *Vogue* or Tiffany's for a role model. A line of frozen food desiring a healthy positioning might look to fitness clubs.

With an external role model identified, the next step is to learn as much as possible: Why is it a good role model? How did it develop authenticity and credibility? What are its stories and internal role models? Its proof points? What is its culture? Is there anything that can be learned or borrowed?

Another tack is to focus on one of your brand's core identity elements (for example, leadership or relationship), then identify a set of brands that also focus on a similar dimension. These brands should be drawn from a variety of product classes to generate the widest spectrum of interpretations of the core identity element as well as possible ways to achieve the sought-after image.

Now ask yourself: Which of these brands are positive role models? Which represent the interpretation of the core identity element that your brand is striving for? Which were effective at communicating the identity? For instance, innovation is a core brand identity element for 3M, Kao, Sony, HP, and Williams-Sonoma; what could each of these companies learn from the others' brand identity efforts? Questions like this almost always lead to fresh thinking and insights.

Similarly, which brands are not good role models, even though they might emphasize the same core identity element? Why not? Which brands were ineffective at communicating the right image, and why? Determining which perspectives on a dimension like leadership or innovation do not fit your brand will help make the correct perspective clearer.

### Boundaries

It is helpful to identify not only external role models that are on target but also those that define the boundaries of the brand identity. In a given role model category, what objects are "too much" and which are "not enough" with respect to brand personality? For example, one snack-food brand clarified its identity by positioning other brands, basketball players, ice cream flavors, and movie stars with respect to its identity.[4] The first table on page 81 shows the results.

In another example, managers thought their department store needed to be revitalized to compete with specialty stores that were encroaching on its market. It was clear that the store's image

*Brand Personality*

|  | NOT ENOUGH | ON TARGET | TOO MUCH |
|---|---|---|---|
| **Soft drink** | Coke | Pepsi | Mountain Dew |
| **Candy** | Plain M&Ms | Peanut M&Ms | Skittles |
| **Basketball player** | David Robinson | Michael Jordan | Dennis Rodman |
| **Ice cream** | Vanilla | Chocolate Chip | Chunky Monkey |
| **Movie star** | Tom Hanks | Mel Gibson | Jim Carrey |

needed more energy and vitality. Programs were put in place to make a difference; they included a sporting goods section with a host of hands-on demonstrations, an audio section with involving demonstrations, and a fashion section with a presentation that had real flair. Now that the brand identity included a dimension of energy and vitality, the question was what *level* of energy and vitality. A spectrum was conceived, and retail brands were positioned on it (see table below).

Wow! would be an audacious and inspiring target, but unrealistic, especially over time. The store would need to continuously renew itself to retain the Wow! label. On the other hand, Delighted did not seem ambitious enough. Excited, though, seemed right. The conception of the scale and the positioning of role models on it helped the store managers refine the execution of their brand identity programs.

An on-line gift-giving brand, Red Envelope, included "authoritative" among its core identity elements. To sort out exactly what

*In-Store Experience*

**Boring**—Subway, Staples, Costco, ALDI, Kmart, CVS

**Pleasant**—Macy's, Toys-R-Us, Pizza Hut, Ethan Allen, ShellShop, Benetton

**Delighted**—Saks, Wal-Mart, Foot Locker, McDonald's, Ikea, Hallmark

**Excited**—Nordstrom, Gap, Victoria's Secret, Hard Rock Café, Williams-Sonoma, Barnes & Noble

**Wow!**—NikeTown, Urban Outfitters, Starbucks, Crate & Barrel, Virgin Megastore, Harrod's

*Authority*

| | PERSONAL | | | PROFESSIONAL | | | |
| | Two-way communication | | | One-way communication | | | |
|---|---|---|---|---|---|---|---|
| **Role Models** | Peer | Mentor | Teacher | Expert | Innovator | Institutional | Religious |
| **Examples** | Kate | Lynette Jennings | Bill Walsh | Martha Stewart | Steve Jobs | Alan Greenspan | The Pope |
| **Character- istics** | Validating Approachable | Aspiration Wisdom | Knowledge Admiration | Skill Credibility | Visionary Innovative | Logical Power | Respect Spiritual Force |

authoritative meant in this context, Prophet Brand Strategy used a scale that went from personal, two-way communication to professional, one-way communication. Seven role models were positioned along the scale and characteristics of each were suggested. As a result, the concepts of insightful, visionary, approachable, and validating were selected as being representative of the desired authoritative posture. Interestingly, they were not clustered in the scale.

## VISUAL METAPHOR DEVELOPMENT

Core identities are defined verbally—that is, a few words or phrases attempt to capture what the brand should stand for. Yet consider the following premises put forward by Gerald Zaltman, a prominent consumer behavior professor at Harvard. Based on his study of research in psychology and linguistics:[5]

- Most communication (70 to 90 percent, by most estimates) is nonverbal. Visual imagery has been shown in a host of contexts to be much more powerful than verbal communication in affecting both perceptions and memory.
- Metaphors (the explication of one thing in terms of another—for instance, as graceful as a cat) are basic to the representation of thought. Linguists have shown that metaphors are powerful communication tools. According to Zaltman, "One implication of this premise is that methods designed to elicit and analyze metaphors systematically could significantly augment knowledge gained from more literal, verbocentric research approaches."

These premises suggest that there is a lot of scientific truth in the adage that "one picture is worth a thousand words." So why not attempt to translate verbal core identities into visual metaphors?

Suppose the core identity of a financial service firm is strength. Potential visual metaphors could be a steel girder, a heavyweight boxer, an Egyptian pyramid, or a fortress. Even though all imply strength, some will probably reflect the desired image more than others. Often, visual metaphors can reveal a considerable spectrum behind what seems to be a simple concept.

On-strategy visual metaphors can powerfully communicate the core identity to those involved in implementing the brand identity. Plus, the process of working with visual metaphors has the side benefit of getting team members to think about what represents their brand and what does not.

### IDENTIFYING RELEVANT METAPHORS

The first step is to identify visual metaphors that either represent the brand or the brand identity, or represent the opposite. Customers, for example, can be asked to suggest visual metaphors representing the core identity element (such as friendship or leadership). These images, drawn from magazines and other sources, could involve a wide variety of stimuli, including animals, books, people, activities, or landscapes. Participants could also be given a camera and asked to take pictures of images that they felt were on-strategy subjects. In addition, they could collect images that were the opposite of the core brand identity—the most off-strategy they could find.

To obtain visual metaphors without involving customers, you might examine brands that have images close to the identity under study. What visual cues are associated with each of these brands? What colors, images, metaphors, or feelings? Gold is a color that is associated with premium in most categories. The Gap uses plain, white designs and layouts to suggest contemporary styling and freshness. Eddie Bauer uses a lot of earth tones, with landscapes, snow, and motion to represent the outdoors.

To prune down a large number of visual metaphors to a manageable set, cluster them into groups. Representative elements from each group can be scaled as to how closely they represent the identity elements.

### ANALYZING METAPHORS

The next step is to analyze the images that you have gathered. What makes them on or off strategy? What characteristics are key? The ultimate goal is not so much to identify a key metaphor but to learn what makes a metaphor right or wrong for the strategy and its communication.

### Visual Positioning

SHR, a Scottsdale design firm, uses a visual positioning methodology to develop and interpret metaphors. They start with a strategic core identity element (like strength, warmth, leadership, or ruggedness), then find a dozen or so images that are relevant to the concept but vary in topic and tone. Subjects are asked to rank these images from the most perfect representation of the target construct to the least, then explain the order they selected. This exercise provides not only a richer vision of the strategic construct but also a set of visual stimuli that can provide direction for later creative efforts. The best result, although rare, is the discovery of an ownable visual metaphor for the brand.

## BRAND IDENTITY PRIORITIZATION

As a multidimensional portrayal of the brand, the brand identity can be complex. A brand might have associations that reflect product attributes, personality dimensions, organizational associations, symbols, and user images. How can such a conceptually messy portrayal be prioritized? Here are some hints.

The core identity plays a key role in providing focus to the brand identity, as does the brand essence—a word or phrase that represents much of what the brand stands for. Another approach to prioritization, however, which is almost always helpful, involves comparing the image to the identity and assessing the ability to leverage each dimension.

### LEVERAGING VERSUS CHANGING ASSOCIATIONS

Each element of the identity should be compared to the current brand image and heritage in order to clearly specify the communication task. What associations need to be changed or added, as opposed to maintained or leveraged? A key decision in setting priorities with respect to the brand identity is whether to leverage owned associations (the current image/heritage) or move toward the new strategic thrust of the brand by changing these associations.

For example, take an oil exploration and production support firm known as the best in the business, a firm that always delivers innovative, problem-solving solutions. One communication option is to reflect the superior performance and people; a brand essence such as "We deliver" or "Innovation and quality" would ring true and remind those delivering the service of the high-quality tradition. Suppose, however, that in the future the firm needs to be more synergistic, operating with cross-functional teams involving customers and different units in the company. Should the brand essence reflect the new strategic thrust, even though the company has not yet acquired this competence? In this case, an aspirational essence such as "The team delivers" would be part of a culture-changing program. Not an easy call.

Many brands with strong heritages (such as Sears, John Deere, Oldsmobile, AT&T, Maytag, Merrill Lynch, L.L. Bean, and Kodak) have associations of being trustworthy, delivering high quality, and being technologically solid, but also a bit old-fashioned and bureaucratic. Most would classify these associations as follows:

Maintain—Trustworthy, responsive, reliable, high-quality, and ethical

Enhance and leverage—Technologically solid, knowledgeable, and global

Reduce or eliminate—Old-fashioned, slow, overpriced, and bureaucratic

Add—Contemporary, energetic, and innovative

Unfortunately, few brand identities can achieve all of these goals at once. What associations should take priority? Again, the choice is not easy.

The decision whether to leverage owned associations or develop new associations rests on two questions. First, can the owned associations carry the load in the current competitive arena, or is it imperative that new associations be developed? Second, is it possible to make a convincing claim that the new associations are deserved, or will the claims lack credibility and substance (and thereby risk damaging the core associations)?

Building on owned associations means reinforcing and reminding customers of something that they already know and believe—a relatively easy task. Staking out new ground for the brand is a much more difficult and expensive job. Leveraging owned associations is thus the preferred course, assuming they are effective. If they are strong but a bit tired and familiar, perhaps they can be refreshed in message and in substance to provide a revitalized competitive advantage. IBM, for example, used the e-business subbrand to make an association it owned, technological leadership, more dynamic, relevant, and contemporary.

In some cases, though, new associations may be so central to the brand's future in the market that pursuing them is vital. It may be absolutely necessary, for example, for Bank of America to be perceived as more human, for TCI to be perceived as more technologically innovative, or for J. Walter Thompson to be perceived as more capable of providing broad communication solutions. If so, it might be worthwhile to emphasize aspirational associations even if the organization cannot yet deliver on them.

Focusing on new associations involves dealing with a credibility issue. Is it possible to make the claim in a convincing manner that the new associations are deserved? In part, the answer depends on substance. Are there programs and assets in place to underlie claims? If not, it may be prudent, indeed even necessary, to wait until programs and results do materialize before attempting to move the brand. In the meantime, develop an internal brand communication program based on the new associations, then introduce these associations into the external communication program after the substance is in place and the internal brand-building programs have borne fruit.

By stretching to include new associations, of course, the brand may risk its core image position. Lexus owned associations of quality, smooth driving, and comfort in its class of car supported by "The Relentless Pursuit of Perfection"; however, the firm felt that a lack of energy and excitement was holding the brand back. The brand thus took a risk by moving from this safe haven into a much edgier direction that suggested a driving experience more like BMW, which was supported by the revised tagline "The Relentless Pursuit of Exhilaration." The gamble was that the brand could retain quality and comfort while stretching the product and image and that the stretch could be made in a credible way. Volvo made an analogous move by stretching its brand identity beyond safety to something more stylish in order to make the purchase more acceptable to a larger audience. The trick often is to stretch without walking away from or being inconsistent with the core image heritage.

### The internal brand image

The brand identity needs to guide an internal communication effort as well. Employees and partners need to be on the same page. When the brand identity lacks consensus and clarity, it is unlikely to be realized. Regis McKenna, the Silicon Valley marketing guru, tells about a critical time in the life of Apple when the organization was internally torn between wanting to be like Sony (lively and fun) and wanting to be like IBM (a serious partner for the business enterprise).[6] It is difficult to build a brand with such a dichotomy in place.

To see if your internal brand image needs support, try the following challenge suggested by Lynn Upshaw, a San Francisco advertising strategist. Ask employees and communication partners two questions:

• Do you know what the brand stands for?
• Do you care?

If the brand identity promise is to be achieved, the answer to both questions must be yes.

The internal communication task should place a higher priority on new associations because they need to be in place internally before they will be a factor externally. The challenge is to communicate, motivate, and inspire employees and partners to understand and care about the new associations. The brand identity is the North Star, and eliminating departures in internal perceptions that are important enough to misguide strategy should be a priority.

### FINDING ASSOCIATIONS THAT DIFFERENTIATE AND RESONATE

The identity elements also need to be prioritized with respect to their ability to differentiate the brand from competitors and resonate with customers. The decision whether to build on the existing associations or to move the associations in a new direction will depend on how much leverage the respective identity dimensions have in creating customer interest and loyalty. This leverage, in turn, will depend on how much each dimension differentiates and resonates with customers. Scaling each identity dimension along these two criteria is a useful exercise.

Some identity elements that are important legs of the brand strategy, however, are neither differentiating nor relevant to customer decisions. They are the price of entry, characteristics that all participating brands are expected to deliver. For example, an acceptable and consistent quality level is absolutely critical, but it is not something that can differentiate a brand. The challenge is to identify or create associations that do differentiate or resonate.

### Differentiation

Using Young & Rubicam's Brand Asset Valuator database in which more than 13,000 brands in 33 countries have been measured on over 35 dimensions, Stuart Agres, a Y&R brand veteran, has persuasively argued that differentiation is the key to strong brands.[7] Successful brands such as Kinko's, Teva shoes, and Swatch start with high differentiation scores and relatively low scores on relevance (personal appropriateness of the brand), esteem (perceived quality and popularity), and knowledge (how well the brand is known by a respondent), and brands that fade or fail seem to lose differentiation first. Some get very sick when differentiation fades even though esteem and knowledge remain high. Thus differentiation is key to the dynamics of brands.

Even two competing brands that share a common brand identity element can be differentiated by diverging interpretations and companion associations. For example, relationship is a powerful core identity element that many financial service firms adopt. One brand's relationship might be based on being a supportive friend, however, while that of another is based on being a competent professional. Thus two very different programs and brand personalities could grow out of the same concept.

In addition to being able to create points of differentiation, a brand must also own those points of differentiation over time. There is little value to differentiation that is not sustainable. Thus each dimension should be evaluated in terms of differentiation:

- Can this association provide a point of differentiation?
- Can this association be owned by the brand over time?

### Customer resonance

An association that resonates with the customer because it is both relevant and meaningful has significant brand-building potential. Ultimately the brand needs to deliver a value proposition—functional benefits, emotional benefits, and/or self-expressive benefits. Thus an identity dimension that provides relevant, meaningful benefits should play a central role in the brand-building efforts. Spectracide (the leading weed killer from Home Depot) and Gillette are among brands that have high customer resonance because their customer value proposition is highly relevant.

Thus, a second characteristic of a high-priority identity dimension is its ability to create customer resonance:

- Does this association resonate with the customer?
- Will it contribute by delivering functional, emotional, and/or self-expressive benefits?

### Differentiation plus resonance

Strong brands often have several associations that are high on both differentiation and customer resonance. In the brand identity of Virgin, for example, the underdog role, delivering innovative customer service, being fun and entertaining, and offering real value are highly differentiating and tend to resonate with customers. An association that has only one of the two properties may not be very powerful. Thus even though Ford's "Quality Is Job One" association is probably important to customers, it may have ceased to differentiate the brand as others have improved their quality. Conversely, an extreme music group or a high-end brand like Rolls-Royce may be differentiated but lack relevance. When prioritizing the brand identity, the goal is to identify associations that both differentiate *and* resonate with customers.

## PRESENTING THE ELABORATED IDENTITY

A key step in implementing a brand identity is communicating it to organizational members and partners. To be effective the communication needs to create exposure, engender understanding, and be motivating. This communication can take several forms, including presentations by brand spokespeople, workshops, videos, books, or manuals.

## CREATING VIDEOS

A video is a powerful way to communicate a brand identity. The marketing team of The Limited, a firm with a dozen or so retail brands including The Limited, Victoria's Secret, Express, Bath and Body Works, and Structure, realized that their people (and those of its partners) needed to develop a deeper understanding of the brand identity of their stores. Accordingly, for each brand a video was created that contained no dialogue, only music and a collage of visuals representing what the brand stands for. The videos play a huge role in communicating the brands to those who must represent them, particularly new salespeople.

Saturn developed a two-hour video on the identity and heritage of its brand, using the CEO, union leader, agency president, manufacturing people, and engineers who helped start the company to capture the philosophy of the brand ("A different kind of company, a different kind of car"). The Saturn effort is somewhat ironic, as the brand is so young that it barely has a history, and it may be the GM brand with the least need to worry about team members not knowing its heritage and philosophy. The video, however, helps make sure that Saturn never has that problem.

## CREATING A BOOK

When Volvo wanted to expand its brand identity beyond safety and security for families, it created a twenty-page glossy book entitled "Communicating Volvo Cars; One of the World's Great Brands." The objective of this book, plus a thirty-page supplement with definitions and guidelines, was to elaborate on what the brand stands for and how its identity should be communicated to the people and organizations involved with the communication process.

The Volvo book starts with a description of where the brand is today, including its strong reputation for safety, quality, and care for the environment. Another section describes the target audience of "affluent progressives" as modern, well-educated, socially conscious, cosmopolitan, and active, with a strong need to express individuality but indifferent to traditional prestige and status symbols. As a subtle indicator of the company's desire to change its identity, there are no images of families. A third section talks about the associations that result from Volvo's Scandinavian origins—nature, human values, security and health, elegant simplicity, creative engineering, and the spirit of stylish/innovative functionality.

The seven elements of Volvo's new brand identity are described in the book along with an elaboration that shows how each element is expressed.

| BRAND IDENTITY ELEMENT | EXPRESSED BY |
| --- | --- |
| Leader in safety and security | Reverence/respect for life/love, care for others, peace of mind |
| World-class quality | Authenticity, integrity, self-esteem |
| Among leaders in environmental care | Responsibility, care for others, self-esteem |
| Attractive and distinctive design | Individuality, sophistication, taste |
| Pleasure to drive | Comfort, control, freedom, enjoyment |
| Pleasure to own | Peace of mind, convenience |
| Maximized perceived value | Economic well-being, satisfaction |

The brand identity summary is:

"style, driving pleasure and superior ownership experience while celebrating human values and respecting the environment."

A far cry from safety and security!

The book also suggests the tone that all communication should employ—namely, the "love of life, humanity, warmth, intelligence, and honesty"—as another part of Volvo's strategy to move the needle on style, warmth, and driving pleasure. The book does much more than communicate this message verbally; of its roughly three dozen often-dramatic photos, two-thirds do not involve the car.

### CREATING A BRAND MANUAL

Some organizations go beyond a book to provide a detailed manual that indicates exactly how the brand is to be communicated worldwide. One brand has a 350-page manual with detailed communication guidelines, including the target audience specification, the brand identity, the core identity, the brand essence, the identity elaboration, and exactly how the logo and other symbols are to be presented—color, typeface, layout, and so on. The visuals to be used and to be avoided are also explained. With respect to global brand building, three categories of guidelines as to what autonomy country managers have are clearly identified:

Nonnegotiable guidelines (such as the logo presentation—no autonomy)

Negotiable guidelines (local implementation of advertising—some autonomy)

Local authority (development of promotions within certain parameters—considerable autonomy)

A manual of this type provides the ultimate guidelines in managing a brand worldwide. It needs, however, to be a permanent work-in-progress—the global brand manager must continually update it as the market evolves and new best practices are uncovered. Moreover, if a brand has not found a strategy that really works, the manual should be less explicit. Only when a brand has hit its stride with a successful identity, position, and execution will it make sense for the manual to be fully detailed, because then it will provide the institutional memory and discipline needed to keep brand identity communication consistent over time.

## PACKAGING THE STORIES

Stories are powerful ways to vividly communicate the brand identity and its heritage. Many are the source of legend and get passed on, while others get lost to posterity unless the organization actively packages them. PriceWaterhouseCoopers has developed a digital storytelling format based on roughly seventy short videos crafted from home movies, still photos, and video tapes.[8] A presenter draws on this database to tell groups of employees stories that reflect the brand identity in an entertaining way.

## HOME STUDY MATERIALS

Berendsen is a Danish company that has bought dozens of small laundry operations and is forming a national organization that will provide not only laundry services but also storage and distribution of textile supplies. The business concept requires that employees understand the new brand identity, value proposition, and customer relationship. Toward this end, Berendsen has created a four-week home study course where employees receive simple study materials with both text and images. Each week employees go through the materials, then participate in a quiz in order to qualify for a reward. The program allows Berendsen to reach all organizational members and get them involved in the revised brand.

## THE BRAND IDENTITY REVISITED

In order to be communicated effectively, a brand identity needs to be punchy, memorable, focused, and motivating. An excessively terse description, however, results in ambiguity and the risk that the identity will not play the guiding role that it should. In addition, jumping directly from identity creation to communication can easily result in programs that are off strategy, without a real link to the identity. By extending and elaborating the identity, an organization can provide the needed richness and texture that will guide effective and consistent communication programs.

### QUESTIONS TO CONSIDER

1. Focus on a brand with a well-defined identity. Elaborate on the identity, using each of the elaboration approaches. Which approach was the most helpful?
2. Do the same with your brand.
3. Focus on a brand identity element such as trust. Identity role models and visual metaphors. Cluster them into groups and interpret the resulting groupings.
4. Design a brand identity elaboration presentation.

# PART III

# BRAND ARCHITECTURE: ACHIEVING CLARITY, SYNERGY, AND LEVERAGE

# 4

# The Brand Relationship Spectrum

You don't get harmony when everyone sings the same note.
—Doug Floyd

The loftier the building, the deeper the foundation must be laid.
—Thomas Kempis, Fifteenth-Century Augustine Monk

## THE GE APPLIANCE STORY

Many mainstream, premium brands face overcapacity and increasing retailer power in their core markets, resulting in smaller margins and added pressure on market share. The onset of a hostile market creates one of the most difficult brand architecture challenges—how to extend brands vertically, either into the super-premium arena or into the value segment. A look at the branding strategy of GE Appliances provides insights into the issues involved and the utility of introducing subbrands in this context.

Most typically, as the premium market becomes more mature, an attractive growth segment emerges at the super-premium end. This segment enjoys much higher margins, and provides interest and product vitality to a tired category. Microbreweries, designer coffees, upscale waters, luxury cars, and specialty magazines all represent attractive target niches that are less price sensitive than the larger market center. Premium brands often struggle to differentiate themselves and credibly communicate a more upscale message to this segment.

When it faced such a situation in the competitive premium appliance market, GE considered various options for entering the super-premium market in order to capture margin dollars. Creating a new brand (as Toyota did with Lexus) was not feasible because the required investment could not be justified in this market context. Another option, to stretch the GE brand up (with a "model 800c," for example), would not provide the needed distinctiveness and impact. Instead, GE decided to leverage its own brand by introducing two new appliance subbrands: the GE Profile line (positioned above the premium GE Appliance line) and the GE Monogram designer line aimed at the architect and designer market.

An organization that uses a subbrand to move upscale runs the risk that the master brand may lack the credibility and prestige needed to compete in the super-premium market. In fact, the GE Monogram line initially struggled largely because it stretched the GE brand too far. However, the GE Profile line was well received from the outset.

Three factors explain the superior performance of the GE Profile brand. First, this new line improved the existing and familiar line, rather than trying to symbolize prestige. By positioning off of the existing brand, GE reduced the credibility problem. Second, the GE Profile line was visibly different from the premium GE Appliance line, with better components and features and a different design, look, and feel. If the product had been difficult to differentiate, like film or fertilizer or motor oil, a subbrand strategy would have been more challenging to implement. Third, the distinct target markets for the three GE lines reduced the potential confusion in the nontarget segments. For example, the GE Profile line's substantially higher price point and distribution strategy made it less visible to mainstream buyers.

At the same time that GE sought to move up in the appliance market, it needed to move down as well. The growth of aggressive value retailers like Circuit City necessitated GE's participation in the growing value market. The use of the GE brand in the value market, even with a subbrand or an endorsed brand, would have risked both cannibalizing GE (by attracting buyers of the premium GE Appliance line to the less expensive alternative) and damaging its image. A new brand for the value segment was deemed prudent, given these risks. Because cost parity is crucial in the value market and margins are slim, however, a new value brand cannot afford much of a brand-building budget. Therefore, establishing a new brand is much more difficult in the value context than in the super-premium market.

GE navigated these challenges by using previously acquired brands. For example, GE had previously purchased the Hotpoint line, a premium appliance brand with substantial equity. Repositioning Hotpoint as a secondary or value line provided the needed market entry without placing the GE brand at risk. In doing so, Hotpoint's perceived quality was reduced, making a return to premium status unlikely in the future. Even so, its entry into the value segment created a stronger total appliance line for GE. The Hotpoint story illustrates the power of using an established brand, whether owned, bought or "leased," when accessing a value segment.

To create a price brand positioned below Hotpoint, GE again made use of an acquired brand by pulling the RCA name off the shelf. This action was less logical, since RCA (although a great name in entertainment) had little credibility in appliances. Risking significant damage to the RCA brand in other markets by making it a price brand in appliances was a questionable call. Perhaps fortunately, its volume was small, so the damage was likely small as well. GE ultimately discontinued the RCA line.

The GE appliance line thus resulted in a four-level coverage created by adding two subbrands and one distinct brand, as shown in Figure 4–1.

FIGURE 4-1
*The GE Appliance Vertical Brand Architecture*

| BRAND | | TARGET MARKET |
|---|---|---|
| GE Monogram | (GE) **Monogram** | Designers/architects |
| GE Profile | (GE) *Profile*~ | Upscale, high income |
| GE Appliances | (GE) *GE Appliances* | Mainstream—quality seekers |
| Hotpoint | **HOTPOINT** | Mainstream—value seekers |

# THE MARRIOTT STORY

The Marriott brand started with a solid franchise in the premium downtown hotel market, then was extended horizontally to create Marriott Hotels, Resorts & Suites, and Marriott Residence Inns. The Marriott organization faced the same vertical extension challenges as GE. The resulting Marriott brand strategy, almost a mirror image of GE's route, provides additional insights into the vertical stretch problem.

Marriott, although a premium brand, did not participate at the highest end of the hotel industry. Because the super-premium hotel market involved prestige and self-expressive benefits, it would have been very difficult to move the Marriott brand into that space. A case in point is the experience of Crowne Plaza, a brand initially endorsed by Holiday Inn, which failed to overcome its association with the more down-market Holiday Inn brand and ultimately had to remove the endorsement after years of trying to make it work.

Further, even if Marriott were successfully positioned up-market, the price expectations of its existing line of hotels might be affected, and its current market segment might be inhibited from considering Marriott hotels. Thus, Marriott chose to move into the luxury segment by buying Ritz-Carlton—and notably decided not to associate the prestigious brand with Marriott even though it would have helped the Marriott brand and created operational synergies.

In the early 1980s, Marriott faced the challenge of expanding its presence through new brands to attract a more price-conscious traveler. The size and growth of the value segment dwarfed that of the premium market in which Marriott was established. Because the value market was attractive and because a more complete product line would provide operational synergies with respect to the reservation and reward systems, entering the value market successfully became a strategic necessity for the Marriott organization.

The preferred choice would have been to enter the value market by creating a new brand or by acquiring an established one as GE had done. However, the available established brands were a hodgepodge of properties lacking consistency and definition. And creating a new brand would have been extremely difficult and expensive because of the clutter in the value end of the hospitality market. Thus, with con-

**FIGURE 4-2**
*A Partial Marriott Brand Architecture*

Marriott Residence Inn

Marriot Hotels • Resorts • Suites

Courtyard by Marriott

Fairfield Inn by Marriott

siderable trepidation, Marriott decided to leverage the Marriott brand by endorsing two new value brands, Courtyard and Fairfield Inn (the resulting brand architecture is shown in Figure 4–2).

After considerable research into the wants and needs of business travelers, Courtyard by Marriott was introduced in 1983 as a businessperson's hotel that had limited dining facilities and was usually located in the suburbs. The Courtyard concept was followed in 1987 by Fairfield Inn by Marriott, a family hotel competing in the value segment and located in suburban areas but easily accessible to major freeways. The endorsement of these two value brands very likely tarnishes the Marriott brand, although there are so many forces influencing the brand that it is hard to isolate the impact of the endorsement strategy alone. Conversely, however, the value of the Marriott brand endorsement to Courtyard and Fairfield Inn is significant. Developers, hotel operators, and communities receive Courtyard and Fairfield Inn proposals favorably because they realize that Marriott will stand behind the concept. Furthermore, the expensive and difficult task of attracting new travelers to try the hotels is reduced, because the Marriott name reduces the risk of an unknown brand.

Three factors reduce the damage to the Marriott brand from the endorsement of low-end hotel brands. First, in each case, the endorsed offerings are distinct from the flagship Marriott hotels, so expectations are managed through different locations, amenities, and look and feel. Second, there are two Marriott brands—Marriott hotels and the Marriott organization. The endorsement clearly indicates that the Marriott organization (not the premium hotels) is standing behind Courtyard and Fairfield Inn. Third, the Marriott core identity elements of consistency and friendliness work in all of the markets and provide a bridge between the brands.

## DESIGNING THE BRAND ARCHITECTURE— ENDORSERS AND SUBBRANDS

Brand architecture organizes and structures the brand portfolio by specifying brand roles and the nature of relationships between brands (e.g., between Citibank and MasterCard) and between different product-market contexts (e.g., between Ford trucks and Ford cars). A well-conceived and managed brand architecture can generate clarity, synergy, and brand leverage rather than a diffused focus, marketplace confusion, and brand-building waste. In Chapter 5, brand architecture will be defined, illustrated, discussed, and applied.

The role of this chapter is to focus on the relationships between brands—a key brand architecture building block—and on the role that endorsers and subbrands play in defining these relationships. What is the relationship between Courtyard and Marriott, between the GE and Profile brands, and between GE and NBC (a GE-owned company)? We start by more formally introducing endorsers, subbrands, and the central concept of the driver role.

### Endorsers

An endorsement by an established brand provides credibility and substance to the offering. In the above example, Marriott is an endorser of Courtyard by Marriott. Basically, this endorsement means the Marriott organization affirms that Courtyard will deliver on its brand promise (which is very different from that of Marriott hotels). Endorser brands usually represent organizations rather than products, because organizational associations such as innovation, leadership, and trust are particularly relevant in endorsement contexts. Moreover, because endorsers are somewhat insulated from the brands they endorse, these associations are likely to be unaffected by the performance of the endorsed brand.

### Subbrands

Subbrands are brands connected to a master (or parent, umbrella, or range) brand that augment or modify the associations of the master brand. The master brand is the primary frame of reference, but it is stretched by subbrands that add associations (for instance, Sony Walkman), a brand personality (Mazda Miata), and even energy (Nike Air Force). One common role of a subbrand is to extend a master brand into a meaningful new segment—as, for example, Ocean Spray Craisins stretches Ocean Spray from juice to snack foods.

Descriptive subbrands (also known as descriptors) simply describe what is offered. In the brand GE Appliance, the brand "Appliance" is a descriptor; it is still a brand, but one with limited responsibility. Similarly, consider a Fisher-Price All-In-One Kitchen Center, where the subbrand "All-In-One Kitchen Center" simply describes the offering.

### Driver Roles

The driver role reflects the degree to which a brand drives the purchase decision and use experience. When a person is asked, "What brand did you buy (or use)?" the answer will most often be the brand that had primary driver role responsibility for the decision. Endorsers, subbrands, and descriptive subbrands can all potentially have a driver responsibility, albeit a minor one in some contexts. ThinkPad, for example, is the driver of the IBM ThinkPad laptop computer—that is, research shows that users will say they own (or use) a ThinkPad rather than an IBM. Similarly, buyers of Hershey's Sweet Escapes will say they bought (or had) a Sweet Escapes bar rather than a Hershey's (which thus is relegated to a minor driver role). Courtyard is the driver of the Courtyard by Marriott offering, because its associations were the primary influence in determining the selection of the hotel (as well as augmenting the use experience by adding richness and emotional or self-expressive content).

Subbrands and endorsers are arguably the most important relationship variables because they fundamentally assert the nature of the *product-market context relationship* between two brands. The use of these context constructs is powerful because they provide tools to:

- Address conflicting brand strategy needs
- Conserve brand-building resources in part by leveraging existing brand equity
- Protect brands from being diluted by overstretching
- Signal that an offering is new and different

Without these context tools, the choice of a new offering would be limited largely to either building a new brand (an expensive and difficult proposition) or extending an existing brand (and thereby risking image dilution).

The balance of this chapter will focus on the *brand relationship spectrum,* a tool to help understand and select product-market context roles. The next chapter will broaden the brand architecture challenge and introduce the brand architecture audit.

## LINKING BRANDS— THE BRAND RELATIONSHIP SPECTRUM

The brand relationship spectrum, portrayed in Figure 4–3, helps to position the various product-market context role options. It recognizes that these options define a continuum which involves four basic strategies and nine substrategies. The four basic strategies are:

House of brands

Endorsed brands

Subbrands under a master brand

A branded house

The position of each strategy on the spectrum in Figure 4–3 reflects the degree to which brands (e.g., the master brand and the subbrand or the endorser brand and the endorsed brand) are separated in strategy execution and, ultimately, in the customer's mind. The maximum separation occurs at the right side of the spectrum in the house of brands where the brands stand by themselves (for

FIGURE 4–3
*Brand Relationship Spectrum*

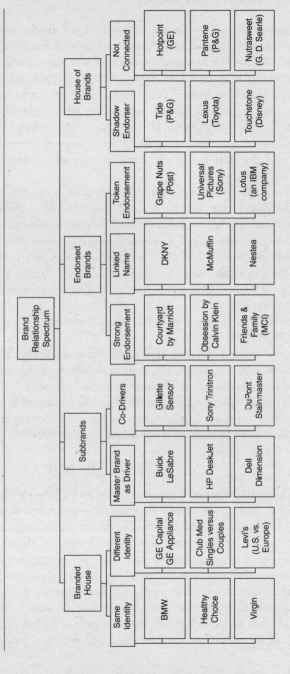

example, GE and Hotpoint). Moving to the left, there is a relationship between an endorser brand and an endorsed brand, but the brands are still very separate—for instance, Courtyard can be very different from its endorser, Marriott. Moving further to the left, the master brand/subbrands relationship is more confining; the subbrand (such as GE Profile) can refine and augment the master brand but cannot stray too far from the master brand's identity. In a branded house, which is at the far left, the master brand is the driver and the subbrands are usually descriptors with little driver responsibility.

The relationship spectrum, as suggested by the figure, is related to the driver role. At the far right, in the house of brands, each brand has its own driver role. With an endorsed brand, the endorser usually plays a relatively minor driver role. With subbrands, the master brand shares the driver role with subbrands. At the far left, in the branded house, the master brand generally has the driver role and any descriptive subbrand has little or no driver responsibility.

### Nine subcategories

Figure 4–3 shows that beneath the four brand relationship strategies, there are nine subcategories. Each of these is positioned on the spectrum based on how much brand separation it implies.

To design effective brand strategies, one must understand the four strategies and nine subcategories in the brand spectrum. Each will be reviewed and explained in the sections that follow.

## A HOUSE OF BRANDS

The contrast between a branded house and a house of brands (illustrated in Figure 4–4) vividly describes the two extremes of alternative brand architectures. While a branded house uses a single master brand such as Caterpillar, Virgin, Sony, Nike, Kodak, or Healthy Choice to span a set of offerings that operate with only descriptive subbrands, a house of brands contains independent, unconnected brands.

In a house of brands strategy, each independent stand-alone brand maximizes its impact on a market. Procter & Gamble is a house of brands that operates over 80 major brands with little connection to P&G or to each other. In doing so, P&G sacrifices the economies of scale and synergies that come with leveraging a brand across multiple businesses. In addition, those brands that cannot support investment themselves (especially the third or fourth P&G entry in a category) risk stagnation and decline, and P&G sacrifices brand leverage in that the individual brands tend to have a narrow range.

The P&G house of brands strategy, however, allows firms to clearly position brands on their functional benefits and to dominate niche segments. Compromises do not have to be made in the positioning of a given brand to accommodate its use in other product-market contexts. Instead, the brand connects directly to the niche customer with a targeted value proposition.

P&G's brand strategy in the hair care category illustrates how a house of brands works. Head & Shoulders dominates the dandruff-control shampoo category. Pert Plus, the perky category pioneer, targets the market for a combined conditioner and shampoo product. Pantene ("For hair so healthy it shines"), a brand with a technological heritage, focuses on the segment concerned with enhancing hair vitality. The total impact of these three brands would be lessened if—instead of three distinct brands—they were restricted to a single brand or even were branded as P&G Dandruff

FIGURE 4-4
*Branded House vs. House of Brands*

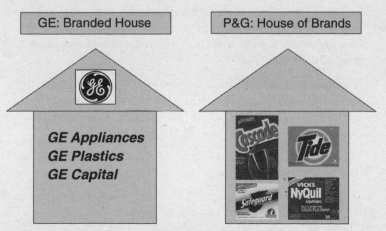

Control, P&G Conditioning Shampoo, and P&G Healthy Hair. P&G detergents are similarly well positioned to serve niche markets: Tide (tough cleaning jobs), Cheer (all-temperature), Bold (with fabric softener), and Dash (concentrated powder) provide focused value propositions that could not be achieved by a single P&G detergent brand.

Targeting niche markets with functional benefit positions is not the only reason for using a house of brands strategy. Additional reasons include the following:

- Avoiding a brand association that would be incompatible with an offering. The Budweiser association with beer taste would prevent the success of Budweiser Cola. Likewise, Volkswagen would adversely affect the images of Porsche and Audi if the brands were linked.
- Signaling breakthrough advantages of new offerings. Toyota's decision to introduce its luxury car under the separate Lexus name differentiated it from any predecessors at Toyota. Similarly, GM decided to create the Saturn brand with no connection to any existing GM nameplate so that the Saturn message ("A different kind of company, a different kind of car") would not be diluted.
- Owning a new product class association by using a powerful name that reflects a key benefit, such as Gleem toothpaste or the Reach toothbrush.
- Avoiding or minimizing channel conflict. L'Oréal reserves the Lancôme brand for department and specialty stores that would not support a brand available in drug and discount stores. When unconnected brands are sold through competing channels, conflict is usually a not an issue.

The unconnected brand subcategory represents the most extreme house of brands strategy, because it maximizes the separation between the brands. Few people, for instance, know that Head & Shoulders and Pantene are made by the same company.

### SHADOW ENDORSER

A shadow endorser brand is not connected visibly to the endorsed brand, but many consumers know about the link. This subcategory in the house of brands strategy provides some of the advantages of having a known organization backing the brand, while minimizing any association contamination. The fact that the brands are not visibly linked makes a statement about each brand, even when the link is discovered. It communicates that the organization realizes that the shadow-endorsed brand represents a totally different product and market segment.

A good example of a shadow brand is Lettuce Entertain You, a Chicago-based restaurant group that has rolled out some thirty-nine restaurant concepts since its first restaurant, R. J. Grunts, appeared in 1971. Each restaurant has its own image, personality, style, and brand name. From Shaw's Crab House to Tucci Benucch, from Brasserie Joe's to The Mity Nice Diner, each is unique and success-ful. Many are trendy, the ultimate restaurant accolade.

Because the master or umbrella brand, Lettuce Entertain You, ini-tially was not included on any of the signage inside or outside the restaurant, it was not an endorser in the normal sense. Patrons needed to discover the shadow endorsement themselves—which, in this case, increased its impact. Knowing about the shadow endorsement repre-sented some intriguing insider knowledge and only added to the mys-tique. The communication vehicle for the first twenty-five years of the group's operation was primarily word of mouth, buttressed by an aggressive public relations effort. Because the Lettuce Entertain You endorsement was subtle or in the shadows, it avoided the stigma of being part of a chain. There was no organizational brand such as Marriott or Westin shouting its association in the patron's ear.

Today, however, existing and potential patrons usually know when they enter a Lettuce Entertain You restaurant. In the mid-1990s, the group conducted a survey of diners at its Chicago restaurants and discovered that the Lettuce Entertain You brand had strong equity in terms of awareness, loyalty, and perceived quality. As a result, they moved the Lettuce Entertain You brand out of the shadows by embarking on a print and radio advertising campaign, establishing a frequent diner program, and prominently displaying business cards at each restaurant that represent all of their restaurant concepts. The individual restaurants maintain their uniqueness but now enjoy a strong endorser.

Lexus is another example of how a shadow endorser can be helpful. People who know that Toyota makes Lexus are reassured, because they know that Toyota's financial strength and reputation support

Lexus. However, Lexus also delivers self-expressive benefits that would be diminished by a visible connection with Toyota. The absence of any such connection makes a statement that Lexus is a brand distinct from Toyota; it also means that there is no memory cue about the connection. Without a memory cue, the connection is less likely to have an impact on the endorsed brand.

Still other examples of shadow endorsements are DeWalt (Black & Decker), Mates/Storm (Virgin), Banana Republic/Old Navy (Gap), Saturn (GM), Dockers (Levi Strauss), Mountain Dew (Pepsi), and Touchstone (Disney). Each of these shadow endorsers has a minimal impact on the image of the brand but provides credibility and reassurance for some customers. Its value can also be significant among those who are not consumers but who are relevant in some other way. For instance, the concierges at major Chicago hotels, who are continually asked to give recommendations for interesting restaurants, are more likely to recommend a Lettuce Entertain You restaurant because of the shadow endorser. The shadow endorsement of Touchstone by Disney helps it attract high-potential scripts, and Mountain Dew gets more attention from retailers and others in the trade because of the shadow endorsement of Pepsi.

## ENDORSED BRANDS

In the house of brands strategy, the brands are independent. Endorsed brands (such as Courtyard or Fairfield Inn) are still independent, but they are also endorsed, usually by an organizational brand (such as Marriott). Even though an endorsement can help to modify the image of the endorsed brand, its primary role is to provide credibility to the endorsed brand and reassurance to the buyer and user.

The endorser brand usually has only a minor driver role. For example, the Hanes hosiery brand endorses the Revitalize collection, a line of sheer hosiery designed to promote leg health. The driver brand is clearly Revitalize because customers believe that they are buying and using Revitalize, not Hanes. As the endorser brand, though, Hanes provides assurance that Revitalize will live up to its quality and performance claims.

The endorser can also affect the perceptions of the endorsed brand. Although people buy and use Obsession, the endorsement by

Calvin Klein gives consumers permission to buy something that might otherwise, on its own merits, seem too tacky. The endorsement is like a wink at the consumer, saying that the name is just a game, a bit of self-expression.

Do endorsers make any difference? A study of confectionery brands in the United Kingdom provides some empirical evidence that organizational brand endorsement pays off.[1] The study involved customers evaluating nine offerings, each of which was endorsed by one of six corporate endorsers (Cadbury, Mars, Nestlé, Terry's, Walls, and a control which was no endorsement). The results showed that all the corporate endorsements did add significantly more value than the control even for Walls, an ice cream brand whose associations are with a different category. Cadbury, which received the highest ratings, consistently endorsed a range of leading confectionery products. Second was Mars (which endorses only a few of its confectionery brands), and third was Nestlé (which endorses a wide range of products). The study concluded that endorsement is helpful and that the best endorsement is from an organization with credibility in the product class.

Making the endorsed brand strategy work involves understanding the role of the organizational brand. Consider the Hobart brand, the Mercedes of industrial mixers used by larger restaurants and bakeries. Purchasing a Hobart provides significant self-expressive benefits to chefs who want only the best brands for their kitchens. Responding to an emerging value segment served by off-shore suppliers, Hobart introduced the Medalist brand, with the Hobart endorsement in small type. A key insight here is that there are now two Hobart brands in the marketplace—the Hobart *product brand,* and the Hobart *organizational brand* used to endorse the Medalist brand.

Because the product brand is distinct from the organizational brand, the integrity and self-expressive benefits of the Hobart product brand are maintained. The Hobart organizational brand, meanwhile, is now an important part of the brand architecture and needs to be actively managed. In particular, the Hobart organizational brand will have its own identity and set of organizational associations to develop and maintain. It is possible to make clear that the endorser is an organizational brand by representing it as "from Hobart" or "a Hobart company." This is not always necessary, however, because the endorser role by itself has an organizational brand connotation.

Another motivation for endorsing a brand is to provide some useful associations for the endorser. For example, a successful, energetic new product or an established market leader can enhance an endorser. Thus when Nestlé bought Kit-Kat, a leading chocolate brand in the United Kingdom, a strong Nestlé endorsement was added. The purpose was not so much to help Kit-Kat as to enhance Nestlé's image in the United Kingdom by associating it with quality and leadership in chocolate. In another industry, the endorsement by 3M of Post-it Notes probably does as much for 3M as it does for Post-it Notes.

## TOKEN ENDORSER

A variant of the endorsed brands strategy is the use of a token endorser (usually a master brand involved in several product-market contexts), which is substantially less prominent than the endorsed brand. The token endorser can be indicated by a logo such as the GE light bulb or the Betty Crocker spoon, a statement such as "a Sony Company," or another device. In any case, the token endorser will not have center stage; the endorsed brand will be featured. Nestlé, for example, puts a seal of guarantee on the back of Maggi brand packages that reads, "All Maggi products benefit from Nestlé's experience in producing quality foods all over the world." The role of the token endorser is to make the connection visible and provide, especially for new brands, some reassurance and credibility while still allowing the endorsed brands maximum freedom to create their own associations.

A token endorser can be especially helpful to brands that are new or not yet established. The token endorsement will have more impact if the endorser:

- Is already well known (such as Nestlé or Post)
- Is consistently presented (for example, if the visual representation—the Betty Crocker spoon or the GE bulb—is in the same location in the visual setting of the ad, a package, or other vehicle)
- Has a visual metaphor symbol (such as the Traveler's umbrella)
- Appears on a family of products that are well regarded (such as the Nabisco product lines), and thus provides credibility from its ability to span a range of products.

A token endorsement is preferable to a strong endorsement when the endorsed brand needs more distance from the endorser. The endorser may have undesirable associations, or the endorsed brand may be an innovation that needs more independence to make its position credible.

Sometimes, a token endorsement is a first step in a gradual name change: A token endorsement becomes a strong endorsement, then a co-brand, and finally a master driver brand. The process involves transferring the brand equity from the endorsed brand to the endorser.

A common mistake is to exaggerate the impact of a token endorsement when the endorser is not well known and well regarded, or when the endorsed brand is well regarded and established in its own right and thus does not need the reassurance of an endorser. The following two studies reinforce these points.

Providian, a major financial services firm, was once a combination of businesses connected by a forgettable phrase (something like "A Capital Holding Company") as a type of endorsement. In a survey of 1,000 customers who had been exposed numerous times to the phrase, only three—not three *percent*, but three *people*—knew the endorser. This sobering statistic led to the decision to rename the firm Providian and adopt a new brand architecture.

Nestlé once conducted a U.S. study to determine the impact of a token endorsement by Nescafé (a strong coffee brand overseas but a weak one in the United States) on Taster's Choice (a strong brand in the U.S.). Because of Taster's Choice's brand strength, the token endorsement had little impact either positively or negatively in terms of image or intention measures. When the Nescafé endorser was elevated to a co-brand status, however, it had a negative impact.

## LINKED NAME

Another endorsement variant is a linked name, where a name with common elements creates a family of brands with an implicit or implied endorser, thereby allowing multiple distinct brands to have their own personality and associations but also a subtle link to a master or umbrella brand.

McDonald's, for example, has Egg McMuffin, Big Mac, McRib, McPizza, McKids, Chicken McNuggets, McApple, and so on. The

"Mc" in each name creates an implied McDonald's endorsement, even though the traditional endorsement is not present. Linked names allow more ownership and differentiation than a descriptor brands strategy (such as McDonald's Ribs or McDonald's Pizza).

Similarly, HP has the Jet series—LaserJet, DeskJet, OfficeJet, InkJet and others—that covers a variety of price points and applications. LaserJet is the strongest brand in this group (the others have little equity), but its associations with quality, reliability, and innovation transfer to the other Jet brands. In effect, LaserJet endorses the rest of the family. The Netscape e-commerce brand, Netscape CommerceXpert, has the same effect on the linked subbrands ECXpert, SellerXpert, BuyerXpert, MerchantXpert, and PublishingXpert. Nestlé's Nescafé, Nestea, and Nesquik (in the United Kingdom) provide a compact but strong link to Nestlé. Even though Ralph Lauren endorses the Ralph and Lauren brands, the fact that they are also linked in name enhances the strength of the endorsement.

A linked name provides the benefits of a separate name without having to establish a second name from scratch and link it to a master brand. Marriott needed to establish the brand name Courtyard (an expensive and difficult process), then link it to the Marriott brand, another nontrivial task. In contrast, the name DeskJet itself accomplishes 80 percent of the task of linking the product to the established brand, LaserJet. Furthermore, the communication of what DeskJet stands for is partially accomplished by what is known about LaserJet. The linked brand name is also more compact—compare "DeskJet from LaserJet" with the simple DeskJet.

## STRONG ENDORSERS

A strong endorser is visually indicated by a bold, prominent presentation. Examples of strong endorsers include Simply Home from Campbell's, Highland by 3M, Polo Jeans by Ralph Lauren, Optiquest by Viewsonic, Lycra only by DuPont, and Paramount's Kings Dominion. A strong endorser usually has more of a meaningful driver role than does a token endorser or linked name relationship; therefore, it should have credibility in the product-market context and associations that fit.

## SUBBRANDS

The subbrand, another powerful brand architecture tool, can play a driver role by adding associations that are relevant to the customer. For example, a subbrand such as the Dodge Viper can create associations that make the master brand seem more differentiated and appealing to customers. A subbrand can also stretch the master brand, allowing it to compete in arenas in which it otherwise would not fit—Uncle Ben's Country Inn Recipes, for instance, provides a vehicle to allow Uncle Ben's to move upscale. Finally, a subbrand can signal that a new offering is novel and newsworthy. Intel developed the Pentium subbrand in part to signal a new generation of chips that were significantly more advanced.

In addition, the subbrand can alter the image of the master brand by adding an attribute or benefit association, by adding energy and personality, or by connecting with a user, as shown in these examples:

- Black & Decker Sweet Hearts Wafflebaker (which makes heart-shaped waffles) and the Black & Decker Handy Steamer (for steaming fresh vegetables) add points of attribute differentiation while offering emotional benefits to the Black & Decker brand.
- Smucker's Simply Fruit strengthens the fresh/healthy/quality associations of the master brand.
- Microsoft Office adds an application association to the Microsoft operating system brand.
- Audi TT adds energy and personality to an established master brand that is considered a quality, reliable brand but one characterized by German stodginess.
- Revlon Revolutionary Lipcolor and Revlon Fire and Ice (fragrance) both add energy and vitality to the Revlon brand.

The link between subbrands and their master brand is closer than the link between the endorsed brands and endorsers. Because of this closeness, a subbrand has considerable potential to affect the associations of the master brand which in turn can be both a risk and an opportunity. In addition, the master brand, unlike an endorser brand, will usually take on a major driver role. Thus, if Revolutionary Lipcolor is a subbrand to Revlon rather than an endorsed brand (Revolutionary Lipcolor from Revlon), it will have less freedom to create a distinct brand image.

FIGURE 4–5

*Descriptive/Driver Subbrand Spectrum*

| | Subbrand Role | | |
|---|---|---|---|
| | **DESCRIPTIVE ONLY** | **MEANINGFUL DRIVER ROLE** | **EQUAL DRIVER ROLE** |
| **SITUATION** | Master brand as dominant driver—Branded house | Master brand as primary driver | Master and subbrands as co-drivers |
| **EXAMPLE** | GE Jet Engines | Compaq Presario | Sony Walkman |

The subbrand can serve primarily as a descriptor, a driver, or some combination of the two. In developing a subbrand strategy, it is important to recognize where on the descriptive/driver spectrum (illustrated in Figure 4–5) the subbrand should be. If the subbrand is purely descriptive, the strategy can be termed a branded house because the master brand is the dominant driver. If the subbrand has a meaningful driver role, however, the strategy involves a true subbrand. If the subbrand is as important as the master brand, a co-driver situation exists. If the subbrand is the dominant driver, it is no longer a subbrand but an endorsed brand.

A purely descriptive name, such as Spicy Honey or Minivan, will rarely have any driver role; however, sometimes a descriptive brand will be inappropriate and a suggestive name will be used (such as Express, Gold, Reward, or Advisor). A suggestive name has more potential to promote an emotional response and thus also has more potential to play some driver role.

### THE SUBBRAND AS A CO-DRIVER

When both the master brand and the subbrand assume major driver roles, they can be considered co-drivers. The master brand is performing more than an endorser role—for example, customers are buying and using both Gillette and Sensor; one does not markedly dominate the other. Usually, for this to be the case, the master brand will already have some real credibility in the product class. Gillette, with its innovation over the years, has become a brand that enjoys loyalty in the razor category. Sensor is a particularly innovative razor, however, and so that brand also merits and receives loyalty.

The cosmetics product Virgin Vie uses the Vie subbrand as a co-driver. While the Virgin brand provides presence, visibility, and attitude, it is associated with a generation older than the target market for Virgin Vie. The use of the Vie subbrand rather than a subbrand descriptor (such as Virgin Cosmetics) helps to make the brand more credible in the cosmetics market and to access a younger target market—twenty-something consumers. The young British celebrity used in the Virgin Vie advertisements creates further separation from the Virgin brand and founder Richard Branson.

Unless the two brands in a co-driver situation represent comparable quality, the association might tarnish the more prestigious brand. When Marriott (a premium hotel name) endorses Courtyard, the risk to Marriott's status and perceived quality standards is reduced because it is an endorser. If Marriott had instead been a co-driver (meaning in part that its name would be just as prominent in visual depictions), the Marriott brand would have been perceived to have been stretched downward, and its perceived quality as a product brand would therefore be in greater jeopardy.

## THE MASTER BRAND AS THE PRIMARY DRIVER

Another subbrand variant occurs when the master brand is the primary driver. The subbrand is more than a descriptor, but it has a minor role in the purchase process and use experiences. For instance, a Dell Dimension customer believes he or she is buying and using a Dell computer, not a Dell Dimension, although the Dimension subbrand can indicate a particular model and may have an impact on the purchase.

When the subbrand has a minor driver role, one implication is that a lot of resources should not be placed into the subbrand; rather, the emphasis should be on the master brand. Too often there is an illusion that the subbrand has equity and a co-driver status, especially when the subbrands have been around for many years. Subbrands like Del Monte's Fresh Cut or Celestial Seasonings' Mint Magic or Compaq's Presario, however, usually have less equity than is assumed. Thus, in sorting out the brand architecture, it is important to ascertain which subbrands have significant equity in order to avoid trying to build brands that lack potential.

## A BRANDED HOUSE

In a branded house strategy, a master brand moves from being a primary driver to the dominant one, while the descriptive subbrand goes from having a minority role to little or none at all. Virgin uses a branded house strategy because the master brand provides an umbrella under which many of its businesses operate. Thus, there are Virgin Airlines, Virgin Express, Virgin Radio, Virgin Rail, Virgin Cola, Virgin Jeans, Virgin Music, and many others. Other branded houses include many of the offerings of Healthy Choice, Kraft, Honda, Sony, Adidas, and Disney. The branded house option leverages an established brand and requires a minimum investment on each new offering.

This strategy, however, also has limitations. When brands like Levi's, Nike, and Mitsubishi are stretched over a wide product line, the firm's ability to target specific groups is constrained; compromises must be made. In addition, a significant amount of sales and profit are affected when the master brand falters. As with a large truck or boat, a broadly stretched brand is hard to turn around once its momentum shifts (and the brand loses its buzz). However, the branded house does enhance clarity, synergy, and leverage, which are the three goals of brand architecture.

A branded house architecture, such as Virgin's, often maximizes clarity because the customer knows exactly what is being offered. Virgin stands for service quality, innovation, fun/entertainment, value, and being the underdog; it also has a heritage of being fun and outrageous. The descriptors, meanwhile, indicate the specific business: Virgin Rail, for example, is a rail service run by the Virgin organization. It could not be simpler from a branding perspective. A single brand communicated across products and over time is much easier to understand and recall than a dozen individual brands, each with its own associations. Employees and communication partners also benefit from greater clarity and focus with a single dominant brand. There should be little question of brand priorities or the importance of protecting the brand when a branded house is involved.

In addition, a branded house usually maximizes synergy, as participation in one product market creates associations and visibility that can help in another. At Virgin, the product and service innovations in one business enhance the brand in other businesses. Further, every exposure of the brand in one context provides visibility that enhances brand awareness in all contexts.

Two anecdotes from GE show how the synergistic value of brand building in one business can affect another. First, GE was the perceived leader (by a big margin) in the small-appliance category years after it had exited the business, in part because of the advertising and market presence of its large appliances. Second, more than 80 percent of the respondents in a survey said that they had been exposed to a GE plastics ad during a time in which no such ads appeared but other GE products had been advertised. Clearly, the accumulation of brand exposures over time and across business units has impact far beyond their intended function.

Finally, the branded house option provides leverage—the master brand works harder in more contexts. The Virgin brand equity, for example, is harnessed and employed in numerous contexts.

When a new offering needs a brand name, the default option should be to house it under the root of an existing brand. This will provide synergy, clarity, and leverage. Any other strategy requires compelling reasons.

### SAME BRANDS BUT WITH DIFFERENT IDENTITIES

When the same brand is used across products, segments, and countries, one of two implicit assumptions is usually made—both of which are counterproductive to creating an optimal brand architecture. The first assumption is that there can be different brand identities and positions in every context, despite the common brand name. The use of dozens of identities, however, creates brand anarchy and is a recipe for inefficient and ineffective brand building. The second assumption is that there can be a single identity and position everywhere, even though the imposition of a single brand identity risks a mediocre compromise that may be ineffective in many of its contexts. In fact, there usually needs to be a limited number of identities that share common elements but have distinctions as well (for example, GE Capital requires certain associations that are inappropriate for GE Appliances). We considered how to deal with this problem in Chapter 3.

FIGURE 4–6
*Selecting the Brand Relationship Spectrum Position*

| TOWARD A BRANDED HOUSE | TOWARD A HOUSE OF BRANDS |
| --- | --- |
| Does the master brand contribute to the offering by adding— | Is there a compelling need for a separate brand because it will— |
| • Associations enhancing the value proposition?<br>• Credibility through organizational associations?<br>• Visibility?<br>• Communication efficiencies? | • Create and own an association?<br>• Represent a new, different offering?<br>• Avoid an association?<br>• Retain/capture customer/brand bond?<br>• Deal with channel conflict? |
| Will the master brand be strengthened by associating with the new offering? | Will the business support a new brand name? |

## SELECTING THE RIGHT POSITION IN THE BRAND RELATIONSHIP SPECTRUM

Each context is different, and it is difficult to generalize about when to use which spectrum subcategory and how to meld sets of brands and their relationships into a composite brand architecture. Addressing the four key questions summarized in Figure 4–6, however, provides a structured way to analyze the issues. Positive answers to the two questions at the left will suggest a leftward movement on the brand relationship spectrum toward a branded house, while positive answers to the two questions on the right imply a rightward movement on the spectrum toward a house of brands.

The brand architecture issues become most graphic when a new offering is added to the existing set of brands. Thus the perspective of a new brand will be the primary frame of reference in the following discussion of the conditions that would suggest a move either left or right on the spectrum. These issues also arise, though, when evaluating an existing brand architecture to identify needed adjustments.

### DOES THE MASTER BRAND CONTRIBUTE TO THE OFFERING?

The master brand needs to add value by becoming attached to a new product offering in the branded house scenario. It can add value by adding associations that contribute to a value proposition, by providing credibility to the offering, by sharing the visibility of the master brand, and by generating communication efficiencies that can result in cost advantages.

### Associations enhancing the value proposition

Most fundamentally, does the master brand make the product more appealing in the eyes of the customer? Do the positive associations of the master brand transfer to the new product context, and are the associations relevant and appropriate? When the answer is yes, the brand equity can be leveraged in the new context. For example, Calvin Klein fragrances are enhanced by the master brand's associations of an authoritative, edgy designer with provocatively sexy clothes and a vivid user imagery. Determining the ability of a brand to lend its associations to a new context requires a brand extension analysis, which is discussed in the next chapter (and detailed in *Managing Brand Equity*).

### Credibility with organizational associations

A brand, especially a new brand, has two tasks. First, a relevant, compelling value proposition needs to be created. Second, the value proposition needs to be made credible, a task that is most difficult with a compelling value proposition that breaks new ground and involves consumer risk—for example, a battery-powered car or a solar home. By attaching a brand with strong organizational associations, however, the credibility challenge can be reduced or even eliminated. Among the most important organizational associations are the following (with examples in parentheses):

Quality (HP home computers)

Innovation (Shiseido skin care products)

Customer concern (Nordstrom's beauty parlor)

Globalness (AT&T news channel)

Reliability and trust (Sears' appliance business)

### Visibility

A brand, particularly a new entry, requires visibility not only to get an offering considered but also to imply a host of positive product and organizational attributes. An existing brand such as CitiGroup may already have visibility, but the problem is how to link it to a new business arena (such as brokerage services). In contrast, establishing visibility for a new entrant (say, Mega Brokers), that is *not* linked to a visible established brand can be expensive and difficult with so much marketplace clutter.

### Communication efficiencies

All aspects of brand building involve significant fixed costs that can be spread over all the contexts in which the brand is involved. The creation of advertising, promotions, packaging, displays, and brochures is costly both in time and in talent. When a brand enters a new brand context, though, prior brand-building efforts can be adapted or used directly. More important is the synergy created by media spillover into adjacent markets. Ads and publicity for GE jet engines and GE appliances are seen by potential buyers of both product lines, giving GE an advantage over more focused rivals. As media such as event sponsorships (for example, sports events and music concerts) and the use of publicity become more important relative to conventional media, such spillover should be more significant.

The potential of economies of scale and synergy will tend to be higher under the following conditions:

- The collective communication budget supporting a brand playing a driver role is significant. The communication budget for a brand used as an endorser will have fewer economies of scale, because in those contexts other brands will still need to be supported.
- Media vehicles work across the brand contexts. An Olympic sponsorship, for example, may need to be spread over multiple business contexts in order to be feasible.
- There is a meaningful brand-building budget. When the numbers get small, the synergy potential also shrinks.

### WILL THE MASTER BRAND BE STRENGTHENED?

The impact of a brand extension (such as Virgin Cola) or brand endorsement (a Sony company) on the master brand equity is often overlooked but can be critical. Some organizations allow access to their brand to business units that are concerned only with the credibility gained by using the name, and not with the equity of the master brand. If the brand will help, they will use it with no regard for any image dilution that may be generated. If there is no organizational unit to prevent this brand extension or brand endorsement promiscuity, real brand equity damage may result.

A brand extension or brand endorsement should support and enhance the key master brand associations. A Healthy Choice offering, for instance, should reflect and reinforce the core identity of Healthy Choice. If Healthy Choice is used to promote a product— even a quality product—that is not positioned as a healthy food, it undercuts the brand. Wherever Sunkist products communicate health, vitality, and vitamin C, they are helping the Sunkist brand; when the brand is placed on candy or soda, the core franchise is placed in jeopardy. The risk is that customers will not separate in their minds orange-flavored Sunkist candy or soda from other Sunkist products that imply real orange ingredients.

It can be difficult but important to say no, to recognize the boundaries of a brand and to resist the temptation to stretch it too far. Clorox means bleach; lending the Clorox name to a cleaning product without bleach is risky. The Levi's name, which means casual clothing, defines boundaries as well. In contrast, Bayer's decision to put the Bayer name on non-aspirin products has diluted its ownership of the aspirin category, a significant cost.

## IS THERE A COMPELLING NEED FOR A SEPARATE BRAND?

The development of a new or separate brand is expensive and difficult. Multiple brands complicate the brand architecture for both the firm and the customer. Using an established brand in a branded house strategy, by comparison, will reduce the investment required and lead to enhanced synergy and clarity across the offerings. Thus a separate brand should be developed or supported only when a compelling need can be demonstrated.

Because of the enormous pressure to create new brands by those who believe (often wishfully) that the latest product improvement merits a new name, organizational discipline is required to make sure that any new brand is justified. This discipline might involve a top-level committee with sign-off authority, as well as a specified set of conditions under which a new brand is justified. Although these guidelines will depend on the context, in general new brands should be absolutely necessary to either create and own an association, represent a totally new concept, avoid an association, retain a customer relationship, or deal with a severe channel conflict issue. The "absolutely necessary" qualification is important to set the right tone and keep managers from picking rationalizations.

### Creating and owning an association

The potential to own a key association for a product class is one rationale for a new brand. Pantene ("For hair so healthy it shines") would not be successful under the Head & Shoulders or Pert brands, because the unique benefit of Pantene could not emerge under the shadow of the existing associations. When an offering has the potential to dominate a functional benefit (as is the case for many of the P&G brands), a distinct brand is justifiable. However, a similar argument is unclear at General Motors, which aspires to be a house of thirty-three brands; the motivating segmentation of key associations is much fuzzier and complex. The GM brands in general lack distinct driving value propositions.

### Representing a new, different offering

A new brand name can help tell the story of a truly new and different offering or signal a breakthrough benefit. Because there is a temptation for all new-product managers to believe that they are in charge of something dramatic, however, a larger perspective is needed. A minor evolution or an empty attempt to revitalize a product will rarely qualify. A new brand name should represent a significant advance in technology and function. For instance, the Viper, Taurus, and Neon all merited new names because their new designs and personalities represented a radical departure from other automotive offerings.

### Avoiding an association

Does a link with an existing brand create a liability? When Saturn was introduced, tests showed that any association with GM would adversely affect its perceived quality, and so a decision was made to avoid any connection between the two brands. Microbrewed beers base their differentiation on uniqueness and personal craftsmanship;

any endorsement or co-brand with a major brewery would undercut that claim. Any hint of a connection between Clorox, the makers of bleach, and its Hidden Valley Ranch salad dressings would raise the specter of the salad dressing tasting like bleach. Thus the label states that Hidden Valley Ranch dressing's owner is HVR Company, and there is no mention of Clorox even on the back of the packages.

Will a link with an existing brand risk damaging that brand? Gap has chosen a house of brands approach for its three principal brands, with Banana Republic at the high end, Gap in the middle, and Old Navy at the value end. Old Navy (one of the most successful retail concepts ever, judged by sales growth) offers energy, fun, creativity, and value with tasteful, stylish clothes sold at affordable prices. Management felt that initial efforts to brand the concept as the Gap Warehouse threatened damage to the Gap brand. It would cannibalize sales and, worse, would associate Gap with lower-priced clothing. Similarly, Nestlé has no connection with any of its pet food brands such as Alpo or Fancy Feast because customers might have visions of pet food when exposed to Nestlé food products.

### Retain/capture a customer/brand bond

When a firm buys another brand, there is an issue as to whether the purchased brand name should be retained. In making this judgment, the strength of the acquired brand—its visibility, associations, and customer loyalty—should be considered as well as the strength of the acquiring brand. The bond between customers and the acquired brand name is often the key ingredient; if it is strong and difficult to transfer, keeping the acquired brand could be a sound decision. The following conditions would make a brand equity transfer difficult:

- The resources required to change the acquired name are not available (or are not justified).
- The associations of the acquired brand are strong and would be dissipated with a brand name change.
- There is an emotional bond, perhaps created by the organizational associations of the acquired brand, that may be difficult to transfer.
- There is a fit problem; the acquiring brand does not fit the context and position of the acquired brand.

Schlumberger, the oil-field service company, has retained several strong brand names that it acquired, including Anadrill (an oil drilling company), Dowell (oil well construction and production), and GeoQuest (software and data management systems). In most cases, these brands became subbrands of Schlumberger with co-driver status. Each of these three brands has its own culture, operating style, product scope, and personality that combine to form the basis for strong customer relationships; to abruptly or even gradually replace those brand names with that of a large diverse brand (Schlumberger), however well regarded, would waste assets. Nestlé also usually retains acquired brand names, although a Nestlé endorsement is sometimes added. Too often a name change is motivated by ego or convenience rather than a dispassionate analysis of brand architecture.

There are circumstances, of course, when a name change is wise. Usually the rationale involves a strong branded house. HP has made hundreds of acquisitions over the years and has consistently changed the name to HP even when the previous brand name had substantial visibility, attractive associations, and a customer following. It is not clear that the HP policy generated the right decision in all cases, but the strong associations of HP and the advantages of a branded house strategy provided defensible reasons.

### Avoiding channel conflict

Channel conflict can preclude using established brands for new offerings; the problem usually is twofold. First, an existing channel may be motivated to stock and promote a brand because it has some degree of exclusivity. When that is breached, the motivation falls. Second, an existing channel may support a higher price in part because it provides a higher level of service. If the brand became available in a value channel, the brand's ability to retain the high-margin channel would be in jeopardy.

Fragrance and clothing brands, for example, need different brands to access the upscale retailers, department stores, and drug/discount stores. Thus L'Oréal has Lancôme, L'Oréal, and Maybelline Cosmetics brands for different channels. The VF Corporation supports four distinct brands—Lee, Wrangler, Maverick, and Old Axe—in part to deal with channel conflict. Purina distributes ProPlan to specialty pet stores and Purina One to grocery stores.

## WILL THE BUSINESS SUPPORT A NEW BRAND NAME?

If a business is ultimately too small or short-lived to support necessary brand building, a new brand name will simply not be feasible whatever the other arguments are. It is costly and difficult to establish and maintain a brand, almost always much more so than expected or budgeted. Too often in the excitement of a new product and brand, unrealistic assumptions are made about the ability and the will to fund it adequately. The will is particularly important; many organizations have deep pockets but short arms. It is futile to plan brand building only to fail to fund its construction and provide a maintenance budget.

## A CLOSING NOTE

The brand relationship spectrum, with its four branding routes, is a powerful tool; however, nearly all organizations will use a mixture of all of them. A pure house of brands or branded house is rare. GE, for example, looks like a branded house, but Hotpoint and NBC are outside; in addition, GE Capital itself has a host of subbrands and endorsed brands. The challenge is to create a village where all the subbrands and brands fit in and are productive.

The decisions concerning brand architecture and the brand relationship spectrum are driven in large part by the business strategy of the firm. As a result, the market environment is also an important driver of brand architecture decisions. Marriott saw a major opportunity in the value segment, which led to the Fairfield Inn and Courtyard brands. It also identified opportunities in the extended stay traveler segments, which led to the Residence Inn brand and others. Brand strategists' assumptions about the market—the trends, unserved needs, alternative segmentation approaches, and industry market structure—are the fundamental issues that need to be evaluated and clarified.

## QUESTIONS FOR DISCUSSION

1. Pick two diverse firms—one that is close to a branded house, and another that is close to a house of brands. Look closely at their

branded offerings and identify the subcategories in the brand relationship spectrum that are represented.

2. Analyze your endorser brands. Should there be more? Fewer? How much of a driver role do they take in each distribution channel? Rate each on a percentage scale. What percent of the buying and use experience does the endorser drive?

3. Analyze your subbrands. What do they add to the brand architecture? Are they confusing and complex? Could they be simplified? Rate these as well on the driver/descriptor subbrand spectrum (shown earlier in Figure 4–5).

4. For what portion of your offerings is a house of brands appropriate? Why? What portion should be modeled as a branded house? Why? Under what circumstances would additional subbrands or endorsers be helpful?

5. Create a brand architecture decision guide that would specify the conditions under which a new or existing offering would use an existing master brand, a subbrand, an endorsed brand, or a new brand.

# 5

# Brand Architecture[1]

We hire eagles and teach them to fly in formation.
—D. Wayne Calloway, former CEO of PepsiCo

The way a team plays as a whole determines its success. You may have the greatest bunch of individual stars in the world, but if they don't play together, the club won't be worth a dime.
—Babe Ruth

## THE POLO RALPH LAUREN STORY

A problem facing many brands is how to access new segments and introduce new products without the risk and expense of creating new brands. Polo Ralph Lauren has addressed this problem by creatively developing a portfolio of brands that are linked together. In doing so, they have emerged as one of the most successful fashion labels in the world.

In 1968 designer Ralph Lauren founded his firm to market quality men's wear under the brand Polo Ralph Lauren. The upscale image

**POLO RALPH LAUREN** of a polo player fits the core identity of Polo Ralph Lauren, which includes a country club lifestyle characterized by good taste; classic, elegant, understated clothing; and exceptional quality and craftsmanship. The Ralph Lauren endorsement helped to personalize and differentiate the brand, but it also began to build a brand around the Ralph Lauren name that would prove valuable in other contexts.

In 1971 a women's wear line was launched under the Ralph Lauren brand name, since the designer's name already had powerful associations in women's fashion. Because the Polo brand was already committed to men's fashions, it might have been a liability in entering the women's wear market. In fact, had Ralph Lauren been the men's clothing brand instead of an endorser of Polo, the ability to use the designer's name in women's fashions might have been hindered.

In 1974 Ralph Lauren accessed the market for moderately priced men's fashion by introducing Chaps, a new brand sold exclusively at department stores. Endorsed by Ralph Lauren, Chaps' accessible American personality was distanced from the more upscale Polo. The endorsement was feasible in part because Chaps products still featured a classic style that one would expect from Ralph Lauren. The new brand provided access not only to a less upscale segment but also to less upscale retail outlets. Had the Polo brand been stretched, a more severe brand dilution problem could have occurred.

During the 1980s, the Ralph Lauren brand was vertically extended into the premium end of the women's fashion world. The Ralph Lauren Collection brand promised up-to-the-moment fashion with Ralph Lauren's trademark understated touch, while a sister brand, Ralph Lauren Collection Classics, featured clothing designs that were slightly less exclusive and current. Distributed only through premier fashion retailers and through the company's own stores, the two new brands enabled Ralph Lauren to span a wide range of price points without an excessive vertical stretch. They also provided credibility for Lauren as a fashion designer and therefore enhanced the Ralph Lauren brand. (Such enhancement can be an important function of premium subbrands.) The 1980s also saw Ralph Lauren extend his design principles to home furnishings using the Ralph Lauren brand, a bit of a stretch and risk for the brand.

In the 1990s Ralph Lauren sought to provide less expensive offerings by introducing separate Ralph and Lauren brands. Like Chaps, the Lauren brand is sold exclusively in department stores rather than in upscale specialty stores; it is intended for women who might be

Ralph Lauren Collection customers but lack the necessary income. In contrast, Ralph's target customer is the young, smart, and sophisti-

# LAUREN
## RALPH LAUREN

cated woman who wants to be cutting-edge but tasteful. Its styling could best be described as Collection Classics with a twist—

the cut is more body-conscious, and details are a little more daring. Ralph is sold in Polo Ralph Lauren stores and upscale department stores. In the fall of 1999, Ralph was renamed RL. The Ralph/RL and Lauren brands allow Ralph Lauren to participate in lower price points and target new segments while still drawing on the equity of the Ralph Lauren brand.

Also in the 1990s, a premium line of exclusive men's suits made in England were sold with a purple label bearing the Ralph Lauren signature. This first attempt to sell men's clothing with a Ralph Lauren brand was notable. Clearly, the line's upscale, fashionable, and British elements combined to make the designer name feel appropriate—the Polo brand, which was associated with a less formal type of clothing, would not have worked as well. The purple Ralph Lauren men's wear brand served a silver-bullet role in that it reinforced the haute couture connotations of the Ralph Lauren name at a time when the brand was in danger of being diffused by its wide-ranging endorsements.

One of the most significant departures for Ralph Lauren in the 90s was the launching of several youth-oriented, more contemporary extensions of Polo. Polo Jeans by Ralph Lauren offers a contemporary

denim line for men and women. Polo Sport by Ralph Lauren is a men's line of fashionable performance athletic apparel. A companion brand, Ralph Lauren Polo

Sport for women, uses the Polo Sport subbrand to stretch the Ralph Lauren brand into casual, youthful, athletic clothing for women. The Polo Sport and Polo Jeans lines broaden Ralph Lauren's potential customer base, effectively extending the Polo brand equity. This brand strategy also provides a way for Ralph Lauren to respond to lifestyle trends toward increased informality and fitness while giving some youth and energy to the Polo brand. The use of the Polo brand on the women's side is a way of making a clear distinction between the upscale fashion (Ralph Lauren) and midmarket casual (Polo) clothing markets, and it reduces the risk of contaminating the Ralph Lauren image in the women's clothing market.

Within its contemporary men's and women's wear collections, Ralph Lauren introduced a premium line of vintage-look denim, Double RL, in 1993. The brand's identity combines the authenticity and ruggedness of outdoor living with American eclecticism. With a weak link to Ralph Lauren and a concept that may have been too late into the market, however, Double RL has struggled and appears to be limited to a niche market.

To tie together the contemporary lifestyle lines (Polo Sport and Polo Jeans) and to differentiate them from the more classic brands, the company created a separate brand symbol to replace the polo player mounted on a horse. The symbol is an American flag, with the stars replaced by the initials RL—clearly moving away from the British association. This new symbol, used in the logos of the new lifestyle brands, suggests that they share a single casual and contemporary brand identity that is distinct from the Polo and Ralph Lauren lines. The new lines are, however, also clearly differentiated from each other. Polo Jeans is a more trendy and fashionable brand. The Polo Sport brand is more upscale, at about the quality tier of Polo by Ralph Lauren, but with more contemporary style and design features. In the spring of 1999 the company introduced the RLX Polo Sport line of men's and women's wear consisting of functional sport and outdoor apparel. The line is sold through athletic specialty stores.

Figure 5–1, which shows how the Polo Ralph Lauren brands are grouped logically, summarizes a complex but cohesive brand architecture. Ralph Lauren has spanned channels, segments, and product categories with brands that are distinct but linked through related names (such as Ralph and Lauren), subbrands (Polo Sport and Ralph Lauren Collection), and endorsed brands (Polo by Ralph Lauren). This strategy has allowed new entries to draw on the established equities of Ralph Lauren and Polo while representing distinct brands with their own personality. The new brands and subbrands not only draw from the existing equities but also add life and energy to them. There is logic and discipline to the structure; Polo is the men's fashion anchor, whereas the designer name Ralph Lauren is the women's core brand equity.

**FIGURE 5-1**
*Polo Ralph Lauren Brand Architecture*

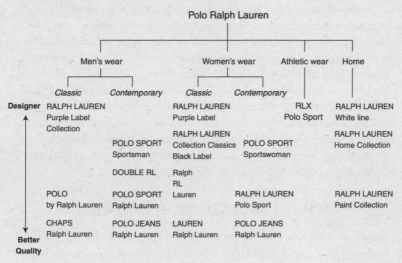

## MARKET COMPLEXITY, BRAND CONFUSION, AND BRAND ARCHITECTURE

The brand-is-an-island trap refers to the implicit assumption that brand strategy involves the creation of a strong brand like Hewlett-Packard, IBM, 3M, or Tide. Creation of strong brands by developing clear, insightful identities and brand-building programs that make an impact is of prime importance, of course. Yet virtually all firms have multiple brands and need to manage them as a team to work together to help each other and to avoid getting in each other's way. Looking at brands as stand-alone silos is a recipe for confusion and inefficiency. Strategic brand leadership requires that team goals be optimized, as well as the goals of the individual brand players.

Brand architecture is the vehicle by which the brand team functions as a unit to create synergy, clarity, and leverage. If you think of each brand as a football player, identity and communication programs are tools or exercises that make the individual player better. The brand architecture, meanwhile, assumes the coach's job of placing the players in the right positions and making them function as a team rather than a collection of players.

Brand architecture becomes especially critical as brand contexts become complex, with multiple segments, brand extensions, a blizzard of product offerings, varied competitor types, intricate distribution channels, and the wider use of endorsed brands and subbrands. Brands such as Coke, Citibank, Nike, Procter & Gamble, Hewlett-Packard, Visa, and Ford all operate in diverse markets and over multiple (sometimes disparate) products and channels. The resulting kaleidoscope can create customer confusion, inefficiencies, and a brand strategy that both employees and partners see as muddled and uninspiring. In the face of competitive pressure, a well-defined brand architecture thus becomes imperative.

## WHAT IS BRAND ARCHITECTURE?

Brand architecture is an organizing structure of the brand portfolio that specifies the brand roles and the relationships among brands (Ford and Taurus, for example) and different product-market brand contexts (Sony Theaters versus Sony Television, or Nike Europe versus Nike U.S.). Brand architecture is defined by five dimensions (shown in Figure 5–2)—the brand portfolio, portfolio roles, product-market context roles, the portfolio structure, and portfolio graphics—each of which will be defined, illustrated, and discussed in this section.

### THE BRAND PORTFOLIO

The brand portfolio includes all the brands and subbrands attached to product-market offerings, including co-brands with other firms. Simply identifying all of these brands and subbrands can sometimes be a nontrivial task when there are many brands, some of which are obscure or even dormant.

A basic brand architecture parameter is the composition of the brand portfolio: Should one or more brands be added? A portfolio can sometimes be strengthened by the addition of brands, but such additions should always be made or approved by a person or group with a portfolio perspective. Decentralized groups that have little feel for (or incentive to care about) the total brand portfolio may damage it by adding brands too promiscuously. Further, a structured framework to consider

FIGURE 5–2
*Brand Architecture*

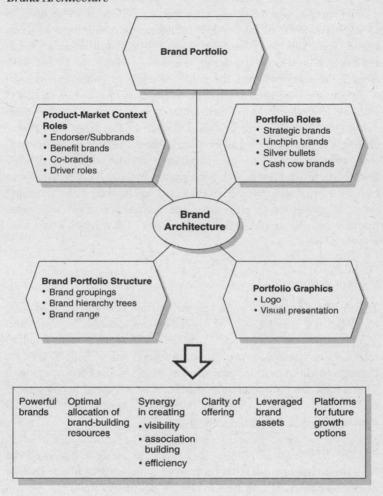

brand addition decisions should exist, drawing on the new brand criteria discussed in the last chapter. Sometimes it is helpful to have a formal flow chart, with the series of criteria to be considered set forth in boxes.

Or should brands be deleted? Each brand requires brand-building resources; if there are an excessive number of brands, there may not be adequate resources to support them. Perhaps worse, superfluous brands can contribute confusion simply by being there. The solution is to prune the brand portfolio, however painful that might be.

For example, when Safeway examined its private-label business, it identified more than twenty-five such brands. Since most of these brands were very weak (largely because they had little brand-building budget or synergy), Safeway decided to eliminate all but four. Among the survivors were the Safeway Select premium brand (usually positioned as equal or superior to the best brands in a category) and the "S" value brands (always priced among the lowest in each category). The other two brands, Lucerne in the diary department and Mrs. Wright for packaged bakery items, were kept on because they were perceived to have significant equity, while the deleted brands simply did not have a good reason to exist. This decision was based on a realistic appraisal of the existing brand equities, the value proposition offered to customers, the economics of carrying extra brands, and the brand-building synergies of having the two base brands all over the store.

## PORTFOLIO ROLES

Treating brands as silos owned by individuals or organizational units can lead to a misallocation of resources and a failure to create and exploit synergy across brands. Portfolio roles, which provide a tool to take a more systems view of the brand portfolio, include a strategic brand, a linchpin brand, a silver-bullet brand, and a cash-cow brand. These roles are not mutually exclusive. A brand could be simultaneously a linchpin and a silver-bullet brand, or it could evolve from a strategic brand into a cash-cow brand.

### Strategic Brand

A strategic brand is one that represents a meaningful future level of sales and profits. It may be a currently dominant brand (sometimes termed a megabrand) that is projected to maintain or grow its position, or a small brand that is projected to become a major one. For the American Automobile Association, AAA Financial Services is a strategic brand because the future of the organization is to move beyond roadside services. Nike All Conditions Gear (ACG) is a strategic brand as it provides the basis for a Nike position in the outdoor-adventure arena. Slates is a strategic brand for Levi Strauss because it lays the foundation for a position in men's slacks for business or casual settings.

### Linchpin brand

A linchpin brand is the leverage point of a major business area or of a future vision of the firm; it will indirectly influence a business area by providing a basis for customer loyalty. Hilton Rewards is a linchpin brand for Hilton Hotels because it represents the future ability to control a critical segment in the hotel industry. If a competitor's rewards program became dominant for any reason, Hilton would be at a strategic disadvantage. Schwab Mutual Fund One Source is a linchpin brand for Schwab, the upscale discount brokerage firm. One Source, which provides customers of Schwab access to over 900 no-load mutual funds with no transaction fee, provides a precious source of differentiation in an industry where all competitors look alike and tend to focus on price.

### Silver Bullet

A silver bullet is a brand or subbrand that positively influences the image of another brand. It can be a powerful force in creating, changing, or maintaining a brand image. Some successful silver bullets include the following:

- IBM ThinkPad. When it hit its stride, this innovative product generated a significant (and rare) boost in public perceptions of the IBM brand. The fact that ThinkPad sales represent a minute percentage of total IBM's sales makes this impact even more remarkable.
- Ernest and Julio Gallo varietal wines. This brand represented a premium wine, supported by an upscale label and substantial advertising, whose only goal was to make the huge Gallo jug wine brand a bit more acceptable.
- San Jose Sharks. This major league hockey team has changed the image of the city of San Jose, which had been stuck in the shadow of San Francisco.
- HP LaserJet's Resolution Enhancement. This branded feature served to make credible claims that Hewlett-Packard had achieved another breakthrough in printer technology.
- Del Monte Orchard Select. This line of bottled fruits, designed to compete with the fresh fruit aisles, enhances the Del Monte claim of quality and taste.

- The new VW Beetle. This product has been the symbol of the resurgence of Volkswagen in the United States.

When a brand or subbrand such as IBM's ThinkPad is identified as a silver bullet, the communication strategy and budget would logically no longer rest solely with the business manager in charge of the silver-bullet brand. The parent brand group (IBM corporate communications) should also be involved, perhaps by featuring the silver-bullet brand (ThinkPad) in corporate communications or augmenting its communication budget.

### Cash Cow Brands

Strategic, linchpin, and silver-bullet brands involve investment and active management so that they can fulfill their strategic mission. A cash-cow brand, in contrast, is a brand with a significant customer base that does not require the investment that other portfolio brands require. Even though sales may be stagnant or slowly declining, there is a loyal core of customers who are unlikely to leave the brand. The role of a cash-cow brand is to generate margin resources that can be invested in strategic, linchpin, and silver-bullet brands that will be the bases for the future growth and vitality of the brand portfolio.

An example of a cash-cow brand is the Campbell's Red & White label. These soups are the heart of the Campbell's equity, but the real vitality of the brand is elsewhere. Another cash cow is Nivea Crème, the original product of Nivea, a brand that has been extended into a variety of skin care and related products. A balanced brand portfolio needs cash-cow brands to provide resources for promising but embryonic strategic brands, linchpin brands, and silver bullets.

### PRODUCT-MARKET CONTEXT ROLES

In general, a set of brands combines to describe an offering in a particular product-market context. The Cadillac Seville with the Northstar system, for example, is a particular offering for which Cadillac is the master brand with the primary driver role; Seville plays a subbrand role, and Northstar a branded component role. Apple-Cinnamon Cheerios from General Mills is a particular offering in which Cheerios is the master brand playing the primary driver role, Apple-Cinnamon the subbrand role, and General Mills the endorser role. There are four sets of product-market context roles that work together to define a specific offering: endorser/subbrand roles, branded benefit roles, co-brands, and driver roles.

### Endorser and Subbrand Roles

A master (or umbrella or range) brand is the primary indicator of the offering, the point of reference. To define a specific offering, an endorser and/or one or more subbrands may augment a master brand. An endorser brand (e.g., General Mills endorsing Cheerios) is an established brand that provides credibility and substance to the offering, while subbrands (such as Porsche Carrera or Apple-Cinnamon Cheerios) modify the associations of that master brand in a specific context. Each of the involved brands might be used in other contexts as well, but they come together to provide meaning (hopefully a clear one) to a distinct offering.

The understanding and use of endorser brands and subbrands is a key to achieving clarity, synergy, and leverage in the brand portfolio. The brand relationship spectrum, discussed in Chapter 4, provides a tool to help use these powerful constructs effectively and appropriately.

### Benefit Brands

The benefit brand is a branded feature, component ingredient, or service that augments the branded offering. Some examples are as follows:

Branded Features

- Ziploc sandwich bags—ColorLoc zipper
- Oral-B toothbrushes—Power Tip bristles and Action Cup shape
- Whirlpool electric range—Whirlpool CleanTop, AccuSimmer Element
- Reebok—3D UltraLite sole design
- Lipton tea—the Flo-Thru bag
- Prince tennis racquets—Sweet Spot, Morph beam, Longbody
- Revlon Revolutionary—ColorStay Lipcolor

Branded Components or Ingredients

- Compaq—Intel Inside
- North Face parkas—Gore-Tex
- GE Profile Performance Refrigerator—Water by Culligan
- Cheer—Advanced Color-Guard Power

- Reebok—Hexalite (lightweight honeycomb-shaped cushioning)
- Kenwood—Dolby noise reduction
- HP LaserJet—Kodak color enhancement
- Diet Coke—Nutrasweet

Branded Services

- American Express—Round Trip (a package of services for the corporate travel office)
- Ford/Mercury/Lincoln—Quality Care
- UPS—Proprietary Mail
- United Airlines—Arrivals by United, United Red Carpet Club, United Mileage Plus, Ground Link, Business One

A branded benefit is powerful when it genuinely adds something to the product or service. Because that something extra is usually relevant (or seems to be relevant) to the brand promise, it contributes to the functional benefit of the brand. It can also work somewhat like an endorser by providing credibility to the offering; for example, Gore-Tex suggests that the garment will deliver on its promise of being effective in wet weather.

Branded benefits have been consistently found to provide a boost to brands, particularly those that are new or less-established. One study found that consumers were willing to pay more for a garment with a branded ingredient, even though they did not know what that ingredient did.[2] Intel Inside, a classic branded component program, has consistently produced substantial price premiums.

Other studies have shown that branded components add value unless they are placed on brands with an already very strong image. For example, in a controlled experiment branded chocolate morsels helped Nabisco but did nothing for Pepperidge Farm, a super-premium brand (presumably because consumers assumed that Pepperidge Farm used only the best ingredients anyway).

Brands can gain preestablished equity and credibility by licensing branded benefits (such as Gore-Tex) that are owned by other firms. Benefits that are ownable are potentially much more powerful, however, because they can represent points of differentiation that lead to a competitive advantage—even if the feature, component, or service is eventually imitated by others. For instance, HP's Resolution Enhancement was only an important source of differentiation during one generation of printers. That brief lifespan, though, was enough to provide a much longer-lasting enhancement of the HP LaserJet reputation for innovation and high quality.

An ownable branded benefit can play a silver-bullet role by helping to communicate the brand concept. For example, the Power Tip feature of Oral-B toothbrushes communicates the innovative nature of the brand. Moreover, the benefit brand need not necessarily be supported with a communication program that will generate awareness and a specific meaning. Sometimes it can contribute simply by being there, particularly if the name is descriptive—as in the cases of Power Tip and Resolution Enhancement.

## Co-Brands

Co-branding occurs when brands from different organizations (or distinctly different businesses within the same organization) combine to create an offering in which each plays a driver role. One of the co-brands can be a component or ingredient brand (such as Pillsbury Brownies with Nestlé chocolate) or an endorser (such as Healthy Choice cereal from Kellogg's). It can also be a composite brand with multiple master brands, as with the three-brand Citibank—American Airlines Visa credit card.

Co-branding has significant rewards and risks. On the plus side, the offering can capture two (or more) sources of brand equity and thereby enhance the value proposition and point of differentiation. Consider the Eddie Bauer edition of the Ford Explorer, which for more than fifteen years has been a notable co-brand effort in automobiles. Because Eddie Bauer means quality outdoor wear used by active people with discriminating taste and style, the Ford Explorer offering gains not only a perception that the leather interior will be stylish, of high quality, and comfortable (like Eddie Bauer clothes) but user lifestyle imagery as well.

The impact of co-branding can be greater than expected when the associations of each brand are strong and complementary. A research study by Kodak showed that for a fictional entertainment device, 20 percent of prospects said they would buy the product under the Kodak name and 20 percent would buy it under the Sony name, but 80 percent would buy the product if it carried both names.[3] The implication was that the combination would represent an advance that could not be credibly claimed by either alone. A study of GE Profile appliances and Culligan Soft Water found a similar result for a co-branded Water by Culligan GE Profile Refrigerator.[4] Such co-branding synergy might also allow greater freedom to stretch—like tying two rubber bands together, the combination goes farther than one.

Co-branding can and should enhance not only the co-branded offering but also the associations of both brands. For example, the way the Eddie Bauer Edition of Ford Explorer is presented in ads and promotions creates visibility and reinforces associations for both the Ford Explorer and the Eddie Bauer brands. In effect, the co-branded car is a high-end, quality, stylish silver bullet for both brands. In addition, the co-brand should not damage the associations of either brand, which is a significant risk when an upscale brand has a higher perceived level of quality and prestige than the brand it is allied with.

One key to successful co-branding is to find a partner brand that will enhance the offering by complementary associations. That is more likely to happen when an organization uses research to search systematically and proactively for that right fit rather than simply evaluating options that come through the front door. What associations are now weak? What brands have those associations? How can a product and surrounding brand-building activities make an impact for a co-branded offering? Will the brand-building resources of both brands be leveraged by the alliance? How would the two brands benefit, and how would it fit into their existing business model?

Co-branding, like any alliance between organizations, has risks. Can the program generate attractive returns (both financial and in terms of brand building) over time for both firms? When one of the partners feels that the return is inadequate or that the program no longer fits strategically, it may withdraw or, sometimes worse, stay in the venture but lose interest. Also, when two different organizations are involved, designing and implementing programs becomes more complex, resulting in inferior brand building and alliance strains. The risk is largely eliminated, of course, whenever licensing is involved (as when Kellogg's licenses the Healthy Choice brand, or when Barbie licenses the NBA name for NBA Barbie) and one brand is in charge.

### Driver Role

Recall that a driver role, introduced in Chapter 4, represents the extent to which a brand drives the purchase decision and defines the use experience. A brand with a driver role will have some level of loyalty; customers would be less comfortable with the product if the brand were missing. Brand architecture design involves selecting the set of brands to be assigned major driver roles; these brands will have priority in brand building. Brand architecture also involves the understanding of the driver responsibility of each brand in a product-market context. Consider, for example, the relative driver responsibilities for the brands involved in the Porsche Carrera Cabriolet.

While a business may have hundreds of brands, usually only some of these have major driver responsibility. These brands are candidates for active management, both individually and as a group. Because a misstep with a driver brand (a brand with a major driver role) is a serious problem, an organization defining its brand architecture should think carefully about the composition of this group. What are the brands that collectively control the relationships with customers? Should some be retired or de-emphasized? Should others be added or elevated? Should some be extended, or have some been stretched so far that they should contract?

A driver brand is usually a master brand or subbrand, but endorsers, branded benefits, and second- and third-level subbrands can have some driver role. In fact, when multiple brands are involved, the driver role of each can vary from zero to 100 percent. The ability of the brand architecture to refine the driver role in this manner is flexible and powerful. It is sometimes productive to divide 100 driver points among the involved brands to represent the relative driver roles.

Subbrands, in particular, can have a variety of roles. Some subbrands, such as Domino Sugar, Ziploc Sandwich Bags, Cadbury Chocolate Biscuits, and Tylenol Extended Relief, have no driver function and are only descriptive. Others, such as United Express, Holiday Inn Express, and Wells Fargo Advantage, have some driver role. Still other subbrands, such as Ford Taurus, Calloway Big Bertha gold clubs, Iomega Zip drives, and Hershey's Sweet Escapes, have major driver roles. In Chapter 4, the driver-descriptive subbrand spectrum was introduced as a way to clarify the decision as to how much driver responsibility a subbrand should have.

The attribution of a driver role to a brand is important because it has direct implications for the value (and, indeed, necessity) of building the equity of the brand. Driver brands need to be actively managed; if a brand has a limited driver role, it should neither receive brand-building resources nor be actively managed.

## BRAND PORTFOLIO STRUCTURE

The brands in the portfolio have a relationship with each other. What is the logic of that structure? Does it provide clarity to the customer, rather than complexity and confusion? Does the logic promote synergy and leverage? Does it provide a sense of order, purpose, and direction to the organization? Or does it suggest ad hoc decision making that will lead to strategic drift and an incoherent jumble of brands? There are three approaches to discussing and presenting portfolio structure: brand groupings, brand hierarchical trees, and brand range.

### Brand Groupings

A brand grouping or configuration is a logical grouping of brands that have a meaningful characteristic in common. In the Ralph Lauren example, the brands were grouped with respect to four characteristics:

• Segment (men or women)
• Product (clothing or products for the home)
• Quality (designer to premium)
• Design (classic or contemporary)

The groups provide logic to the brand portfolio and help guide its growth over time. The first three groupings used by Ralph Lauren—segment, product, and quality—often play a role in many portfolios, since they are dimensions that define the structure of many product markets. The hotel industry, for example, is structured according to segment (for example, Courtyard for business travelers versus Fairfield Inn for leisure travelers), product (Marriott Residence Inns for extended stays versus Marriott for single-night stays), and quality level (Marriott for luxury versus Fairfield Inn by Marriott for economy). Portfolio brands grouped along such basic product-market segmentations tend to be more easily understood by consumers.

Two other useful categorical variables are distribution channels and applications. L'Oréal uses the Lancôme and Biotherm brands for department and specialty stores, the L'Oréal and Maybelline brands for

FIGURE 5–3
*Brand Hierarchy Tree for Colgate Oral Care Products*

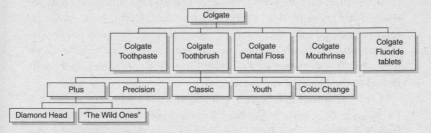

drug and discount stores, and another set including Redken for beauty salons. Nike has a set of brands grouped around applications—in its case, individual sports and activities (basketball, hiking, and so on).

### Brand Hierarchy Trees

Sometimes the logic of the brand structure can be captured by a brand hierarchy (or brand family) tree, as illustrated in Figures 5–3 and 5–4. The hierarchy tree structure looks like an organizational chart, with both horizontal and vertical dimensions. The horizontal

FIGURE 5–4
*Brand Hierarchy Tree for Toyota*

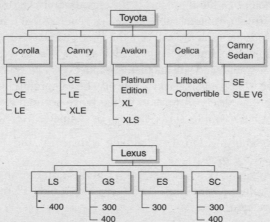

dimension reflects the scope of the brand in terms of the subbrands or endorsed brands that reside under the brand umbrella. The vertical dimension captures the number of brands and subbrands that are needed for an individual product-market entry. The hierarchy tree for Colgate oral care (Figure 5–3) shows that the Colgate name covers toothpaste, toothbrushes, dental floss, and other oral hygiene products. It also shows that Colgate Plus has two distinct subbrands linked to the shape of the toothbrush.

A firm with multiple brands will require trees for each; in effect, a forest may be needed. Colgate, for example, has three toothpaste brands (Colgate, Ultra Brite, and Viadent) and dozens of other major brands, such as Mennon, Softsoap, Palmolive, Irish Spring, and Skin Bracer. In Figure 5–4, Lexus and Toyota represent two different trees. In addition, some trees may be too extensive to present on a single page and thus will need to be broken into major trunks. The Colgate oral care products, for example, will be difficult to display in one tree structure, and so it may be useful to consider the toothbrush trunk separately.

The brand hierarchy tree presentation provides perspective to help evaluate the brand architecture. First, are there too many or too few brands, given the market environment and the practical realities of supporting brands? Where might brands be consolidated? Where might a new brand add market impact? Second, is the brand system clear and logical, or confused and ad hoc? If logic and clarity are inadequate, what changes would be appropriate, cost-effective, and helpful?

A successful brand architecture makes a range of offerings clear both to the customer and to those inside the organization.[5] Having a logical hierarchy structure among subbrands helps generate that clarity. When the subbrands are each indicators of the same characteristic, the structure will appear logical. When one subbrand represents a technology, another a segment, and still another a product type, however, an organizing logic will be missing, and clarity may be compromised.

There are a variety of ways to define portfolio brands with logic and clarity. For example, subbrands can be defined by the following:

- Product family—L'Oréal's Plenitude (skin care) and Preference (hair coloring) brands
- Technologies—HP's LaserJet, InkJet, and ScanJet printers
- Quality/value positioning—Visa's Classic, Gold, Platinum, and Signature cards

## EXPANDING THE RANGE OF THE ENDORSER BRAND

There are two reasons to add endorsements: first, to provide credibility and associations to the endorsed brand; and second, to provide brand-enhancing exposure contexts to the endorser. Both reasons motivated Kraft to change its endorser brand strategy in 1997.

Until the late 1990s, Kraft was the master brand for cheese, barbeque sauce, salad dressing, and mayonnaise (Miracle Whip), and the endorser of Philadelphia, Cracker Barrel, and Velveeta cheeses. In addition, the Kraft portfolio contained over a dozen stand-alone brands, (such as Minute Rice and Post) that were diffusing the brand-building resources. The decision was made to add the Kraft endorsement to these brands in order to leverage the Kraft name. As part of the strategy, these stand-alone brands were evolved toward the Kraft image of everyday, easy-to-prepare good meal solutions for the American family and the Kraft personality of wholesome, family oriented, and reliable. A major $50 million campaign to enhance the Kraft name supported the move to unite these brands comfortably under the Kraft umbrella.

As a result, Kraft became a strong endorser for Stovetop Stuffing, Minute Rice, and Shake & Bake. In addition, it became a token endorser for Oscar Mayer, Tombstone, Post, Maxwell House, Breyer's, Cool Whip, and Jell-O. Interestingly, all of these brands (and especially the three that received a strong endorsement) are also everyday, all-American products, not that much of a stretch from Kraft. Some brands such as DiGiorno pizza and Bull's Eye Barbeque sauce were left as standalone brands in part because they were positioned as upscale and in part because their companion brands, Tombstone pizza and Kraft Barbeque Sauce, were regarded as closer to the core Kraft identity. The net result was more coherence among the Kraft family of brands and subbrands so that they can more effectively create synergy with cross-brand programs and promotions.

- Benefits—Prince's Thunder (for power) and Precision (for accuracy) tennis rackets
- Market segments—Lee Pipes (cutting-edge cool for preteens and young teens), Dungarees (a retro/authentic style for older teens

and twenty-somethings) Lee riveted (classic jeans for the general audience) and casuals (for adult women).

### Brand Range

A key architecture issue is the range of the portfolio brands, particularly the endorser brands and the driver brands. How far should they be stretched horizontally across markets and products? How far should they be stretched vertically into upscale markets or into value arenas? How can endorser brands and subbrands extend brand leverage, but also protect the associations of a brand that needs to be leveraged?

The brand range can be described for each brand in the portfolio that spans product classes or has the potential to do so. The basic issues to explore are how far the brand is stretched now and how far it should be stretched. In analyzing these issues, organizations should distinguish between the brand in its role as an endorser (where it can be stretched further) and its role as a master brand (where it might be more confined), and recognize that subbrands and co-brands can play a key role in leveraging brands.

The description of the brand range can take many forms. Using the Kraft example described in the boxed insert, Figure 5–5 specifies the range for Kraft in its roles as master brand, strong endorser, and token endorser. The brand identity, shown in the second column from the left, helps to underscore the nature and quality of the logic of the brand range (that is, the products to which the brand has been applied). The column on the right lists issues representing the brand's problems and opportunities.

The concept behind Figure 5–5 is to have a compact representation of the range of each brand in its role as either endorser or driver. With this information, organizations can ask whether a brand is currently stretched too far or underleveraged. Overstretched brands can cause a fit problem or undesirable associations. Underleverage, in contrast, occurs when the brand can be helpful in contexts in which it is absent.

### PORTFOLIO GRAPHICS

Portfolio graphics are the pattern of visual representations across brands and contexts. Often the most visible and central brand graphic

FIGURE 5–5
*Kraft's Brand Range*

| BRAND | BRAND IDENTITY | PRODUCT SCOPE | ISSUES |
|---|---|---|---|
| Kraft as master brand with a driver role | Everyday, easy-to-prepare, good-quality meal solutions for the American family. Personality—wholesome, reliable. | Cheese, Mayonnaise, Barbeque Sauce, Salad Dressing | Weakness in noncreamy dressing, as well as upscale markets. |
| Kraft as strong endorser | (Same as above) | Stovetop Stuffing, Shake & Bake, Minute Rice | How to leverage the Kraft brand when it is used as an endorser. |
| Kraft as token endorser | (Same as above) | Oscar Mayer, Post, Maxwell House, Jell-O, Cool Whip, Tombstone, Breyer's | Will the Kraft endorsement help or hurt the offerings? |

is the logo that represents the brand in its various roles and contexts. The primary logo dimensions, color, layout, and typeface, can be varied to make a statement about a brand, its context, and its relationship to other brands. Portfolio graphics are also defined by visual representations such as packaging, symbols, product design, the layout of print advertisements, taglines, or even the look and feel of how the brand is presented. Any of these can send signals about relationships within the brand portfolio.

One role of portfolio graphics is to signal the relative driver role of sets of brands. The relative typeface size and positioning of two brands on a logo or signage will reflect their relative importance and driver roles. For example, the size and location of the Ralph Lauren endorsements clearly show a strong endorsement of Ralph and a much weaker one for Polo Sport when the brands' respective logos are examined. The Marriott endorsement of Courtyard is visually larger and stronger than its endorsement of the more downscale Fairfield Inn. The fact that the ThinkPad brand name appears in a smaller typeface than IBM tells the customer that IBM is the primary driver of the product.

Another portfolio graphics role is to signal the separation of two

## THE MAXFLI BRAND GRAPHICS

Maxfli's redesign of its golf ball packaging illustrates some brand graphics issues. Maxfli's 1995 packaging was more consistent with videotapes than with golf balls (see Figure 5–6). Further, consumers felt that the typeface was boring. With the help of a design firm, Maxfli redesigned

FIGURE 5–6
*Maxfli Before and After*

its packaging to differentiate its premium golf ball offering from leading competitors such as Titleist, Top-Flite, and Wilson and to create separation within its product line (which ranged from standard to super-premium golf balls). As the No. 4 brand in the market, the challenge for Maxfli was to create a style that was differentiating, reflected its brand identity, and still suggested a structure within the line.

The package shot in Figure 5–6 shows the revised brand graphics. A soft-focus, monochromatic photograph of a golf ball was added to make a visual link to the category. Name and color separated the three performance-level subbrands. The top-of-the-line product retained the gold color and the name HT. The midmarket line, renamed the X-Series, had three variations—XD (distance), XF (feel) and XS (spin)—and was dressed in plain black, which suggested both premium and masculine qualities. The value line was termed MD and used white, which signaled value to most golfers.[6]

brands or contexts. In the case of John Deere lawn tractors, color and product design played a key role in separating a value product (branded as Sabre from John Deere) from the classic, premium John Deere line. Because the Sabre line removed the yellow from the familiar John Deere color scheme, customers received a strong visual signal that they were not buying a premium John Deere product. The product was also visibly different, lacking the substantive feel of the parent John Deere line. To visually separate its home products from other lines, HP uses a different color set (purple and yellow), a unique package (people are portrayed, which they are not on the white package used for business customers), and a different tagline ("Exploring the possibilities").

Still another portfolio graphics role is to denote the brand portfolio structure; the use of color and a common logo (or part of a logo) can signal a grouping. The use of the Maggi color and package layout, for example, provides a very strong master brand impact over its subbrands, indicating that they form a grouping with common brand associations.

An illuminating exercise—which is part of the brand architecture audit discussed at the end of the chapter—is to collect all the brand graphics for all contexts, then put all the visual portrayals of the brand on a large wall. Do they have the same look and feel? Is there visual synergy (that is, do the graphics in one brand context support the graphics in another)? Or is the brand presented in an inconsistent, cluttered manner? This visual test is a good complement to the logical test of the brand structure presentations. It is also useful to compare the brand graphics to those of competitors.

## BRAND ARCHITECTURE OBJECTIVES

Earlier in this chapter, Figure 5–2 summarized the five dimensions and six objectives of brand architecture. The goals of the system are qualitatively different from the goals of individual brand identities. Creating an effective and powerful brand impact is still a prime goal, but others are also essential to achieving brand leadership. The six objectives of brand architecture are detailed below.

- **Create effective and powerful brands.** Strong brand offerings that resonate with customers and have a point of differentiation and customer appeal are the bottom line. New subbrands or brands often help toward that end by adding or refining associations, even though they add cost and complexity to the existing brand architecture. It would be self-defeating not to have strong brands as a brand architecture goal.
- **Allocate brand-building resources.** If each brand is funded solely according to its profit contribution, high-potential brands with modest current sales will be starved for resources, and brands with linchpin or silver-bullet roles will receive inadequate resources to fulfill their portfolio roles. The identification of brands that can play portfolio roles is a key first step in making optimal allocation decisions.
- **Create Synergy.** A well-conceived brand architecture should result in several sources of synergy. In particular, the use of brands in different contexts should enhance the visibility of the brands, create and reinforce associations, and lead to cost efficiencies (in part by creating scale economies in communication programs). The brand architecture should also avoid the negative synergy that can result from conflicting brand identities in different contexts and roles.
- **Achieve clarity of product offerings.** A brand system should clarify product offerings not only for customers but for employees and partners (retailers, advertising agencies, in-store display firms, PR

firms, and so on). Strong brands project a clear brand identity among employees and partners.

- **Leverage brand equity.** Underleveraged brands are unused assets. Leveraging brands means making them work harder—increasing their impact in their core market and extending them into new product markets. One job of brand architecture is to provide a structure and discipline to deal with brand extension opportunities. Brand extensions have risks, of course, that need to be addressed. Of particular sensitivity is the vertical extension of a brand, as the most downscale version will tend to define the brand.
- **Provide a platform for future growth options.** Brand architecture should have its eye on the future and support strategic advances into new product markets. This might mean creating a master brand with significant extension potential, even if such a brand is difficult to justify on the basis of current sales.

There are significant issues surrounding each of the five dimensions of brand architecture. Some (such as the endorser and subbrand roles) were covered in Chapter 4, while others (such as the silver-bullet and strategic brand portfolio roles) were detailed in *Building Strong Brands*. In the balance of this chapter, another key brand architecture issue, that of brand range, will be discussed, followed by a presentation of the architecture audit, a methodology for diagnosing brand architecture problems and opportunities.

## EXTENDING THE RANGE OF A BRAND

A central and strategic brand architecture question involves the range of each of the brands. Extensions help fulfill two objectives of brand architecture: leveraging brand assets, and creating synergy by generating brand exposures and associations in different contexts. Poorly considered extensions can dilute brand associations, however, thereby weakening brands and reducing the clarity of the offerings.

### ARE THERE HORIZONTAL BRAND EXTENSION OPPORTUNITIES?

How far can the brand stretch with respect to its driver role? The answer is simple. The brand should only travel where it fits, where it can add value, and where the new association enhances its equity. Each of these three criteria can be explored with market research.

### Fit

Customers must be comfortable with the brand in the new setting. There can be a variety of bases of fit, including product association (Ocean Spray Cranberry Juice Cocktail), an ingredient (Arm & Hammer Carpet Deodorizer), an attribute (Sunkist Vitamin C tablets), an application (Colgate toothbrushes), user imagery (the Eddie Bauer edition of Ford Explorer), expertise (Honda lawn motors), or designer image (Pierre Cardin wallets).

Whatever the link, the customer should sense a fit rather than a discordant association (McDonald's Photo Processing, for instance, would conjure the image of greasy fries instead of fast, consistent, convenient service). Although such problems can sometimes be managed by altering the perspective (by creating a visual image of a McDonald's photo-processing outlet that is sharply dissimilar from the restaurants, for example), the possibility of such counterproductive associations is very pertinent to decisions whether to stretch a brand.

The rules for such decisions, however, are not written in stone. An intervening extension or two may make a previously excessive stretch feasible and even desirable. A successful extension can help alter perceptions of a brand, which in turn may help the brand fit elsewhere. Virgin, initially a music company, extended its brand to start an airline, which was not a good fit. Once the airline was successful, however, the fit proposition changed completely. The brand evolved into much more of a personality brand—an underdog, feisty and irreverent, but dedicated to high quality—that can work in many arenas.

When a brand is tied closely to a product class, its potential to extend is limited. Thus even though the name Campbell's Soup has many positive associations, the brand has not done so well when it has strayed from soup. Similarly, brands like A–1 Steak Sauce, Kleenex, and Clorox Bleach cannot stretch too far beyond their basic product areas because they are so connected to a specific product and its attributes. In such cases there is a certain irony in that the stronger the brand is, the harder it is to extend. In contrast, brands that have credibility in intangible associations—such as weight control (Weight Watchers), healthy eating (Healthy Choice), and fashion

(Ralph Lauren)—are more able to extend to new categories because those intangibles work in a wide variety of contexts.

The frequent secret to gaining leverage, therefore, is to evolve a brand from a product focus to a deeper relationship with customers. Maggi was a firm that made soup and products to enhance food: it was very product oriented. When it evolved into a partner and friend who helped make cooking fun, its image and ability to extend broadened.

Consumers who have a functional relationship with a brand tend to evaluate extensions more negatively than consumers who have an emotional relationship. Visa customers who perceive their card as simply an efficient way to make payments (a functional relationship) respond more negatively to brand extensions outside the payment category than do customers who perceive Visa to be an information-technology-based global brand.

### Adding value

Wherever the brand goes, it should help the offering. Thus, if a brand such as Campbell's, Williams-Sonoma, or Saturn is placed into a new product market (for example, Campbell's fresh mushrooms, Williams-Sonoma spices, or a Saturn sport utility vehicle), the brand name alone should help customers articulate why the offering is superior to other brands. Where this is the case, the brand offers associations that will be relevant, credible, and valued by customers.

A brand should not detract from or harm the offering by providing unappealing associations. Thus the GM relationship was downplayed in the Saturn offering because it detracted, at least at the outset of Saturn's life. If the Campbell's name were used as a master brand or even an endorser for a line of Italian food, the presumption might be that the products would taste and feel like soup.

### Enhancing brand equity

Conversely, the brand equity should be enhanced by the brand's presence in another context—not only from increased visibility but also from the associations generated. Virgin Cola's outrageous plan to attack Coca-Cola (supported by creative publicity), for example, strengthens the feisty, underdog image that is at the essence of the Virgin brand.

## WHAT ABOUT VERTICAL EXTENSIONS?

There is often considerable incentive to move a brand down to partic-ipate in a large and growing value market, or up to enjoy the product vitality and margins in the upscale market. As the Marriott and GE Appliance cases discussed at the outset of Chapter 4 noted, a vertical stretch is particularly tricky because perceived quality is involved, and also because the use of subbrands and endorsed brands needs to be considered. The safe course is usually to keep the brand at a con-sistent quality level.

Many brands lack both the credibility and the prestige to move upscale. Black & Decker, makers of superior tools for the do-it-your-selfer, failed with its Professional line for construction tradesmen who were "above the home handyman tools"; the line had to be relaunched under the DeWalt name. When upward stretches do work (as with the GE Profile appliances), they tend to be modest in nature. The brands are positioned as better than their established position rather than as one of the best, and the upward stretch is based on functional superi-ority or improvement rather than prestige. In addition, the new offer-ings usually are visibly different, and use subbrands and endorsed brands to separate themselves from the master brand.

In contrast, the value market is much easier to access—as any mountain biker can tell you, it is easier to go down than to go up. Accessing a value market usually poses a significant risk to the brand's reputation and customer base, however, because existing customers will be attracted to the less expensive offering. Further, the value claim may lack credibility coming from a more upscale brand, in part because competitors usually respond by lowering their prices further. Thus Kodak Funtime, a low-priced film offering, enticed mainly loyal Kodak buyers rather than the value-conscious consumers who were targeted. Downward extensions that work, such as Courtyard by Marriott, tend to be clearly separated product offerings aimed at a distinct segment and tend to participate in the value market as an endorser.

# THE BRAND ARCHITECTURE AUDIT

A brand architecture audit provides a systematic way to examine the current brand architecture and to identify problems or issues that merit further analysis and responsive programs. In Figure 5–7 are some two dozen questions to provide a structure and agenda for the audit. Each question is potentially important and can lead to significant analysis and change, but this set of questions is not meant to be exhaustive. As the agenda is pursued, additional questions will appear helpful and relevant.

## BUSINESS ANALYSIS

In the first audit stage, which precedes the examination of the five actual brand architecture dimensions, the business areas are identified and evaluated with respect to their importance to the firm. Two outputs of the business analysis are particularly crucial to the brand architecture audit—an assessment of current and proposed business arenas, and an understanding of the segmentation strategy.

An assessment of what business areas will be most financially significant to the organization is central to many brand architecture issues. One key architecture issue is to identify a plan for strategic, linchpin, and driver brands, so an understanding of each business arena's potential is important. What is the business vision? What are the key strategic initiatives? How is the market defined from a competitive point of view? What is the current market structure, and how is this structure likely to evolve? What is the relative attractiveness of the various submarkets?

An understanding of segmentation and segmentation strategy is similarly important, because the brand portfolio structure needs to overlay the segmentation strategy. (Segmentation had a significant impact, for example, on the Ralph Lauren portfolio structure.) To create a portfolio structure, it is therefore necessary to identify the segmentation variables, the most important segments, the unmet needs of those segments, and how the brand will connect with them.

## BRAND ARCHITECTURE

### Brand Portfolio

With the business analysis in place, the audit should inventory the existing brands and subbrands, the fundamental building blocks of the brand architecture. Which are candidates to be deleted from the active portfolio?

FIGURE 5–7

---

## THE BRAND ARCHITECTURE AUDIT

**BUSINESS ANALYSIS**
- What are the current and potential sales, profits, and growth in the brand's product portfolio?
- What are the strategic initiatives?
- What businesses are important financially and strategically, now and in the future?
- What segments are important financially and strategically, now and in the future?

**BRAND ARCHITECTURE**

**Brand Portfolio**
- Identify the brands and subbrands in the portfolio.

**Portfolio Roles**
- Which brands are the strategic brands (that is, brands representing substantial future profits)?
- Are there (or should there be) any linchpin brands that will leverage important business arenas?
- What brands or subbrands are playing (or should play) silver-bullet roles? Are additional silver bullets needed?
- Are strategic, linchpin, and silver-bullet brands being supported and actively managed?
- What brands should be playing cash cow roles? Do they require the resources they now receive?

**Product-Market Context Roles**
- Identify the brands and subbrands with substantial driver responsibility. How much equity do they have? How strong is each one's link to customers? Which brands need active management and brand building?
- Identify the subbrands and scale them on the driver-descriptive subbrand spectrum. Given that appraisal, are they all receiving an appropriate amount of resources and management?
- Do the existing endorser brands add value as endorsers? Do they detract? Is their identity appropriate for that role? Should their role as endorsers recede or be deleted in some contexts? Are there other contexts in which an endorser should be added or made more pronounced?
- Identify co-brands. Are they well-conceived? Should new ones be

---

considered? What types of partners would serve to enhance the brand?
- Identify the branded components, features, and services. Should these be given a greater or lesser role?
- Are there other components, features, and services now being offered that could be packaged and branded?

**Brand Portfolio Structure**
- Portray the brand portfolio structure by one or more of the following methods:
  —Show a grouping of brands, using logical descriptors such as segment, product type, application, or channel.
  —Diagram all the brand hierarchy trees.
  —Specify the product/market range and potential range of all the major driver and endorser brands.
- Evaluate the brand portfolio structure (and meaningful subparts) as to whether it generates clarity, purpose, and direction versus complexity, ad hoc decisions, and strategic drift.
- Should existing brands be deleted or given a greater or lesser influence in existing contexts? Should new driver brands or subbrands be created?
- Are some brands overextended? Are their images being jeopardized?
- Are the driver brands and subbrands adequately leveraged? What are some possible horizontal brand extensions? Does the potential exist to extend brands vertically (with or without a subbrand)?

**Portfolio Graphics**
- Lay out a sample of the way that the brands are presented visually, including logos and communication material. Is it clear, consistent, and logical, or is there confusion and inconsistency? Is the relative importance of each brand reflected in the visuals? Is there visual energy?
- Does the visual presentation of the brand across the portfolio support the portfolio structure? Does it support the context roles? Does it support the brand identities?

**MANAGING THE BRAND ARCHITECTURE**
- What is the process by which a brand or subbrand gets added to the portfolio? What criteria are used?
- Is the brand architecture periodically reviewed?
- Who is in charge of the visual presentation of the brand? What is the process by which the visual presentation of the brand is managed?

### Brand Portfolio Roles

Identify those brands within the brand portfolio that are playing strategic, linchpin, cash-cow, or silver-bullet roles. Are the strategic, linchpin, and silver-bullet brands getting the resources they need, or are they being starved? Are these brands successful, and does their access to resources reflect the importance of their role? Are the cash-cow brands receiving an appropriate level of brand-building resources, or are they getting excessive support because of their current sales and profit levels? Should any brands be assigned portfolio roles? In particular, are additional silver bullets needed to assist brands with image problems?

### Product-Market Context Roles

The audit then turns to the use of endorsers and subbrands, branded benefits, co-brands, and driver brands. What are the driver brands? Are they receiving adequate support? Are the endorsers adding value or getting in the way? Are there brands that could contribute as endorsers? Are subbrands contributing enough to warrant the resources they require? Are the current branded benefits fully exploited? Are more needed? Would co-brand partnerships with other organizations be helpful?

### Brand Portfolio Structure

The brand portfolio structure portion of the audit starts by asking whether there is a logical structure to the brand portfolio that can be portrayed with a brand grouping, a hierarchy tree, and/or a specification of the range of each brand. Does the portfolio suggest clarity, purpose, and direction? Should the brand portfolio be pruned? Are some brands overextended? Are others underleveraged? Should some be extended?

### Portfolio Graphics

The analysis of portfolio graphics is best done with a visual summary—perhaps using a large wall—of the visual representations of a brand in all its contexts. Does this visual presentation of the brand across the portfolio create clarity or confusion? Does it support the portfolio structure? Does it support the context roles? Does it support the brand identities? A problem might suggest that design work is needed to create a graphical system. It might also suggest that the management of the graphics is out of control, and so the management system should be reviewed.

## MANAGING THE BRAND ARCHITECTURE

Procedures and organizational structures to create, review, and improve the brand architecture should be available and working. There should be a periodic brand architecture audit to uncover emerging problems with the architecture, as well as an audit of all or part of the brand portfolio when a new product is being considered or an acquisition is made. In fact, an acquisition that introduces a set of brands into the portfolio almost always raises serious architecture issues.

Problems that are detected in a brand architecture audit should prompt analysis and action programs. For example, if the brand architecture is creating confusion, the contributing elements of the architecture (such as the number of brands, or the level of subbrands) should be identified and responsive programs developed.

Management of brand architecture also involves mechanisms to communicate the architecture to those in the firm whose decisions will affect it. The visual presentation, in particular, needs to be communicated. Having a logo cop, however, is not all there is to managing the architecture. There is also a need to be concerned with the way brands are being used: What product extensions are being considered? What new markets? How are new offerings branded? Brand architecture includes visual presentation but goes way beyond it.

## QUESTIONS FOR DISCUSSION

1. Conduct a brand architecture audit.
2. Identify programs to address the emerging issues.

# PART IV

# BUILDING BRANDS:
# BEYOND ADVERTISING

# 6

## Adidas and Nike— Lessons in Building Brands

You don't win silver, you lose gold.
There is no finish line.

—Nike ads

Every player, every level, every game.
Earn them.

—Adidas ads

The stories of Adidas and Nike offer some instructive lessons in building brands. The Adidas story centers on Europe, where innovations in the 1950s, 1960s, and 1970s helped create a dominant brand. Adidas faltered in its key European market in the 1980s in part due to the Nike challenge, but rebounded during the 1990s because of paradigm-breaking efforts. The Nike story centers on the United States and features its own brand-building success stories—first during the 1970s, and again in the 1980s and 1990s when it recovered from the Reebok challenge and enjoyed a remarkable growth record. The strategy and execution of the brand-building programs of these two organizations is a fascinating story.

Our goal is not to provide comprehensive biographies of these two brands; rather, it is to highlight some of their brand-building programs and put them in a historical context. By exploring not only what was done but why it was done and why it was successful, we hope to generate insights that have value for other brands as well.

This is the first of four chapters that address the challenge of creating brand-building programs. Chapter 7 will discuss how sponsorship can be used to build a brand. Chapter 8 will turn to brand building on the Web. Many firms struggle with sponsorships and the Web because, unlike advertising and promotions, how these two avenues work to build brands and how they should be managed is not well understood. Further, the discussion of brand building in those two specific contexts will illustrate issues and principles that apply to other contexts as well. Finally, the case studies in Chapter 9 will illustrate other successful approaches and discuss the highest level of brand building—building deep relationships and core groups of committed customers.

Many of the major observations, insights, and guidelines detailed in this part of the book will be listed at the end of each chapter. One theme is that brand building is not just advertising, and so the management of a brand should not be delegated to an ad agency. Instead, with the brand identity and brand position as guides, the task is to create an integrated assortment of communication and association-building media. The challenge is to access alternatives and to manage them so that they create a coordinated synergistic impact—not an easy task, given the conceptual and organizational realities of the real world.

## ADIDAS—THE GROWTH PERIOD

Adidas was founded in 1948 by Adi Dassler, a German shoemaker and dedicated amateur athlete. Dassler had been in business since 1926, when his family set up a factory to produce special lightweight track and soccer shoes. Following a family dispute, the Dassler Company split in 1948 into two firms. One, named Puma, was owned by Adi Dassler's brother; the other became Adidas.

Adi Dassler was to Adidas what Phil Knight later became to Nike, and much more. Not only an athlete and a sports enthusiast, he also was an inventor and entrepreneur who valued craftsmanship, quality, and a dedication to innovation. He listened to top athletes, attended track meets, and sat on the bench with competitors to assess their needs. "Function first" became the company's leitmotiv, and its slogan was "The Best for Athletes." Over time, Adidas developed a reputation as the company that made shoes for serious athletes.

From the outset, the strength of Adidas was its product innovation. Adi Dassler was the genius behind many of the breakthroughs, registering more than seven hundred patents. The first shoe for use on ice; the first multistudded shoe; and a special lightweight, molded-rubber studded soccer shoe—all were born at Adidas. The screw-in studs on Adidas soccer shoes were such a revolutionary concept that they were considered one of the key reasons why the German soccer team won the World Cup in 1954.

In many ways, Adidas was run as a family firm: Adi Dassler's wife helped to manage the business, and all five children worked there. Horst Dassler, the oldest son, stood out as having a knack for marketing and promotions. He became the pioneer of visibly linking a brand with sports—athletes, teams, events, and associations. He made Adidas the first firm to give free shoes to top athletes, and the first to sign long-term agreements to supply entire sports teams with footwear (thereby ensuring that Adidas footwear was worn by many of the world's greatest athletes in the top venues of the world). But the most important marketing breakthrough was the active promotion of global sporting events, especially the Olympics.

The connection of Adidas to the Olympics has a rich heritage. Dassler shoes were first used in the 1928 Olympics and first worn by a gold medal winner in 1932. The American sprinter/jumper Jesse Owens won a record four gold medals in Germany in 1936 with an irritated Adolf Hitler in the audience; photos featuring Jesse Owens in Dassler shoes were reprinted around the world. The Olympics is an ideal sponsorship for Adidas because it is prestigious, showcases the best athletes, and provides a vehicle to demonstrate the performance of the shoes across a broad range of sports. Unlike the products of other sponsors (such as Visa and Coke), the Adidas shoes are used during the competition to enhance performance. The continuing association of Adidas with Olympic athletes and the event itself over a long time period made it feasible for Adidas to create a strong link to the Olympics. Brands that only sporadically become Olympic sponsors find it difficult to develop such a link.

One of Horst Dassler's innovative ideas was to time new product introductions with the occasion of specific sports events. Adidas began this practice with the Melbourne subbrand, an innovative multiple-studded shoe that was introduced at the 1956 Melbourne Olympics. What better way to link Adidas with the Olympics and create a strong performance subbrand. Seventy-two medals were won and thirty-three records broken in Adidas footwear in that year.

Backed by the Dasslers' innovations, Adidas used a pyramid of influence model of brand building, which worked on three levels. First, the serious athlete was enticed to use the brand not only by incentives but also because it delivered innovation and quality supporting the highest performance standards. Second, the visibility of the brand being worn by these top athletes in major competitions established demand among a larger layer of potential customers: weekend warriors and amateur athletes. Word-of-mouth communications and products that delivered to their needs played key roles at this level. Third, the preferences of athletes at both levels filtered down to casual users.

The active promotion of Adidas-sponsored professional athletes, sports clubs, and major events such as the Olympic games was geared to all three levels, but was especially focused on the professional athlete, the first tier. Free exposure on television of major competitive events translated directly into brand-building visibility for Adidas with casual users, the third tier.

The pyramid-of-influence model worked particularly well because Adidas was the dominant player for many contexts during the 1960s and 1970s. The market size differential allowed Adidas to pursue its strategy much more aggressively and effectively than smaller competitors; it also was able to dominate the endorsements of the major visible athletes.

By 1980, Adidas had sales of $1 billion, with market shares as high as 70 percent in some key product categories. The company offered roughly 150 different shoe styles, producing 200,000 pairs per day in twenty-four factories in 17 countries. Its diversified product line (including clothing, sports equipment, and athletic gear) sold in more than 150 countries.

In the early 1980s, however, the Adidas brand-building model began to lose power. In America, the world's largest sports market, Nike had built a successful business in part by riding the explosive growth of running and jogging among casual users, the lowest layer of the pyramid. It is hard to imagine how the trend toward jogging could have been missed by Adidas; a late-1970s survey showed that more than half of all Americans had tried it. The number of contestants in the New York City Marathon increased from 156 to 5,000 between 1970 and 1977.[1]

While Adidas had a strong presence in running among athletes, it did not take either the jogging fad or Nike seriously because things were going so well. It was the familiar curse of success: why invest in new, uncertain business areas? As neither a team nor competitive activity, jogging was very different than the markets the company was used to. Further, the Adidas brand-building model did not work for joggers. There were few teams, clubs, or associations (and no national or global federations) for jogging with which Adidas could build relationships.

There was also a bit of arrogance involved. The shoe design that worked for joggers was foreign to Adidas designers, who felt that anything that would cushion the runner was somehow a professional compromise. In fact, when they finally came out with a running shoe, it was nicknamed "the Crippler," because it would cripple anyone wearing it. This Adidas attitude is somewhat reminiscent of the reaction of German car firms to the appeal of the Lexus automobile: Good cars for serious drivers do not have soft rides and cup holders.

## THE NIKE STORY

Phil Knight founded Blue Ribbon Sports in 1964 with the intention of importing low-price Onizuka athletic shoes from Japan to the United States. Associated with Knight in this venture was Bill Bowerman—a track coach at the University of Oregon, a student of running and shoes, and an innovative shoe designer. Their goal was to improve shoes for competitive runners as well as create a business. A brand graphic was established that can best be described as a combination of the Adidas and Puma logos. The shoe brand name, however, changed several times during these early years, from Onizuka to Onizuka Tiger to Tiger to Asics. Quality problems, delivery problems, and business disputes abounded.

In 1972 Blue Ribbon Sports began to manufacture its own line of products in Korea and established both the name Nike and its swoosh trademark (which by the way, was designed for only $35). During the 1970s, Nike's sales revenues doubled or tripled almost every year, from $14 million in 1976 to $71 million in 1978, $270 million in 1980, and more than $900 million in 1983. In 1979, Nike sold almost half of all running shoes purchased in America. A year later, it even surpassed Adidas, the longtime U.S. market leader in athletic shoe sales. The engine behind this phenomenal sales growth was the running, jogging, and health craze that began in the mid-1970s and swept through the United States (and, soon after, much of the rest of the world). Because of its track and running heritage, Nike was well positioned to take advantage of this trend. In addition, Phil Knight, as a former track athlete and active runner, was sensitive to the growing interests and needs of the participants.

Phil Knight wanted Nike, like Adidas, to be a serious sports shoe brand—from jocks for jocks. The Nike philosophy was that better technology leads to better performance, and the company gained the respect of the serious running community by creating a string of innovative products and features. Among its 1970s inventions were the Waffle Sole (named after a waffle iron used to make a prototype) and the Astrograbbers (designed especially for use on Astroturf), both of which made an immediate difference in the performance of athletes.

Following the Adidas model, the early Nike brand-building efforts consisted of encouraging athlete endorsements. In the early years, rising stars and the Olympic trials were a focus because Nike's resources were inadequate to attract the top athletes; as revenues grew, however, so did the scope of the endorsement program. The goal was to get the Nike logo in the winner's circle and on television—not only to gain credibility and free exposure for the shoe but to create emotional and self-expressive benefits. Tapping into the emotion in sports has been a part of the Nike mystique from the beginning.

The type of athlete sought by Nike was very different from the Adidas athlete: edgy, provocative, aggressive, independent, someone with an attitude—in short, his or her own person. The original athlete associated with Nike, Steve Prefontaine, was a star distance runner who was highly competitive and embodied this iconoclastic personality. He tragically died in a car accident in 1975 and is memorialized in a statue at Nike headquarters. Tennis great Ilie Nastase, who was nicknamed "Nasty" with good reason, also fit the mold; Nike signed him away from Adidas in 1972 (for what turned out to be a short-lived association). John McEnroe, another brilliant tennis player well known for temper tantrums on the court, signed in 1978.

The Nike McEnroe ad showed a picture of a shoe with the text: "Nike, McEnroe's favorite four-letter word." This pun nicely expressed the essence of the Nike brand.

The Nike personality was also captured in the company's early print advertising. Among its first ads in magazines like *Runner's World* in 1977 was a photograph of a woman running across a bridge in a traffic jam, with the headline "Man vs. Machine." Another ad showed a picture of a lone runner on a narrow two-lane road flanked by towering trees; the headline read, "There is no finish line." The image took the reader away from the hectic urban environment into a place where the air was clean and the challenge was from within. The experience shown was a high for a committed runner. This ad resonated with the audience and became a widely distributed poster displayed in thousands of bedrooms, dorms, and living areas. The advertising and posters contributed to making Nike appear cool, especially in contrast to the more mechanistic, authoritarian Adidas.

Because of the relatively small size of Nike in the mid-1970s and the high endorsement costs of pro athletes, its advertising and endorsement programs had to be modest. Looking for the most impact with a small budget, Nike established its advisory board. College coaches on the board would receive free shoes for their teams, support for the summer camps they sponsored, a modest honorarium, and a first-class annual trip to Nike headquarters. The coaches could not believe it—they got paid to receive free shoes! During the first year (1978), ten top coaches signed on. The program subsequently got fifty coaches involved and resulted in the Nike logo appearing in the NCAA Final Four (the semifinal and final rounds of the men's college basketball tournament), a prime television event.

Another cost-effective program was Athletes West, a training center in Eugene, Oregon, for Olympic competitors who lacked facilities and resources to train in the off-season. Private help of this nature was especially appreciated by Americans in an era when Eastern European athletes were subsidized by their governments. Athletes West, which opened in 1977, provided significant publicity and sent a bonding message to top athletes. Nike was on their side.

One more important program at Nike, Ekins (whose name was based on "Nike" spelled backwards), combined a technical rep and sales person, with grassroots brand-building activities. New Nike hires who joined the Ekins program received extensive training about the technology of the shoes, as well as the Nike philosophy. The Ekins team members then went into their assigned markets and provided sales consulting services to sports stores, educated orthopedic doctors at a highly sophisticated technical level about how Nike shoes helped prevent injuries, organized sales clinics and road shows, and interacted with athletes during weekend competitions (road races, track and field trials, and so on). Anything they learned was filtered back to Nike headquarters to guide research.

The Ekins program was unique and even revolutionary at that time. No other shoe company had such an extensive army of highly competent technical and sales consultants in the field who loved sports and understood it—this belly-to-belly brand-building effort created relationships with key influentials. The program had roots in the earliest days of Nike, when its managers hung out at track meets.

## NIKE FALTERS

In 1983 there was a crisis at Nike: inventories were bloated, sales and profits were down, some key people left, Knight withdrew from the day-to-day running of the company, and downsizing began. There was a variety of causes, including an aggressive move into apparel that was accompanied by weak design and inferior merchandise. The brand was drifting, and there were some ill-advised extensions—into women's casual clothing, for example. Recent efforts to enter Europe had siphoned off important management and financial resources. The new product machine was not producing big winners. But the most visible cause was the fact that Nike was blindsided by Reebok.

Reebok grew from $35 million in annual sales in 1982 to more than $300 million in 1985 by exploiting the fitness and aerobics craze among women, especially in the United States. Reebok introduced comfortable athletic footwear constructed of soft, pliable leather in a variety of bold fashionable colors. The Reebok shoes became a hit with style-conscious consumers, especially women. Actress Cybill Shepherd anointed them as a fashion statement when she wore a bright orange pair of Reeboks with her formal evening dress to the Emmy awards ceremony. Reebok in effect stepped into a remarkable void in the athletic footwear industry, and Nike (along with Adidas) was hurting as a result.

Nike's failure to recognize and respond to this trend was remarkably similar to how Adidas reacted to the running craze nearly ten years prior. Nike was doing well, thank you very much, so it was not interested in trends involving new markets (namely, women's aerobics) and new business models in which endorsements and college advisory board programs would not work. There was also arrogance once again, as Nike designers perceived Reebok shoes to be a bit frivolous and shoddy—not shoes for the serious runner or athlete.

## NIKE COMES BACK

As Nike struggled to come back, Phil Knight took charge again and set about redefining its brand identity. He concluded that Nike was about sports and fitness and performance, a statement that helped to refocus the brand in terms of what Nike was and was not (see Figure 6–1). Casual shoes and clothing did not fit; basketball shoes did. Another conclusion, that Nike is about emotional ties to the consumer, implied that the Nike brand should move beyond the product

FIGURE 6–1

---

### NIKE BRAND IDENTITY—AROUND 1984

**CORE IDENTITY**

Sports and fitness
Performance shoes based on technological innovation
Top athletes and serious sports enthusiasts
The exhilaration of winning

**EXTENDED IDENTITY**

Brand personality of being:
- aggressive, provocative, in-your-face
- spirited, cool
- masculine

Swoosh symbol, athletic personalities
Heritage of running shoe innovation, and the Oregon setting
American country of origin for non-U.S. markets

---

to the experience of using it in athletics (as opposed to casual living settings).

Knight also changed the rules of the brand-building game. For twenty years Nike had relied on endorsements and a lot of them; by 1983 it had roughly two thousand track and field athletes, half of the National Basketball Association, and a host of others under contract. And the cost of obtaining these endorsements was going up each year, consuming most of the Nike communication budget. In contrast, advertising had been minimal, limited mostly to specialized magazines. This communications approach was about to change. The endorsement strategy would focus on impact rather than on numbers; a very limited number of influential athletes would carry the ball. Meanwhile, Nike would step up its commitment to advertising in order to push the brand to the front of the crowd. Michael Jordan was both an instrument and symbol of this new policy.

After three difficult years, sales started to grow again. In 1986 Nike finally became a $1 billion company and began an incredible run of sales and profit growth. Sales went to $2.2 billion in 1990, $3.8 billion in 1994, and $9.6 billion in 1998. During this time three brand-building policies and programs contributed to Nike's success: the endorsement focus strategy (starting with Michael Jordan), a commitment to use national advertising to create a dominant presence, and the development of NikeTown stores.

### MICHAEL JORDAN—THE ENDORSEMENT FOCUS STRATEGY

In late 1984, Nike signed Michael Jordan to a five-year contract plus Nike stock and an unprecedented royalty on shoes with the Jordan name; the total value was estimated to be $1 million per year. This amount was more than five times that offered by Adidas or Converse, both of whom thought of Jordan as just another athlete endorsing products rather than the centerpiece of a marketing program and line of shoes and clothing. In a cover story, *Fortune* called the contract a big mistake, given Nike's financial problems. It turned out to be an all-time bargain, however, in large part because Michael Jordan exceeded everyone's expectations.

Jordan turned out to be, in the opinions of many, the best basketball player ever. His worldwide impact had as much to do with the style of his play as with the quality—rather than dominate through sheer size and strength, Jordan used his quickness and leaping ability to float through the air and improvise spectacular plays. People were captivated by his seemingly supernatural talents, and the youth of the world had a hero. In addition, Jordan turned out to be a poised, smart person with an engaging personality, an enviable work ethic, and a visible will to succeed. Ultimately, he was a rare athlete who was able to transcend countries and sports, a quality that paid off as Nike leveraged Jordan's many assets into the basis for a substantial business.

The impact of Jordan on Nike was huge. The epitome of performance, excitement, energy, and prestige, Jordan was bigger than life and an ideal symbol for Nike. He provided the opportunity for Nike to create Air Jordan, a line of distinctively colored basketball shoes and a coordinated collection of clothing. The Air Jordan launch was a commercial as well as a branding success, selling nearly $100 million the first year. When Jordan wore the shoes for the first time, NBA officials banned them because they violated league dress regulations. Sensing a public relations opportunity, Nike ran an ad declaring that Air Jordan was "NBA banned because of its revolutionary design." When Nike and Air Jordan received enormous press coverage as a result, the NBA surrendered, creating a pro-Nike ending to the story.

Air Jordans not only leveraged the magnetism of Jordan but also provided a new way to showcase a technology that Nike had owned since 1974—sealed gas bladders incorporated in the soles of the shoes. (The Air technology, by the way, had been offered to Adidas by a NASA engineer before he went to Nike, but Adidas passed on it.)

While the shoes sold well initially, sales leveled off quickly. Believing that the public did not understand the Air technology, Nike developed the Visible Air shoe (with a see-through window at the sides of the soles), as well as the Air Max line of shoes. The new line was launched in 1987 with a $20 million ad budget; it was Nike's first use of TV advertising. The functional benefit of the Air technology was copied by competitors, but the association with Jordan and the ownership of the "Air" brand allowed Nike to own the perceived technological advantage.

Jordan also allowed Nike to break out of the running shoe niche and build a business around basketball, which just happened to be surging in popularity in the United States. Nike almost overnight became the premier basketball shoe in prestige, if not in sales.

The Jordan endorsement validated the star endorsement philosophy as well. Only a few years after Jordan was signed, Bo Jackson (at that time the only athlete skilled enough to excel in both professional football and baseball) was signed to represent cross-trainers, an important new athletic shoe category that Nike created in 1987. The "Bo knows football" and "Bo knows baseball" ads and posters that were created quickly became part of the popular culture. When Jackson became incapacitated by a hip condition, he was eventually replaced with Deion Sanders, also a football and baseball star. In 1995 Tiger Woods was signed to do for Nike in golf what Jordan did in basketball—create a presence in the sport and support a line of equipment and clothing.

### ADVERTISING—CREATING A DOMINANT MEDIA PRESENCE

Many brands ask the question: What would happen if we stepped up and developed an aggressive advertising campaign and maintained it consistently over a long time period? How much equity would be built? Would it make a difference? Would it allow us to dominate the industry? Would the benefit outweigh the costs? Nike did exactly that, and so it is an excellent case study. The firm made a commitment to advertise at a significantly higher level, obtained excellence in execution, and had the patience to stick to its executions through time. In essence, Nike changed its brand-building model by deciding to market directly to the large customer base rather than relying on the trickle-down model whereby accomplished and serious athletes would influence the larger market.

Nike's first major advertising effort to consumers was $20 million spent before the Los Angeles Olympics in 1984. That year, Nike's U.S. sales decreased by 12 percent and profits dropped by 30 percent. Between 1985 and 1987, Nike's problem worsened. Its share in the U.S. market dropped from 27.2 to 16 percent—mostly to the advantage of Reebok, which grew from nothing to more than 32 percent of the market. Nike was undeterred, however, and aggressively increased its annual advertising spending to $45 million by 1989 and $150 million by 1992.

### *The Cities Campaign*

In a breakout campaign in the mid-1980s, Nike quickly created a dominant media presence in several trend-setting United States cities. TV ads linking Nike to a city were used, but the real drivers were huge, oversized billboards and murals on buildings (see Figure 6–2) that blanketed cities with messages featuring key Nike-sponsored athletes (not products).[2] Carl Lewis's legs extended past the natural frame of billboards for a special attention-getting effect. This visual presence was supported by an in-store effort to translate the advertising into sales.

The centerpiece of the program was Los Angeles during the 1984 Olympic Games. The effort included an "I love L.A." commercial with clips of key sponsored athletes in action—Carl Lewis leaping through the sky and landing in the sands of Venice Beach, for example, and John McEnroe arguing with a traffic cop. These scenes were

FIGURE 6–2
*Nike Painted Building*

also captured on billboards and murals. The resulting visibility and presence for Nike spilled over into the Olympic media coverage, causing Nike's perceived association with the Olympic Games to be several times that of Converse, the official sponsor. While Converse spent money on sponsorship and Adidas poured money into teams, Nike captured the eyes of the consumers.

### Media advertising

It was through national media advertising that Nike really stepped out of the field in the consumer's mind. Nike did it both with media weight and by quality of execution. For example, an early Michael Jordan commercial showed him soaring through the air on the way to dunking the ball, with the tagline "Who says man was not meant to fly?" This image became the symbol of Michael Jordan and was one of the most popular posters ever. The personal side of Jordan was exposed in a series of humorous ads developed by Spike Lee, at that time a relatively unknown avant-garde director.

Nike advertising hit a home run with the "Just do it" campaign

FIGURE 6–3
*The Just Do It Campaign*

launched in 1988 (see Figure 6–3). This Nike effort was named the fourth best advertising campaign in the century by *Advertising Age*, behind only the famous Volkswagen "Think small" campaign of the 1950s and 1960s, the Coca-Cola 1920s advertising with "The pause that refreshes," and the long-running Marlboro Man campaign.[3] It ranked ahead of campaigns by McDonald's ("You deserve a break today."), DeBeers ("A diamond is forever."), Miller Lite Beer ("Tastes great, less filling"), Avis ("We try harder.") and Absolut vodka (the bottle).

The first "Just do it" ad showed wheelchair racer Craig Blanchette and the slogan in white letters on a black background. The tagline was never spoken; however, it resonated with an entire generation. As the Nike advertising director, Scott Bedbury, noted: "We can't put it on pencils and key chains; this thing has become much more than an ad slogan. It's an idea. It's like a frame of mind."[4] It connected with overweight men putting off an exercise program, busy executives becoming diverted from fitness, and people of all types with a dream on hold. It associated Nike with making fitness actually happen, setting the right priorities, and living (as opposed to thinking) the dream.

The "Just do it" slogan had a long run. It was supplemented for a short time in 1997 by the "I Can" slogan, which challenged athletes to set their own limits and suggested that achievement is up to the individual. The change was an effort to influence consumer perceptions and to make Nike fit better with the major trends of caring and sharing of the 1990s. It was confused and failed to resonate, however, in part because the creative execution did not break through. It may have also been the right idea at the wrong time. The lack of success of the "I can" campaign reinforces the view that to have a great campaign, a host of factors must all work.

## NIKETOWN—FLAGSHIP STORE

Nike opened the first NikeTown store on Chicago's North Michigan Avenue in 1992. There had never been anything quite like it in brand building: a major retail presence with nearly 70,000 square feet of selling space on three floors, using eighteen individual product pavilions to showcase the total Nike line. Much more than anything else, though, it communicated the essence of Nike by capturing its energy, its "Just do it" philosophy, and its in-your-face attitude. The air is

FIGURE 6–4
*Nike Flagship Store*

filled with MTV-style music and huge TV screens with replays from important games, the huge poster of Michael Jordan flying through the air, and a Michael Jordan shrine. The store's architecture, layout, people, displays, and overall look and feel all say Nike.

In 1996, the NikeTown store surpassed the Art Institute as Chicago's number one tourist attraction, with more than 1 million visitors and $25 million in annual sales. Within six years after the Chicago NikeTown opened, a dozen more NikeTowns appeared, including one in New York City. These stores all provided customers with a Nike experience unfettered by competitors or by the conflicting needs of other retailers. Most alternative ways to reach customers are fragmented and cluttered; further, most retailers presenting Nike material are not motivated to devote significant store space to building the Nike brand (as opposed to displaying Nike merchandise). Thus NikeTown plays a key role as the centerpiece of Nike brand building, the anchor to which all other efforts are connected.

### NIKE IN EUROPE

Nike set up shop in Europe in 1981 and quickly developed a presence (helped by the struggles of Adidas); its success in Europe helped to soften the difficulties Nike faced in the United States. In 1984, for example, overall Nike sales grew, even though U.S. sales dropped more than 10 percent.

The challenge to Nike in Europe was largely one of positioning. Nike's brand strategy in Europe was basically to build the brand on its traditional emphasis of performance and technological excellence for the serious athlete. These core identity elements had served Nike well in the United States, but Adidas also owned these associations in Europe. Nike therefore needed to differentiate itself, and it did so with the Nike personality and its American heritage.

Nike's American associations provided credibility and depth to the brand. Because many Europeans saw jogging and fitness as trendy activities that came from America, it was easy for Nike to develop a position in these key areas. Among Europeans, particularly younger ones, there is a love for all things American; Coca-Cola, Harley-Davidson, McDonald's, Marlboro, and Levi's have benefited from this love, and so did Nike.

Nike's European brand-building effort used the same American athletes as its U.S. ads, even touting American sports such as basketball. All ad copy was written in English; there was no adaptation for any country except France.

Nike's personality was also a key driver of the brand identity and the brand position in Europe. Nike's provocative, in-your-face attitude, coupled with its underdog position in the marketplace, especially appealed to the key youth segment, who felt that Nike was cool in part because it made irreverence acceptable—even celebrated it. In sharp contrast, Adidas was more mainstream, soft spoken, and inclusive. It was the shoe your father and grandfather wore. Not coincidentally, Nike was one of the first advertisers on the European

## FLAGSHIP STORES*

The use of a flagship or theater or event store has been adopted by other brands since NikeTown first appeared. Brands such as Sony, (shown in Figure 6–4), Polo Ralph Lauren, Warner Brothers, Disney, Sega, Virgin, Bass Pro Shops, and REI have recognized the power of creating a brand theater where the sets, props, and players all support the brand. The Bass Pro Shops Outdoor World in Springfield, Missouri, which draws 4 million visitors a year, includes a four-story waterfall, rifle and archery ranges, four aquariums, an indoor driving range, a putting green, and a wildlife museum. The REI store that opened in Seattle in 1996 is true to the company's image as a premier source of outdoor gear. It includes a 470-foot mountain biking trail, a fireplace for testing camp stoves, a shower chamber for testing raingear, a hiking trail, and the centerpiece—the world's largest free-standing indoor climbing wall.

The flagship store not only provides the ultimate commercial opportunity by immersing customers in a brand experience, it also lets those inside the organization see the brand identity and its implementation come together. What are the critical elements of creating a successful brand-building flagship store environment? Research by Prophet Brand Strategy suggests six guidelines:

1. **Have a clear brand identity.** Make sure that there is a clear brand identity that will guide the flagship store. All elements of the organization need not only to contribute to the store but also to coordinate with it. Everything needs to be consistent, and it all flows from the brand identity. The integrated synergistic impact of the store, combined with other brand-building efforts, creates the real payoff.
2. **Provide a brand-related consumer benefit.** Avoid making the store a museum to the brand, or an entertainment center unrelated to the brand. The REI store, for example, is designed around educating the consumer by demystifying complex products; in this environment, customers can touch, use, and experiment with a variety of outdoor gear.
3. **Leverage brand assets.** A flagship store has the potential to present all forms of brand assets, including symbols, color, music, heritage, and unique product lines. At Sony stores, for example, products are

---

displayed by modeling complete home and office environments featuring Sony products.

4. **Create a superior shopping experience.** The flagship store is still a store, and so it should be designed for a shopping experience that is fun, productive, and exciting. The challenge is to be a functional store and still do the brand building.

5. **Continuously innovate to keep the experience fresh.** Without freshness, the store will have a been-there, done-that feeling. New products are, of course, the lifeblood of retail vitality, but a flagship store needs more change and innovation than new products provide.

6. **Leverage the store and its learning.** Do not treat the store as a silo; leverage it to gain publicity. During the first six years of NikeTown, there were some 1,900 stories in the press about it. And learn from the shoppers—experiment to find out what works and what appeals to them, then apply it elsewhere in the system.

*Source: Flagship Stores, Prophet Brand Strategy.

---

MTV music channel, spending significantly more than all established sports brands combined.

## GOOD MORNING, ADIDAS

Adidas did not participate in the boom of the 1980s; it slept through it. With Adi Dassler's death in 1978, it lost its primary source of technological innovation. With the untimely death of his son Horst Dassler in 1985, it lost its brand visionary. The Adidas brand began to drift and lose focus, and in 1989 the company was sold to a controversial French businessman, Bernard Tapie. Three years later Tapie, endowed with more political ambition than business acumen, found himself in financial difficulties and ceded control of Adidas to a consortium of French banks.

The picture could not have been gloomier for Adidas. Between 1988 and 1992 its total annual sales dropped from nearly $2 billion to $1.7 billion; in the same time period, Nike's sales mushroomed from $1.2 billion to more than $3.4 billion. From being the U.S. market leader in the late 1970s, Adidas's market share dropped to 3 percent in 1992. In Germany, Adidas's key European market, its market share dropped from 40 to 34 percent between 1991 and 1992, while Nike's share grew from 14 to 18 percent. In the same year, Nike's European sales grew by 38 percent, while Adidas sales decreased by almost 20 percent and the company lost over $100 million.

There were a host of causes for this predicament. Adidas was late to recognize the jogging craze and, later, the aerobics movement. And when it did belatedly respond, its new products and appeals lacked direction and deviated from the brand's core values (Adidas no longer "stood for something, so it fell for anything," as Aaron Tippin reminds us in one of his songs). In addition, the Adidas marketing program continued to be based on 1970s models while Nike was innovating and creating new best-practice approaches. It is no wonder that Adidas had an image problem, particularly among the young—it was perceived as being conservative and functional, but not trendy.

### ADIDAS TURNS THE CORNER

In the spring of 1993, amid worsening financial difficulties, the French banks that owned Adidas sold the company to an investor group headed by Robert Louis-Dreyfus, who had just completed a turnaround of the advertising agency Saatchi & Saatchi. The arrival of Louis-Dreyfus, who became the CEO, was preceded by the hiring of Rob Strasser, a former Nike executive, and Peter Moore, a creative talent with substantial Nike experience. This new management team gets much of the credit for turning Adidas around.

One of their first moves was to scale back the many different directions of Adidas and to cut the bloated product line. They then carefully developed an Adidas brand identity and brand-building initiatives. The initiatives included a new high-end equipment subbrand, a new brand management structure, revitalized advertising, a refocused sponsorship program, and Adidas-branded grassroots events.

### THE ADIDAS BRAND IDENTITY

The new executive team realized that the Adidas brand, once strong and focused, had drifted. They wanted to bring the brand identity

FIGURE 6–5

---

**ADIDAS BRAND IDENTITY—1993**

CORE IDENTITY

- Performance
  - Innovative equipment
  - A partner that enhances performance
- Active participation—not just competing to win
  - Not just top athletes but ordinary people
  - Excelling, stretching limits
- Emotion
  - The thrill of achieving goals
  - The excitement of competing

EXTENDED IDENTITY

- Quality products you depend on
- Serious athletes dedicated to sport (not fashion driven)
- The best for the athlete
- The original sports shoe since 1926
- Personality of being:
  - Genuine, unpretentious, and competent
  - Energetic
  - Supportive teammates

---

back to its roots, to recall what it had once stood for and at the same time bring more emotion and a contemporary feel to it. As a result of this process, a clearer picture of Adidas emerged to help guide the brand-building efforts. Among the key dimensions of the identity (summarized in Figure 6–5) were performance, active participation, and emotion. These dimensions can be elaborated as follows.

*Performance.* Adidas is fundamentally a company and brand that delivers superior, innovative products. Its heritage is innovation that enhances the performance of top athletes. Adidas is authentic in that it understands athletes and their sports; it is a partner who helps them to achieve their personal best.

*Active Participation.* Whereas Nike equates performance with winning and top athletes, Adidas is more about participation. To Adidas, performance is overcoming limitations and crossing boundaries, and it can be manifested by an athlete in competition with himself or with the environment. Adidas is inclusive and supports every player, every level, every game, every gender, and every age. Everyone can and should participate, not just the top athletes. Adidas is about teams, teamwork, and team spirit rather than stars and individuals.

*Emotion.* At the core of every sport is excitement—whether it be the thrill of victory, the exhilaration of excelling, the emotion surrounding a team effort, or the thrill of meeting a physical challenge. Whereas Nike is associated with aggressive, almost angry emotion (encapsulated by the phrase "Just do it"), Adidas is connected to positive emotions that relate more to competing than to winning. For Adidas, challenging oneself is exciting; winning is the reward, not the reason, for playing well.

This brand identity effort gave Adidas a personality goal for the first time. It was to be a brand that was genuine, energetic, competent, and a supportive teammate. The personality, in a way, reflects true sportsmanship—a person who is fair and plays by the rules, a player with a strong work ethic, a good team player.

The new Adidas identity made a powerful brand statement in 1993, creating focus for the brand and clarifying how it differed from Nike. It retained the Adidas heritage of technology, innovation, and performance while also stretching the brand in some positive directions.

## CREATING A BRAND-BUILDING FOCUS AROUND THE ADIDAS BRAND IDENTITY

### A New Performance Subbrand—Equipment

Like other athletic shoe and apparel companies, Adidas has a classic vertical extension problem. It needs to appeal to a wide audience, from the serious athletes and top competitors to casual participants—but while serious athletes need the highest-performance equipment, the larger segment does not. Thus, in most product categories from soccer shoes to warm-ups, Adidas (and Nike and Reebok) will have a rather wide vertical range of products and prices. The problem with supporting such a wide range is that the very top end loses both credibility and prestige; the brand name does not mean the best, because it is attached to products that are far from the best.

To address this problem, Adidas introduced a new performance subbrand in 1990 to serve the highest-end products for all categories of shoes and apparel. (Actually, the idea came from Strasser and Moore just before they joined the Adidas team.) The Equipment subbrand would thus represent the best, whether it was a basketball shoe, a soccer shoe, or a warm-up outfit. Communications would focus on the Equipment products because they represented exciting news and the technology-based performance that is the essence of Adidas. In effect, Equipment was a silver bullet for the Adidas brand.

As users realized that Adidas reserved the best product for the Equipment brand, the Adidas brand took on a different meaning—it still meant participation, emotion, and performance, but the performance was now defined relative to its context. Low-end product was effectively insulated in a branding sense because it lacked the Equipment subbrand. The high performance level of the Equipment subbrand was maintained by migrating older technology to the casual user market products, whereas high-end new products (such as the Feet You Wear technology) were made available only in the Equipment line.

In 1998, Nike paid this subbrand idea the ultimate compliment by copying the strategy, introducing the Alpha line as a coordinated line of shoes, apparel, and equipment (including watches and eyewear). The Alpha line features its own symbol, an ellipsis of five dots, in addition to the traditional swoosh. This line had the advantage of an excellent name; Alpha is the universal symbol for the best. In contrast, the name Equipment is a descriptor (you buy, own, and use equipment of all types) that has no natural implication of being better. A name with desirable associations makes the brand-building task easier.

## THE ORIGINALS SUBBRAND

Adidas, of course, had a wonderful heritage of its shoes being worn at memorable events through athletic history—How can Adidas capture that heritage in a product? That question led to a new product line with the subbrand Originals, whose concept was to profit from the heritage by picking a shoe from Adidas's glorious past, rebuilding it, redesigning it, and relaunching it. The Adidas Rome, for example, the shoe that commemorated the Olympic Games and the Italian city, was relaunched as an Original.

The Originals subbrand has become so successful for Adidas today that it accounts for nearly 15 percent of all shoe sales. More important, every sale of an Originals brand shoe enhances Adidas's credibility as an authentic shoe company with a rich heritage. Nike has again taken action, if a bit belatedly, by relaunching products like the Cortez, a running shoe from the days of Blue Ribbon Sports and the Onizuka business partnership.

### A NEW WAY TO MANAGE THE ADIDAS BRAND

Between 1991 and 1992, Adidas made a significant change in how its organization was managed. Until then, the company had been organized into three major business divisions: footwear, apparel, and hardware or equipment that athletes use (such as balls, clubs, and rackets). The new organization called for a division by business units or sports categories. The soccer business unit for example, was staffed with a team exclusively dedicated to that sport. Responsibilities for business units were also allocated according to where the market expertise resided; for example, soccer was managed from Germany, while basketball was managed from the U.S. office.

The reorganization into business units was key to making the brand strategy work. It created focus in a particular sport. It also helped the Adidas staff to learn about and stay on top of any developments in a sport, and it helped the Adidas brand to reclaim credibility as the best performance brand.

### ADVERTISING

In the late 1980s and early 1990s, Adidas was neither seen nor heard against the media onslaught of Nike, which occurred in Europe as well as the United States. Thus a first priority in the Adidas turnaround was to level the playing field, which it did by doubling advertising spending to match Nike on an advertising-to-sales ratio basis.

Consolidation of all advertising efforts centrally and within one agency created further efficiencies. Like Nike, though, Adidas was not simply deciding to spend more money—it made an impact with brilliant executions.

Consider, for example, the advertising campaign based on the TV commercial "The Wall," which used Nike-like surrealistic images to show a runner pushing through the "wall of pain." It was produced by cult filmmaker David Lynch and narrated in English, with the tag line "Earn it." This campaign focused on the performance associations of Adidas. The message itself is inner-directed; the competition is you. "Earn it" is inspirational for the individual athlete, saying, "There is nothing between you and success, so exceed your own expectations and limitations."

Another ad campaign communicated the heritage of Adidas. In this 1995 campaign, the company made explicit use of its endorsed athletes for the first time. One ad featured Emil Zapotek and his double life as a Czech runner and as a soldier; the young Muhammad Ali was featured in another. The campaign's tagline was "We knew then—we know now," a message that communicated Adidas's claim to authenticity, heritage, and leadership. The ads, which suggested that Adidas was honest and genuine and would not engage in hyperbole, supported the target brand personality.

Still another campaign focused on the Adidas reputation for technology and performance by promoting the innovative Feet You Wear system. This new technology was heralded as the most natural shoe ever developed for athletes, a claim that may have involved too much hype for Adidas. In any event, the company spent significantly to support the launch, hoping to break out of the clutter at a time when competitors were introducing their own new product technologies (such as Nike's Air Zoom system and Reebok's DMX system).

## SPONSORSHIP PROGRAMS—TEAM AND EVENTS

Although Adidas does have the endorsement of top individual athletes, including L.A. Lakers basketball player Kobe Bryant, tennis star Anna Kournikova, runner Emil Zapotek, and Zinedine Zidane (a famous soccer player), the focus of the company's sponsorship program is toward major global events, sports associations, and teams. Nike, in contrast, is much more associated with individual athletes and focused on their success. As one of Nike's ads notes, "You don't win silver, you lose gold," clearly suggesting that winning is paramount.

Adidas thus has a continuing interest in sponsorship of key properties like the Olympics, the European soccer championships, and the soccer World Cup. This strategy allows Adidas to associate itself with the most emotional events in a sport. In addition to these global events, the company also sponsors national and local teams around the world. Among the teams that have been sponsored by Adidas are the national soccer teams of Germany, Spain, and France; the Bayern Munich, AC Milan, and Real Madrid professional soccer teams; the New York Yankees baseball team; and the San Francisco 49ers football team. A sports team can be an intense and meaningful part of the life of its followers, and team sponsorship thus provides a unique opportunity for connection.

### THE ADIDAS STREETBALL CHALLENGE

In the summer of 1992, in the Marx-Engels Platz of Berlin, Adidas tested a novel event sponsorship—a local three-person team basketball tournament in a visible urban location. It was a success. For 1993, sixty-six basketball tournaments were organized in the major metropolitan cities of Germany; the events were branded the Adidas Streetball Challenge. For a day or a weekend, the centers of major European cities made space for basketball courts, slam-dunk and free-throw competitions, street dance, graffiti events, and extreme sports demonstrations, all accompanied by live music from bands from the hip-hop and rap scenes.

The Adidas Streetball Challenge was turned into a celebration of the Adidas brand, a way to provide consumers with a powerful use experience with the company's shoes, sportswear, and equipment (see Figure 6–6). Participating teams that played in the competitions—without a referee—were clad in exclusive caps, shorts, tank tops, and jackets, courtesy of Adidas. Specially designed streetball decorations helped to create the desired atmosphere of fun and intense physical effort. A basketball-playing cartoon figure wearing the three-striped shoes became the official Streetball Challenge mascot and brand symbol.

One of the key features of the Adidas Streetball Challenge was that it stressed participation. Spectators were welcomed, but every effort

FIGURE 6–6
*The Adidas Streetball Challenge*

was made to get everyone involved in some form of activity. Extra courts were available for those who wanted to play but were not competing; special areas were set up where young people could try their skills; and Adidas-sponsored stars were on hand to play a demonstration round, sign autographs, and talk shop.

The brand-building potential of the Adidas Streetball Challenge would have been significantly less and the cost more were it not for Adidas's cosponsors. Their participation was instrumental not only in creating and financing the event but also in generating associations. The sponsors included Sony, Coca-Cola (Sprite), Lufthansa, Siemens, Sat 1 Jumpran (a TV station), MTV, and *Sport Bild* magazine. Sony and the media sponsors were especially important. Sony and MTV joined forces to launch a Streetball CD, and the coverage by MTV, *Sport Bild,* and Sat 1 ensured that the event achieved broad awareness across Germany.

The Adidas Streetball Challenge was taken to other European countries. Teams in each country competed for the national championship; the winning teams then went on to the European finals. The inclusion of local retailers was particularly effective. Adidas offered them the opportunity to participate in a number of ways—for example, retailers could choose to "rent" a tournament and organize smaller competitions before the actual events.

Five years after that first test, more than five hundred thousand people participated in the Adidas Streetball Challenge. The German finals in Berlin attracted 3,200 players and forty thousand spectators. At the world finals in Milan, teams from more than thirty countries participated, some coming from as far away as Brazil and Taiwan. Germany's leading basketball magazine, *Basket*, provided effective media coverage.

Adidas extended the Streetball Challenge brand in several directions. In soccer, it created the Adidas Predator Challenge, which was especially targeted at young people between the ages of six and eighteen. The Predator Challenge featured four-on-four competitions and was organized together with the thirteen thousand soccer clubs in Germany. Renamed the DFB-Adidas Cup, it attracted more than 6,500 teams, and attendance at the events was more than three hundred thousand people; co-sponsors were Mercedes-Benz, Lufthansa, Coca-Cola, and Kaercher, as well as *Kicker* soccer magazine and the youth magazines *Bravo* and *Tween*. Then came the Adidas Adventure Challenge, which focused on mountain biking, trail running, rafting, and other outdoor sports.

The Challenge series not only provides an on-strategy experience, associations, and visibility, but it is unique and owned by Adidas. It is not another golf tournament or soccer championship—there is only one Streetball Challenge, and it belongs to Adidas. Because Adidas is part of the name, any experiences and associations from the event will be linked to the brand. Moreover, Adidas can carry it forward without some other entity such as the Olympic committee deciding that the sponsorship cost should double.

## THE PAYOFF

The combination of media advertising, new subbrands, sponsorship, and the branded grassroots sponsorships (as well as a set of other key brand strategy decisions) produced an astounding success for Adidas. Sales grew from $1.7 billion in 1992 to record sales of $4.8 billion in 1998. After the last year of losses (1993), profits grew steadily to $425 million in 1998.

The success of the Adidas brand strategy looks especially impres-

FIGURE 6–7
*Brand Building Lessons from Adidas and Nike*

sive in two specific countries: the company's home market of Germany, where it enjoys market leadership, and the United States, where Adidas is a niche competitor compared with Nike. In Germany, Adidas's market share had fallen to just above 30 percent in the early 1990s. By 1998, however, the footwear market share had rebounded to more than 38 percent, reaffirming the company's leadership. In the United States, market share quadrupled from less than 3 percent to more than 12 percent in some categories in 1998.

For Adidas, these sales results reflected its improved image. One image study of consumers found overall positive improvements across all associations. Significantly, three of the top associations consumers noted with the Adidas brand were trendy, modern, and cool—a dramatic change in just a few years. Another survey showed that more than 50 percent of all athletes perceived Adidas to have changed in the last two years by becoming more modern, more contemporary, and more youthful. Athletes also noted that Adidas had improved its advertising and ways of communicating with consumers.

## THE LESSONS

The story of brand building at Adidas and Nike provides some lessons that are worth summarizing here (see also Figure 6–7).

1. **Brand building is not just advertising.** Advertising played an important role, especially for Nike in the mid-1980s and Adidas in the 1990s; however, their brand-building efforts involved many other elements. These included sponsorships, endorsements, subbranded products, flagship stores, and grassroots events such as the Adidas Streetball Challenge, the DFB-Adidas Cup, and the Adidas Adventure Challenge.

2. **Brand building involves innovation.** When the breakthrough brand-building programs (including NikeTown and the Adidas Streetball Challenge) were invented, they represented new directions not only for the firm but for the industry. Such breakthroughs do not just happen. They require an organizational capability of assessing, evaluating, and assimilating new ideas. When an organization is so lean that anything out of the ordinary must be outsourced, this is not easy; both Nike and Adidas had people capable of stretching the envelope.

3. **Excellence in execution creates huge payoffs.** Several studies have shown that the quality of advertising is about four or five times more important than the amount spent; great advertising, in short, can tell a $50 million story for only $10 million. The successful programs of both Nike and Adidas were executed with brilliance, from the early Adidas sponsorships to the Nike "Just do it" advertising to the Adidas Streetball Challenge.

4. **Products are key to the brand.** There has to be substance behind the brand. From the outset, both Adidas and Nike had a heritage of innovation—creating products that were exciting, and offered real functional benefits—that was not just smoke and mirrors. From the Waffle shoe to Air Jordans to Feet You Wear and beyond, products and advances mattered and were delivered by both brands.

5. **The brand is more than products.** A strong brand has personality, organizational associations, emotion, and self-expression. Nike developed a strong personality—provocative, aggressive, even in-your-face. This personality served it well not only in connecting with customers but also in maintaining a position, and

Nike was all about emotion and self-expression. The Adidas emphasis on functional benefits worked well in the early days, but less so as the market matured; when it added some personality and emotion in the 1990s, the brand started connecting and winning.

6. **Know the brand identity.** A clear brand identity must guide the development and execution of programs over time. (The Adidas identity was very stable through the 1990s.) Note that both Nike and Adidas began their turnarounds by developing a brand identity. In each case, this exercise led to a refocusing of the brand and initiatives that built the brand in new directions.

7. **The brand team should run the brand.** At both Adidas and Nike, the category or business unit teams ran the brand strategy and were closely involved in the development of innovative brand-building programs. The leadership of the brands was not delegated to outside partners. In fact, the Nike brand team got so involved in the creative and media decisions that the agency got frustrated—at one point, it ran a full-page ad with a letter to Nike saying, "Peace."

8. **Connect with customers on an emotional level.** These two brands found ways to connect to the customer beyond delivering functional benefits. The Nike advertising, NikeTown, and the Adidas Streetball Challenge connected with customers by touching their emotions.

9. **Use subbrands to tell a story and manage perceptions.** Nike and Adidas showed how powerful subbrands can be in brand building. The use of a high-end brand (such as Adidas Equipment and Nike Alpha) isolated this line from the mass market products where most of the volume resides. In addition, a host of silver-bullet subbrands (such as Air Jordan) or branded technologies (such as Air and Feet You Wear) helped Nike and Adidas tell the story of their brands.

QUESTIONS FOR DISCUSSION

1. Evaluate the brand-building approaches presented in this chapter. Which do you admire the most? Why? What was the key to getting that approach implemented?

2. Why did Adidas and Nike both miss the aerobics trends? How could they have been so careless?

3. What are the success models of building brands in your industry? How can these success models be improved or refined?

4. Do you have a brand identity statement that provides a clear road map for building the brand? Does your brand identity statement provide sufficient guidance for deciding on communications alternatives and executions that build the brand, and those that are not on target?

5. Develop some new brand-building options that are not currently being successfully employed in your industry. What are the problems in implementing them? How could those problems be overcome?

# 7

# Building Brands—
# The Role of Sponsorship

There's nothing remarkable about it. All one had to do is hit the right keys at the right time and the instrument plays itself.

—Johann Sebastian Bach

## THE MASTERCARD WORLD CUP SPONSORSHIP STORY[1]

MasterCard was established in 1966 to provide a credit card vehicle for banks that were not part of the Bank Americard system (the predecessor to Visa). It now involves well over twenty thousand member financial institutions and operates a family of global products all driven directly or indirectly by the MasterCard brand.

Competing with Visa was (and is) a major MasterCard challenge. In 1993 MasterCard's worldwide volume was only 60 percent of that of Visa, and MasterCard had been losing ground over the years. The third player in the market, American Express, remained significantly smaller, with only half the volume of MasterCard.

Visa was well positioned; its "Everywhere you want to be" tagline generated a strong association with key credit card attributes of being available in most outlets (so users would rarely be disappointed by having the card refused) and being global (so world travelers or potential world travelers can expect their cards to be accepted as well). Further, Visa owned the Olympics within the credit card category by virtue of its visible sponsorship since 1986. In addition to being the best vehicle to convey the attributes of performance and being global, the Olympics taps strongly into patriotism and its associated emotional benefits.

MasterCard not only had the challenge of Visa and other competitors in the United States but needed to develop global associations. Credit cards in particular need a worldwide brand strategy, because they are among the few products whose use is inherently global, especially for the most influential target segment. Further, Europe was a significant growth opportunity, as the number of cards per person and level of card usage were considerably lower there than in the United States.

Thus the opportunity for MasterCard to be one of the eleven worldwide sponsors—and the exclusive credit card sponsor—of the 1994 World Cup, at a cost of $15 million, was appealing. It had the potential of enhancing public awareness and thereby invigorating the MasterCard marketing program throughout the world. The World Cup, which in 1994 would be a tournament of twenty-four soccer teams to be held in the United States, was the only truly global sporting event besides the Olympics. In addition, the sponsorship applied to fifteen other major soccer tournaments to be held between 1991 and 1994.

As a worldwide sponsor, MasterCard received a variety of benefits. Highly visible, strategically placed signage was positioned around the soccer fields at each of the 269 matches played during the sponsored events from 1991 to 1994. (Visa's Olympic sponsorship did not permit such signage.) In addition, a full-page ad was provided in the event programs. For World Cup '94 and the other events, MasterCard had the exclusive right in its category to use the designations "Official Sponsor" and "Official Card" and to use the official emblem, mascot, and music of the events. At all events, MasterCard also could display its products on-site and have access to tickets.

One significant risk to the sponsorship of an event such as the World Cup is ambush marketing, whereby a competitor (such as Visa or American Express) associates itself with the event by other means. To reduce this risk, MasterCard also sponsored the U.S. national team and bought exclusive advertising rights to the events, including those broadcast on a Spanish-language network.

### THE SUPPORTING MARKETING PROGRAM

MasterCard developed a full-scale marketing campaign and promotion plan to exploit the World Cup sponsorship. In addition to advertising, a variety of promotions were employed, many to be implemented by affiliate banks. A decal program included a sweepstakes (with winners getting free trips to one of the four qualifying nations), and a Watch-n-Win

FIGURE 7–1
*A MasterCard World Cup Visual*

World Cup promotion featured free World Cup tickets. A thirty-six–city family soccer festival, the Legends of Soccer Tour, was co-sponsored with several other brands. At each event 90 percent of the attendees (2,300 on average) passed through a MasterCard booth. Pelé, one of soccer's most famous stars, was retained for $2 million to support the MasterCard effort by appearing in posters and advertising, as well as participating in personal appearances. Banks and retailers ran promotions featuring prizes such as posters and Pelé instructional videos.

Publicity was systematically obtained. A MasterCard team received an estimated $500,000 of free local radio coverage, and a "Kickin' for Kids" TV special reached 197 markets. There was also media attention for the Ambassadors Cup ceremony, which honored twenty-four people who brought the love of soccer to the United States. An estimated 36 million impressions were created by local coverage of these and other efforts. In Los Angeles, a MasterCard hot air balloon alone obtained more than five hundred thousand impressions.

Other programs sought to establish personal connections to MasterCard. Nine MasterCard Welcoming the World seminars were attended by more than 7,500 merchants. A showcase Main Street USA area received more than 3.6 million people over the course of fifty-two matches. Forty-two MasterCard/Coca-Cola welcome centers, located in high-traffic areas at airports or near the matches, provided more than ten thousand hours of assistance to over one million people; visitors sampled Coke and received World Cup Master Values booklets (which provided discounts at eighty participating merchants). The world's largest soccer theme park, called SoccerFest, was set up in Los Angeles.

Since the World Cup sponsorship was a global venture, Master-Card sought to encourage its affiliates throughout the world to exploit it. A World Cup advertising campaign was prepared, including a TV commercial featuring Pelé that appeared in more than forty countries. The global effort was also supported by newsletters, promotion-execution guides, sponsorship manuals, a promotional video, Pelé photos, corporate hospitality invitations, and welcome kits. The effort was more extensive in countries where soccer was popular and the national team was participating.

Affiliates outside the United States followed MasterCard's lead in sponsoring regional events and national teams. In Europe, where the World Cup is as important or more important than the Olympics, the interest was very high. More than $19 million was spent by member banks in eighteen European countries, and an estimated combined audience of 7.8 billion watched the fifty-two final-round matches.

Encouraging and supporting the efforts of affiliated member banks globally was not easy, in part because of the differences in cultures and relative abilities to implement a sponsorship program. To overcome these obstacles, MasterCard assigned a U.S. promotions executive to Europe to assist partners who were not experienced with event sponsorship. Later, the company formed a global World Cup product team, (consisting of a member from each region) to transfer knowledge and expertise on a regular basis.

## RESULTS

One objective of MasterCard's World Cup sponsorship activities was to build the presence of the brand beyond paid television advertising. Certainly there were documented exposures of the MasterCard ads and signage (see Figure 7–1). The World Cup achieved a cumulative worldwide television audience of 31.2 billion (twice that of the Olympic games in the summer of 1992); the exposure of the brand signage averaged eight minutes during each of the dozen telecasts and was more than twelve minutes for the final match. To achieve the same length of exposure, purchased media advertising would cost an estimated $493 million; even if the value of exposure was only 5 percent of an ad, it would still be worth $25 million. In addition, an estimated 8.5 billion impressions were created by street banners, billboards, buses, kiosks, and bus shelter ads. Still another one billion impressions were estimated to come from appearances and magazine articles by Pelé.

MasterCard hoped to accomplish two goals with all of these impressions. The first was to build brand awareness (especially in comparison to Visa) and to create a high level of sponsorship awareness (higher than or equal to the Visa Olympics link). Measures reflecting this objective were generally positive in France, Germany, the United Kingdom, Argentina, and Brazil, where soccer is very popular, but less so in Japan, Mexico, and the United States. The second goal was to enhance the worldwide imagery and the attitudes toward the brand. Success on this objective was found in Brazil, Mexico, and Argentina, and more modestly in the United States, Japan, Germany, and the United Kingdom.

Surveys of member banks showed that the sponsorship helped MasterCard significantly in three areas: (1) providing member banks with business opportunities supported by enhanced brand awareness and global imagery; (2) stimulating card acquisition and usage; and (3) enhancing MasterCard's image as a strong marketing organization. Success on these criteria led to considerable support for maintaining the World Cup sponsorship.

The last chapter examined the use of sponsorship by Adidas and Nike. Adidas, in particular, was a pioneer in sponsorships, and its early connection to the Olympics was an important factor in building a strong brand during the 1950s, 1960s, and 1970s. Chapter 6 also showed the power of owned sponsorships by describing the role that the Adidas Streetball Challenge played in the brand's recovery in the 1990s.

In this chapter, the use of sponsorship as a brand-building tool will be explored in more detail. The goal is to understand how sponsorships work to support the brand and how this insight can translate into effective sponsorship programs. This structured discussion will make clear that sponsorship is a very different brand-building tool than advertising and needs to be managed accordingly.

Sponsorship entails the commercial association of a brand with a property such as a sporting event, a team, a cause, the arts, a cultural attraction, or entertainment. Thus it goes beyond event sponsorship, to include, for example, the sponsorship of a basketball team by a Japanese car company or a cancer charity by a clothing brand. Sponsorship does not imply an endorsement of the brand. An endorser, such as Tiger Woods, puts his or her name on products and appears in advertising and elsewhere as an advocate for a brand. In contrast, a sponsored event or group does not deliver (although the sponsorship might imply) an endorsement of a brand.

Sponsorship has been around for a long time. The brand Bovril reportedly sponsored the Nottingham Forest Football Club in 1898, Gillette was sponsoring baseball in 1910, and Coca-Cola was sponsoring the Olympics back in 1928. In the last few years, however, sponsorship's role in brand building has increased dramatically.

According to the Chicago-based *IEG's Sponsorship Report,* in the year 2000 sponsorship expenditures are expected to be over $7 billion in North America, with nearly 67 percent involving sports, another 19 percent covering entertainment tours and festival or fair events, 8 percent going to causes, and about 6 percent to arts sponsorships. Worldwide expenditures have been estimated to be three times those of North America. Further, reported expenditures on event sponsorship understate its impact, because most event sponsorships derive perhaps one to three times their dollar volume in associated advertising, promotions, and other vehicles.

Sponsorship offers unique advantages in brand building. Whereas advertising is intrusive and is clearly a paid message overtly attempting to persuade or change attitudes, a sponsorship can become part of people's lives. Advertising is good at communicating attributes and functional benefits, yet most strong brands go beyond these to provide emotional and self-expressive benefits, to have a personality, and to differentiate themselves on intangible attributes. Sponsorship can be very effective at extending brands beyond tangible attributes because they develop associations that add depth, richness, and a contemporary feel to the brand and its relationship with customers.

Even so, sponsorship is surprisingly underused. Most firms have infrastructures that make advertising and promotions easier media to access; support firms such as agencies are better suited and more oriented to advertising and promotions than to event sponsorship. Further, even when the media alternatives are well known, there are no departments with an inventory of events, programs, or institutions from which to select. And even if there were, there are so many alternatives and variants that the selection and management of sponsorships become an art that requires some out-of-the-box thinking, which is never easy in most organizations.

## HOW SPONSORSHIP BUILDS BRANDS

Sponsorship has the potential to contribute to brand building in a variety of ways, several of which are unique to sponsorships (see Figure 7–2). The primary goal is usually to create exposure for the brand and to develop associations. Three other brand-building bene-

FIGURE 7–2
*Sponsorship as a Brand Builder*

fits, however, can be very relevant to the selection and evaluation of sponsorships: mobilizing the organization for brand building, providing an event experience to customers, and demonstrating new products or technologies. Connecting the brand to the event/customer bond is another aspirational goal.

## 1. MOBILIZING THE ORGANIZATION FOR BRAND BUILDING

Both the process and the result of a brand-building effort often have a key payoff internally to employees and other brand partners, as well as externally to customers. This phenomenon is particularly common in sponsorships.

Employees and other brand partners can receive emotional benefits that result from pride in being associated with the sponsorships, as well as the link between the sponsorship and their own lifestyle and values. For example, people working as part of the MasterCard sponsorship effort felt excited about the World Cup and the fact that they had a direct link to it.

One research study specifically sought to determine the impact of sponsorship on employees.[2] The Bank of Ireland wanted to know the impact on its staff of its two flagship sponsorships, the Bank of Ireland Gaelic Football Championship and the Bank of Ireland Proms (a classical music event that is televised live). Even though these sponsorships were primarily directed toward the bank's customers, more than 80 percent of all employees—from senior managers to bank assistants—expressed pride in the bank's sponsorship of sports; 75 percent expressed pride in the bank's arts sponsorship. Getting employees to attend events can enhance these emotional benefits.

A team sponsorship can be particularly successful at generating emotional benefits because there is an attachment to a goal and a winner, as well as an activity. A firm sponsoring a race car reported that its employees followed the success and failures of the car closely and were enormously proud of their association. When the basketball finals in Japan pitted a team locally sponsored by Toyota against an Isuzu-sponsored team, there was intense interest in the outcome among the employees of both companies. To consider how powerful this benefit can be, imagine channeling the interest and intensity of an Ohio State or Texas football fan to the members of an extended brand team.

An event sponsorship can also act as a catalyst to create a global brand-building implementation process and team. For example, in its sponsorship of the World Cup, MasterCard had to generate consistency and synergy among very different regions and thousands of banks. Making the sponsorship a success required an enormous effort to share information and coordinate advertising and promotions worldwide. The channels of communication created and experience gained, however, went a long way toward solving this previously intractable problem in areas beyond the sponsorship itself.

## 2. PROVIDING AN EXPERIENCE FOR CUSTOMERS

An event experience (such as playing in the pro-am of a golf tournament or being entertained in a Wimbledon facility) can provide a customer with a unique opportunity to develop a link to the brand and its organization. Simply providing customers with an event experience, especially when the event is prestigious, says a lot about the brand and its organization—(for instance, that it is a big-time player). Further, it represents a tangible and unique way to reward a key customer. Assuming that the event is sponsored over time, the reward can be provided year after year, giving the customer an incentive to nurture the relationship. In addition, the event provides a way to interact with key customers in a relaxed setting; access can be obtained that would not be possible without the event as a backdrop.

Involving a customer in an event can also make that customer become a part of the same family or team as the brand. Especially when the experience is duplicated over several occasions (annually, for instance), an intense level of loyalty can be created. Such a bonding is a real payoff, and is most likely to occur when the customer is treated as an insider in the brand's organization and/or when the event is related to the customer's own identity, personality, or lifestyle.

## 3. DEMONSTRATING NEW PRODUCTS AND TECHNOLOGY

As noted earlier, a new product or technology subbrand can be a silver bullet for the brand, representing the brand identity to target audiences. Thus a new product or technology might reflect a brand's ownership of a customer benefit, or show that the brand is innovative or customer driven.

The most powerful way to introduce a new product or technology is by publicity. If it is novel, interesting, and important enough to receive press coverage, its brand-building goals will be much more likely to be achieved. Publicity is not only more cost-effective than advertising, it is also more credible. A sponsorship can be the necessary lever to elevate the news value of a product or technology so that press coverage results. Even if press coverage is not forthcoming, the sponsorship can provide a context to make a demonstration more interesting and vivid. As a bonus, the visibility of the product or technology can also enhance the link between the brand and the event.

M&M's, for example, introduced a new color at the New York City marathon. The concept of a candy company making such a big deal about a new color and connecting the introduction to a New York event was so offbeat that it generated significant publicity, including a prominent mention during the TV coverage of the event. Similarly, demonstrations of the new Visa Cash card at the 1998 Olympics attracted press coverage.

An event can also be used to showcase technology that represents a key association of an organizational brand. For example, Panasonic installed the largest video display in a U.S. stadium at the Atlanta Olympics in 1996. *Sports Illustrated* applied new publishing and photographic technology to print and distribute a daily Olympic issue for the first time. Motorola provided the largest digital system ever created for a sports event, also at the Atlanta Olympics. And Sprint has showcased its voice technology by branding the headphones NFL coaches wear during games.

### 4. CREATING BRAND EXPOSURE

Often, the cost of a sponsorship can be justified solely by the brand name exposure achieved through event publicity or signage. One way to measure the effect of this exposure is to conduct pre-event and post-event surveys of brand awareness. A host of examples show that awareness increases substantially as the result of a sponsorship, especially when brands follow up the sponsored activity with other marketing activities. For instance, a previously little-known computer firm found that its soccer team sponsorship developed high levels of unaided sponsor awareness (which correlates to brand awareness) among people attending the team's games (53 percent), as well as those attending other league games (22 percent).[3]

A second approach is to quantify the brand exposures that a sponsorship generates from the signage placed at the site or worn by the participants. Joyce Julius & Associates breaks down television coverage of events to count "clear, in-focus exposure time"; the value of that time can then be ascertained. This firm found that the top sporting event for 1992 was the Indianapolis 500 with 307 sponsor mentions, which would be valued at $72 million of advertising using that same time.[4] The second-rated event was also a car race, the Daytona 500, followed by the *Newsweek* Championship, a part of ATP Tennis, and the Federal Express Orange Bowl (not coincidentally, two of these four were "named" events).

The impact of on-site event signage can be estimated by sampling the number of people exposed at the event. As noted above, MasterCard estimated more than 8 billion exposures from its World Cup signage. Of course, advertising with a focused message is undoubtedly more effective (even though it is more overtly commercial), so some discount factor needs to be applied. Still, it is not uncommon for the exposure value to exceed the total cost of the sponsorship even if an event-based exposure is deemed to be worth only 10 percent of an exposure to paid advertising.

A distinction should be made between sponsor status (such as being an Olympic sponsor) and named events (the Buick Open), since the latter have two additional benefits. First, the publicity of a named event will help build brand presence, depending on the amount of press coverage. Second, associating the brand with the event is much more feasible when it is a named event rather than one for which the brand is simply a sponsor at some level.

A named stadium is a particularly powerful way to gain awareness and presence. 3Com is the world's second largest data/network company, but few people had heard of it until it paid $4.5 million over four years to put its name on the stadium that is the home of San Francisco 49ers football and Giants baseball. After the stadium name change, TV commentator Al Michaels spent five minutes talking about the deal on a Monday night broadcast; the same amount of advertising time would have cost as much as 3Com paid for the naming rights. In addition, the name-change story was picked up by newspapers around the world, and 3Com is mentioned prominently every time there is a game (around two hundred times per year). There may be a short-term downside to buying naming rights to a facility, however. At least one survey showed that more than 30 percent of respondents are actively hostile to a company that changes the name of a facility to its own name.[5]

Linking the name with a sponsorship property has the further advantage that it is harder to sever the relationship; both the sponsor and the property have a greater need and incentive to make it work. In title sponsorship, sponsors frequently drop out of coverage for many reasons, and so the brand-building impact may not be realized.

A rather unique natural experiment in India in the mid-1980s suggested that sponsoring events can affect awareness.[6] One of the three tire firms in India, MRF, converted its advertising budget for three years almost entirely into sports sponsorships (there was some advertising for the events and their link to the MRF brand); its competitors (Ceat and Dunlop) both continued with traditional advertising during that period. MRF's top-of-mind awareness grew from 4 to 17 to 20 to 22 percent over the four years, and its unaided awareness grew from 39 to 72 to 70 to 76 percent. Clearly, the awareness sharply improved during the first years, and the higher levels did not decay but actually increased as more time passed.

## 5. DEVELOP BRAND ASSOCIATIONS

A fifth and often dominant reason for sponsorships is to gain an association among a target segment. The creation of the desired association will depend on the strength of three links, as shown in Figure 7–3 and detailed below

### The associations connected to the sponsored property

The same qualitative and quantitative techniques used to determine brand associations can be used to determine the associations connected to the sponsored property and their relative strength. For major sponsorships, an in-depth understanding of the image of the sponsored property among target groups—one that goes beyond tangible attributes—can be critical to maximizing the effectiveness of the sponsorship.

Like a brand, a sponsored property can have a host of associations. Some events (such as bowling) are considered downscale, while oth-

FIGURE 7–3
*Developing Brand Associations Through Sponsorship*

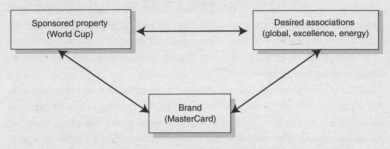

ers (such as an opera event) are very upscale. Some are old and have a long heritage (Kentucky Derby), and others young and energetic (the Swatch events). Some are perceived as macho/male (auto racing) while others are very female (women's figure skating). The events can have very different personalities as well: a ski race is exciting, a football team is rugged, an urban development project can be competent, and a beauty contest can be sophisticated. The location, whether it be a city or a building (such as the Transamerica Pyramid), a country (Spain), or a region (the south of France) can also be relevant, especially for a travel company or hotel group.

Five associations are worth highlighting because of their importance for many brands, and because sponsorships can play a unique role in creating them. The first are associations driven by the functional characteristics of the property itself. For example, a golf tournament will have strong associations with golf, golfers, golf equipment, and golf professionals; a golf equipment or accessory manufacturer will benefit from these associations. The remaining four are organizational characteristics that brands (especially organizational brands) aspire to, yet find difficult to achieve: leadership, being global, being local, and being socially involved. Sponsorship often provides a uniquely effective vehicle for developing these associations.

Many brands state explicitly that they are leaders in their category, which usually means that they are innovative, successful, and reliable. It is awkward and ineffectual, however, to make this claim oneself; "I am a leader" has a hollow ring to it. A sports event sponsorship can help to enhance the brand's leadership association in several ways. First, some events themselves have an image of being the best or most prestigious—the Masters, Wimbledon, the Kentucky Derby, the Indy 500, and the Olympics are all in this category. Second, because all sports events have winners, the association with winning and the determination and talent needed to pull it off should reflect on anything connected to the event.

A second organizational association important to many brands is to be global. A sponsor's association with a truly global property such as the World Cup or the Olympics is one way to make the claim that the brand is global. This was certainly one of MasterCard's goals in sponsoring the World Cup, since it had to compete with Visa's "Everywhere you want to be" claim and its Olympics association. The worldwide association, in fact, is one of the attractions of the Olympics. UPS sponsored the 1996 Olympics, for example, in part to develop an association of global competence in order to become a viable competitor against FedEx and DHL.

Sponsoring local events is an excellent vehicle for linking to the community and thereby developing stronger local associations. In one survey, two-thirds of respondents felt more favorably toward corporations that participated in community or grassroots events, versus only about 40 percent who had the same reaction to corporate sponsorship of national events.[7]

To create a greater presence and synergy, multiple local sponsorships should be linked together. The Adidas Streetball Challenge and the DFB-Adidas Cup, described in the previous chapter, are illustrative. As noted in Chapter 6, Adidas organizes dozens of events every year in Germany, with several hundred local events duplicated in other European countries. Local tournaments are organized with the help of local associations, sports clubs, and retailers. Retailers also can "rent" a tournament and stage additional events of their own. All local events are linked to national events and other European events.

Sponsoring a visible activity that contributes to the public good (perhaps by helping the environment or community) is an excellent way for an organization to communicate that it has values and beliefs that go beyond making products. For instance, McDonald's sponsors the Ronald McDonald House, a place for families to stay while their children undergo medical treatment. Tanqueray sponsored an AIDS bike race benefit that attracted 1,800 entrants and raised more than \$5.5 million; on a retail level, it also held 180 AIDS Ride awareness nights at thirty bars in California. The American Express Charge Against Hunger campaign donated three cents from each transaction to an antihunger organization and was promoted with an eleven-city tour by Stevie Wonder.

### Linking the brand to the sponsored property

A brand does not automatically get linked to the sponsored property. Perhaps the biggest mistake that sponsors make, in fact, is failing to create and support the link between the brand and what is being sponsored.

DDB Needham's SponsorWatch uses a consumer panel to track sponsorship effectiveness.[8] Monthly, five hundred to eight hundred households are contacted by mail, and the head of the household is asked to complete a questionnaire. The data are analyzed for a period of three to twelve months surrounding an event or sport season.

The SponsorWatch data shows that the link between sponsors and the sponsored property is lower than might be expected. Sponsor-Watch uses "exclusive awareness" as a measure of the link—the percentage of the target market who recognize the link between the brand and the property, minus the percentage who mistakenly believe that there is a link between the property and the strongest competitor brand. Obviously, a competitor link detracts from the advantage created by the property—in fact, in cases of excessive confusion, promoting the property and its associations could benefit the competitor.

Some sponsorships provide surprisingly low exclusive awareness. Coca-Cola has been the official soft drink for the NFL for several years and in 1993 paid \$250 million to obtain a five-year extension. According to SponsorWatch, though, 35 percent of respondents thought that Pepsi was the sponsor, only 1 percent lower than the number who named Coke. Only 15 percent correctly named Hilton as the sponsor of the 1992 Summer Olympics; the same number thought the sponsor was Holiday Inn. Other Summer Olympics sponsors such as Crest, Oscar Mayer, Panasonic, Maxwell House, and Nuprin had a similar fate. In contrast, more than 50 percent recognized Visa as a sponsor, while the recognition level of its competitors MasterCard and American Express was just under 30 percent, which is, of course, still a large number.

Of the 102 official Olympic sponsors tracked by SponsorWatch since 1984, only half built a successful link, which was defined as having sponsor awareness of at least 15 percent (and at least 10 percentage points higher than the nearest competitor)—hardly a demanding criterion. In other words, if the objective was to create awareness and a link with the Olympics, many of the sponsors basically wasted their money.

Why is this number so low? The first of three key reasons is that the Olympic sponsorships do not include signage in stadiums or program ads (like the World Cup does), so creating awareness of the sponsorship is not easy. Second, there is little fit or natural association that exists between some brands and the Olympics. Third, sponsors may not invest toward creating the link because their budget is used up by the sponsorship fee.

One direct approach to building a link is to advertise on the televised event. For the Summer Olympic Games in 1984, 1988, and 1992, SponsorWatch data showed that 54 percent of the fifty-eight brands that advertised were successful in creating a link, while only one brand (*Sports Illustrated*, which is, of course, itself an Olympics media vehicle) of the twenty-seven that did not advertise was successful.

The duration and strength of the link are also important, because the impact of the association can be multiplied severalfold for an event that is not restricted to a short time window. J.C. Penney, for example, established a rather strong link with the Olympics, but only during the event itself. Before the games its link was actually below that of Sears, and afterward it was only 6 percent better. Visa, in contrast, had a link from 16 to 20 percent higher than its competition three months before the Olympics and one month afterward. The link, in fact, is probably strong even in off years.

SponsorWatch data showed that of the fifty-one sponsors that did successfully link themselves to the Olympics, only 60 percent maintained the link before and after the event as well; the other 40 percent had the link only during the games themselves. Clearly, an investment in making the association over a period of years makes a perceived link much easier to attain. Visa has done so well in part because it has been associated with so many Olympics that it does not have to fight confusion each time the games are held; it only has to remind audiences that Visa is the official sponsor.

### IBM SPONSORS THE ARTS*

IBM sponsorships are intended to build positive awareness, to promote the company as an exciting leader in a constantly changing industry, and to demonstrate that the organization and its people are contributing to the community. IBM has learned from systematic research that its sponsorships are much more effective when supported by other media.

A sponsorship of a Leonardo da Vinci exhibition in London was evaluated through a survey. All attendees were given a short questionnaire that provided an incentive to list their names and telephone numbers. Several of these respondents were subsequently called and asked a series of questions, including if they knew who the sponsor was, how they learned of the sponsorship, the suitability of the sponsor, the nature of the contribution of the sponsor to the exhibit, and attitudes toward IBM. The unaided mention of IBM as a sponsor was 28 percent (lower than the norm of 41 percent), and the aided mention was 57 percent (also lower than the norm of 66 percent). Further, most learned of the sponsorship at the exhibit, which meant that there was a low payout among those not attending.

A few years later IBM sponsored the Pompeii exhibit, also in London. In this case a substantial advertising campaign announced the IBM sponsorship, and interactive IBM computers were featured in the exhibit. The recall was much higher, unaided at 45 percent and aided at 74 percent. Further, 34 percent knew about the sponsor before they came, above the norm of 25 percent. Nearly 60 percent said they felt more favorably toward IBM, while only 1 percent were less favorable in their perceptions.

*Source: Peter Walshe and Peter Wilkinson, "Pompeii Revisited: IBM Digging for Success," *Marketing and Research Today*, February 1994, pp. 89–95.

### Changing or enhancing the brand image

Given that a sponsored property is visible, has desired associations, and is linked to the brand, the final step is to connect those associations to the brand so that its image is improved or strengthened. Two types of processes might be conceptualized. First, it might be assumed that the process is driven by the desire for consistency.

Psychologists have found that when a strong association (such as being global) is connected to an event which in turn is connected to a brand, people tend to strengthen the perception that the brand is global in order to have a more consistent cognitive understanding. Second, an attempt to persuade someone that a brand is global might be easier in a context such as at the Olympics, where the concept is more likely to come to mind and to be salient.

There is some good evidence that a sponsorship can affect a brand image. SponsorWatch found, for example, that among respondents Visa's lead over MasterCard with respect to which brand offered the best service went from 15 percent prior to the 1992 Olympics to 30 percent during the event and 20 percent one month afterward (Figure 7–4 shows these results). Research in late 1997 showed that the number of consumers worldwide who rated Visa the best on a variety of characteristics (such as merchant acceptance or overall value) averaged 10 percent higher than among those who were unaware of the sponsorship.[9] Similarly, the best-product gap for Seiko versus Timex jumped from 5 percent to nearly 20 percent during the Olympics and 10 percent a month afterward; not coincidentally, Seiko's link with the Olympics went from a negative 2 percent (that is, Timex was named as the Olympic sponsor more often than Seiko) one month before the Olympics to 18 percent during the games and 8 percent one month afterward.

FIGURE 7–4
*Perceived Superiority of Credit Cards*

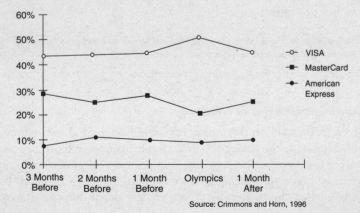

Source: Crimmons and Horn, 1996

In the experiment involving the Indian tire firm MRF, the conversion of the advertising budget to sport sponsorships affected image and preference as well as awareness. All seven image items steadily increased during the four-year period being examined, as did brand preference—the percentage of customers preferring MRF grew from 4 to 9 to 21 to 22 percent while the competitors stayed stable. One image dimension, innovation, was extremely low prior to the test, and it sharply increased during the first year even though there was no factual advertising during that period. Why? In addition to an overall halo effect, sport sponsorship may give a brand some energy and excitement that translate into perceptions of innovativeness.[10]

### Associations need to click

When event associations really click with the brand and its associations, everything becomes easier. It is easier to link the brand with the event, and it is more likely that the brand image will be enhanced as a result. Following are three examples of a good fit:

1. A golf club manufacturer (like Calloway) sponsors a golf tournament where its product will be used and where those following the event will be potential users of its product. If a player using Calloway equipment does well, so much the better.
2. Sony sponsored the total entertainment provided by several of the Celebrity Cruise Lines ships. Each ship became a demonstration of Sony technology, including the TVs in the staterooms, the sound system, the Sony movies shown on the video-on-demand center, the Sony concept area (with a gift shop), the Sony PlayStations for kids, the twenty-foot Sony video display, and the 1,000-seat movie theater. To cap it all off, a 1,200-guest premiere was arranged for the release of a major Sony movie on board.
3. DuPont, makers of thermal underwear, sponsored the exploration of the Bering Straits, which involved a dozen U.S. and Russian explorers climbing through twenty-foot snow drifts in extreme cold.

One study documented the role of sponsorship fit by comparing it with several other variables to understand their relative impact on purchase of a ticket to a theme park. The variables included sponsorship (Children's Miracle Network and Kennedy Center for the

Performing Arts—both equally liked, but a very different fit for theme parks), driving distance (forty-five or ninety minutes), number of rides (thirty-two or forty-six), food quality (fair or good), price ($24.95 or $34.95), and hours open (twelve or sixteen).[11] The impact of sponsorship fit on ticket purchase was over twice that of price, distance, or hours and more than 1.6 times that of number of rides and food.

### Creating your own event

An ideal event in terms of fit may not exist or be available; there is a shortage of good-quality events.[12] The solution thus may be to create one and own it. Some examples are as follows:

- Chase Bank's Chase Corporate Challenge, started in 1977, is a series of 3.5-mile running races (now in nineteen U.S. cities, plus London and Frankfurt) culminating in a championship race in New York in October. The races draw over 150,000 runners from more than 6,000 corporations; Chase has attracted national and local sponsor partners as well.
- The PowerBar CEO Challenge Race invites other CEOs to beat the PowerFoods CEO. The winner gets $5,000 to donate to a favorite charity.[13]
- The Stoli Vodka Ski Classic is a series of five ski races that are strictly limited to food service and bar professionals. The event includes a recipe context and tasting following each race and was an important factor in introducing Stoli's six new flavored vodkas in 1997.
- The Sta-Bil National is a twelve-city series of races for power lawn mowers, sponsored in part by Sta-Bil (an additive that helps keep gasoline from degenerating during storage), Dixie Chopper (a leading mower), and Citgo lubricants. Sales of Sta-Bil have increased 50 percent every year since 1992, when the event was created.
- The Black Velvet Smooth-Steppin' Showdown is the country's largest amateur two-step dance competition. The brand reported a 320 percent pourage increase associated with six regional events.
- Harley-Davidson's Anniversary Reunion celebrations are comprehensive events that attract more than 100,000 Harley riding enthusiasts to Milwaukee, Wisconsin. An international promotion

(including TV spots in collaboration with Miller Brewing Company's Miller Genuine Draft) further mobilizes millions of customers around the globe to participate in local events in their countries. These celebrations have significant brand-building value.

- Nike organizes a series of soccer matches among its sponsored national teams. These matches amount to a sort of mini–World Cup, providing a revenue stream through ticket sales, broadcast rights sales, and sponsorship sales to Nike.[14]

## 6. BECOMING PART OF AN EVENT/CUSTOMER BOND—THE AFFILIATION EFFECT

For almost any sponsored event, team, or other property there is a segment of heavily involved people who make time for the activity and are knowledgeable and current about it. The sponsored property may be a significant part of their lives and a vehicle to express their identities—for some, being a patron of the opera or a Jets season ticket holder is a prominent part of their self-concept. The existence of a reference group (such as other 49er season ticket holders or other participants in Ironman races) solidifies the bond between a person and the event.

The pride factor can also be related to a self-identity effect. Some people may be intensely proud of the national Olympic team, a local museum or event, or a company program. (More than 95 percent of Americans and 90 percent of those in the United Kingdom agreed that the Olympic games were a source of national pride.[15]) This emotion can be an important driver in providing a bond between a person and the sponsored property.

Can a sponsor of an event become part of that emotional commitment, self-expressive effect, and social bond? Is there an affiliation effect, whereby a brand becomes not only associated with, but also a part of that involvement? The payoff of such an effect could be large not only among the involved segment, but also among others connected to them.

Three factors might predict when an affiliation effect could occur. First, the brand likely would need to be tightly associated with a named team or event (such as the Adidas Predator Cup, the Toyota Wildcats, or the Transamerica Open) over an extended time. It would not be enough to put a Chevron sticker among ten others on a race car; the car would have to feature Chevron colors and a logo and represent the Chevron racing team. The brand should also be connected to a product that plays a role in the activity. Pennzoil motor oil or Porsche automobiles are logical contributors to a racing team, for example, whereas Kool-Aid is not.

Second, the activity would have to be an involving part of people's lives (rather than, say, a casual concert that is attended if convenient). Indicators of such involvement might include attendance levels, the tendency to follow news about the property, and making the involvement visible to others so that it becomes a badge. To consider an extreme case, passionate followers of the Texas Longhorns football team do not go to games if it is convenient—rather, their lives are organized around the Longhorns' schedule.

Third, some feeling that the brand was taking a risk by making a commitment to an activity should contribute to the affiliation effect. Barclays Bank stepped in to sponsor English soccer after Canon backed away, perhaps in part because of the hooliganism that the sport experienced.[16] Barclays felt that the sponsorship had a high profile and was closely connected to the British fabric, as well as a link to a young audience. Sponsorship research revealed that soccer fans felt that Barclays had taken risks by its commitment and that its sponsorship was critical to the health of the sport. In fact, the endorsement of a national financial institution was found to help the league's image—which, of course, then made the sponsorship more valuable.

### Affect transfer

A rationale for sponsorship of many events is that since the audience likes and enjoys the event, this positive feeling may get transferred to the brand. It is the same logic that has made liking an ad an important construct in explaining why some advertising is effective. There is substantial evidence that people liking an ad does more than create attention and interest; the liking also gets transferred to the brand. It seems likely that the same phenomenon should happen with events.

## WHAT CAN GO WRONG

Some sponsorships are little more than exercises in management ego at best, while others are dramatic successes. What discriminates between these two outcomes? Stepping back to look at how things can go wrong provides some insight.

### THE EVENT FAILS

When the event bombs the sponsorship will be a waste and may even taint the sponsor. Kodak once sponsored a Kodak Liberty Ride Festival where people in 100 cities were going to pay $23 to ride their bikes, have picnics, and watch a broadcast of a Huey Lewis concert. The problem was that the organizers delivered only a tiny fraction of the 500,000 people they promised; weak organization and a poor concept to begin with were at fault.[17] Golf tournaments and other events featuring individual performers always have the threat that the top players will not participate or will drop out early (either by losing or by getting injured).

### BAD ASSOCIATIONS EMERGE

The worst happens when a bad association emerges and the brand is damaged. An insurance company once sponsored a race car that crashed. IBM's sponsorship of the 1996 Olympics in Atlanta was meant to showcase the company's technology at its best by delivering instant information. The bugs that surfaced in the IBM system, though, drew negative publicity worldwide.

A mix of corporate sponsors might generate confusion or even damaging associations. Sprint, for example, was a second-tier sponsor of the World Cup in 1994, while MasterCard was the official card sponsor of the same event. When Sprint offered prepaid calling cards with the World Cup logo, MasterCard filed a lawsuit and won. While the Sprint event sponsorship was not an outright failure, the negative publicity against the telecommunications company hampered its success.

### GOOD ASSOCIATIONS FAIL TO EMERGE

Sometimes there is a natural fit between the brand and the event, but a good part of the audience simply misses it. In that case, it might be worthwhile to help them by making the fit more explicit. Seiko ran ads during the 1992 Olympics to make sure the connection between the timing of the races and Seiko performance was clear: "We are the clock, and we stand behind everyone who races to greatness in the games of the 25th Olympiad. We're Seiko, the measure of greatness."[18]

Since car racers cannot wear fashion sunglasses under their helmets, Revo foresaw little payoff from its racing sponsorship. Thus the company decided to rework the car's windshield by inserting Revo's brand name so it would be visible for TV cameras and audiences. Through this extra R&D, the company significantly improved the value of its sponsorship because it associated Revo with windshield glass technology.

## LOSS OF FUTURE RIGHTS

If a link to a sponsored property has successfully been created, it is wasteful to walk away from that property. Long-lasting sponsorships will logically have a stronger link, require less investment to create, and have an impact over a longer time period. If a sponsorship is lost because there was nothing (legally or morally) that tied the property to the sponsor, the investment will be wasted. Worse, some of the sponsored property's sought-after associations might become owned by a competitor. As a result, it is very useful to obtain an agreement to have the right to return to the sponsorship in subsequent years. American Express is still paying a price for having lost the Olympics to Visa before the 1988 games; the percentage who rated Visa as the best card for international travel went from 11.5 percent beforehand to 27 percent afterward.[19]

## SPONSOR CLUTTER

Sometimes attaching a brand to a sponsored property is difficult because there is simply too much clutter, too many sponsors, and too much signage. Clutter and its role in interfering with linkage and exposures should be a consideration in evaluating a sponsorship. One way to attack clutter is to use a variety of media such as promotions and the Web to build linkages.

When TV is involved, one way to create brand exposure in a cluttered setting is to use virtual signage—that is, a sign superimposed on TV coverage in the middle of a football field or tennis court, a prime space that would stand out and improve the association with the event. Such signage has the capability of being in 3-D, as well as appearing at critical points in a way that is not intrusive to the contest.

## AMBUSH MARKETING

One risk that sponsors of major events face is that competitors may engage in ambush marketing, attempting to associate themselves with an event they did not sponsor. In these cases, the competitor's brand reaps the rewards that the sponsoring brand paid for.

One ambush approach is through media advertising connected to the event. Nike had an aggressive billboard campaign in Barcelona during the 1992 Olympics, for example, and in Atlanta during the 1996 Olympics. These efforts were so successful in creating the incorrect impression that Nike was a sponsor that the Olympic organizing committee decided to require Athens, the next site, to turn over all of its outdoor advertising facilities to the committee six weeks preceding the 2000 Olympic Games. Similarly, Federal Express ran a series of spots during the 1992 Winter Games in Albertville, France, that led 61 percent of the viewers to believe that Federal Express was the official sponsor. The actual sponsor, the U.S. Postal Service (which only 13 percent thought was the sponsor) was not thrilled.[20] Another ambush tactic is to sponsor a subcategory; for example, Fuji undercut the Kodak worldwide sponsorship of the 1988 Olympics by sponsoring the U.S. swimming team.

Ambush marketing can be defended against by investing more in the link with the event and pre-empting event-connected advertising and promotions. An extreme approach is to explicitly note that competitors are not there. Thus in 1996 Visa defended its Olympic sponsorship by running ads proclaiming that American Express was not accepted at the Olympics. This campaign helped Visa's effort to increase its exclusive awareness and reduced the ambush marketing effort of American Express; it also helped position Visa toward American Express (with all its self-expressive benefits) and away from MasterCard, the real competitor.[21]

## OVERPAY FOR PROPERTY RIGHTS

Sponsorship can have excellent returns for the investment, as Sprint showed by earning an estimated 2.5 times its investments on incre-

---

### THE IEG SPONSORSHIP VALUATION SERVICE

Each year, IEG surveys 3,000 sponsorship opportunities and audits more than 500 sponsorship programs and contracts. By analyzing patterns between the rights fees sponsors pay and the benefits they receive, IEG codifies values for the entire gamut of sponsorship benefits. Using a proprietary formula, it calculates the recommended sponsorship fees by analyzing five broad categories of factors: tangible benefits (impressions in measured and nonmeasured media, televised signage, tickets, and so on), intangible benefits (such as levels of audience loyalty, category exclusivity, and prestige of the property), geographic reach/impact (local impact versus global reach), cost/benefit ratio (including return on investment analyses by property type), and specific factors unique to sponsors (such as length of sponsorship commitment and competitiveness of category).

The IEG valuation is very comprehensive and offered by a respected impartial organization that does not sell sponsorship opportunities—as a result, a high degree of objectivity is delivered. Over 130 of the most active sponsors in the United States have endorsed the IEG valuation.

---

mental calling revenue alone through its successful 1994 World Cup sponsorship.[22] But there are times when the benefits and values of the sponsorship disappoint the sponsor, because the cost is too high. When costs escalate over time, the likelihood of overpaying increases.

How can you assess the value of the sponsorship to know whether it is a sound investment? The ability to link a sponsorship to sales, as Sprint did, is rare. It is possible, however, to compare the impact of a sponsorship with baseline measures using standard industry valuation methods. One such valuation is the IEG Sponsorship Valuation Service described in the box.

## THE SEVEN KEYS OF EFFECTIVE SPONSORSHIPS

How can a firm locate and manage sponsorships successfully? Drawing on the experience of successful and unsuccessful sponsors,

FIGURE 7–5
*Seven Keys to Effective Sponsorship*

it is possible to identify seven key guidelines, shown in Figure 7–5, that should improve the chances of effective sponsorship experiences.

**1. Have Clear Communications Objectives for the Brand.** A sponsorship strategy should be responsive to the communication objectives for the brand. There are often three types of objectives: visibility/awareness, association development, and relationship development. Each of these could be an important driver of the sponsorship strategy.

Having clear communication objectives, of course, starts with an understanding of the brand essence, the core identity, the extended identity, and the value proposition. It also involves setting priorities. Is the goal to enhance existing owned associations, to change existing associations, or both? A knowledge of the associations that are needed should drive the sponsorship strategy—not only the selection of sponsorships, but how they are managed and exploited.

**2. Be proactive.** The temptation in sponsorship is to simply choose from what is offered, especially since some firms get thousands of requests each year. Sponsorship selection, however, needs to be managed proactively by developing a set of criteria for the ideal sponsorship, then listing possible choices that score well on these criteria. Being proactive increases the likelihood that the sponsorship will be original and break out of the clutter. To gauge potential sponsorships accurately, some basic information as to target audience and associations will need to be obtained. Scaling a wide variety of sponsorships as to their personality and matching those to the personality reflected in the communication task is often a helpful way to screen sponsorship options.

A simple decision framework like that in Figure 7–6 may also be useful in the short-list selection. The framework requires an evaluation of the fit of the sponsorship opportunity with the brand identity; what associations of the core identity does the sponsor develop? The second dimension is the degree to which the opportunity provides interactivity; to what extent does the sponsorship provide an opportunity for a brand identity use experience?

**3. Look for exceptional fit.** An exceptional fit between the event and the brand is much better than a good fit, and a forced fit or lack of

FIGURE 7–6
*Sponsorship Evaluation Matrix*

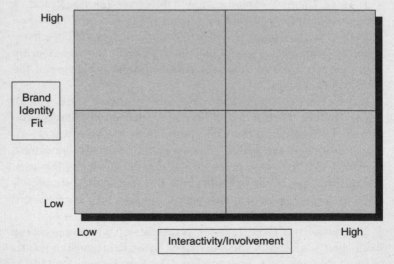

fit is a significant handicap. One mark of an exceptional fit is when the product can be demonstrated in a way that is integral to the core essence of the sponsorship. The fit between DuPont thermal wear and the Bering Straits venture is a good example. For the Olympics, the roles of Seiko in timing the events, UPS in delivering tickets, and Champion in providing the parade and award uniforms for the U.S. team made it easier for the sponsors to link themselves to the Olympics.

**4. Own sponsorships.** The key task of a successful sponsorship is to connect the brand to the event associations, and this task becomes much easier and more cost-effective when the brand is an inseparable part of the event itself. As noted earlier, the real key to success is to own the sponsored event over time and not just during the event; recall the Olympics study in which fewer than half of the sponsoring brands were connected to the event in a meaningful way. Event ownership has several implications:

   a. Consider focusing on one or a few events rather than forming a loose association with many.
   b. Go for long-term relationships and contracts; beware of situations where, if it works out well, a competitor can move into your place.
   c. Consider a named sponsorship.
   d. Beware of sponsorship clutter.
   e. Consider the threat of ambush marketing, and have a plan to deal with it.

**5. Look for publicity opportunities.** These are a mark of most effective sponsorships. The rule of thumb is that the budgeted cost of an effective sponsorship should be three to four times the sponsorship cost per se; this added budget is needed to help connect the brand to the event and to fully exploit the event's potential. Publicity will make the task of achieving brand-building objectives more effective and efficient. Further, an event or a product demonstration strategy within an event having publicity potential means that it has inherent interest—you do not have to create the event.

**6. Consider multiple sponsorship payoffs.** Some sponsorships pay for themselves by creating exposure and creating and strengthening certain brand associations. The sponsorship, however, can achieve meaningful brand-building objectives in other ways—by providing event experiences to key customers, by demonstrating new products, by mobilizing the organization for brand building, and by interjecting the brand into the event/customer bond. Again, a thorough evaluation of the sponsorship is beneficial.

Strong brands with large financial resources benefit more from sponsorship; small brands are at a disadvantage. Often, the property rights are too high. In order to make a sponsorship pay off, consider co-marketing with other strong brands. Ocean Spray, for example, chose to co-sponsor Dale Jarrett's Busch Series race team with Polaroid and Gillette to make the sponsorship affordable and to increase its impact with retailers and customers.

**7. Actively manage the sponsorship.** An effective sponsorship does not just happen—goals need to be set, programs put in place to achieve the goals, and the results measured. Consider sponsorship to be a co-branding experience; a co-brand needs to be created by consistently using a composite logo and actively creating brand awareness and associations. The co-brand is the ultimate asset from the sponsorship. Active management also means the involvement of the extended organization, as shown by the MasterCard case study in which the World Cup sponsorship was leveraged by having much of the extended organization play a role.

Sponsorship can be powerful. Consider how Virgin expresses its personality through the Virgin Balloon Challenge, the visibility and involvement of the Adidas Streetball Challenge, the relationship building of Saturn's Homecoming Event, and the associations created by the Hallmark Hall of Fame. These effective sponsorships were not ad hoc; rather, they were owned, actively managed, integrated into other brand-building programs, and on target as far as furthering the strategic objectives of the brand. Like any other element of brand building, there is a significant difference between good and great. The bar should be set high.

QUESTIONS FOR DISCUSSION

1. Evaluate the sponsorships with which your brand has been involved. What are the associations of those sponsorship properties? How did they contribute to brand building?

2. Take one of the priority items from the core identity. Identify properties that will have similar associations; consider sports, entertainers, and cultural events or entities.
3. Sponsorship can be particularly effective in reinforcing elements of the identity. Do your sponsorship efforts complement other brand-building approaches by developing or reinforcing elements of the core identity or the extended identity?
4. Identify sponsorships of competitors that have achieved a perfect fit with the brand. Identify sponsorships outside your industry that have a perfect fit. Consider owned events as well.
5. How are your sponsorships managed? Could that be improved? How do you coordinate sponsorships across the organization?

# 8

# Building Brands—
# The Role of the Web

Online gives us a way to meet customer needs unmatched since the days of the
door-to-door salesmen.
> —George Fisher, CEO of Kodak

The Web represents the convergence of media and commerce in a way that
may fundamentally destabilize existing communication channels.
> —Martin McClanan, Internet guru, Prophet Brand Strategy

Take a chance and try my fare;
It will grow on you, I swear;
Soon it will taste good to you;
If by then you should want more,
All the things I've done before will inspire things quite new.
> —Friedrich Nietzsche, an early Internet guru

## AT&T AND THE OLYMPICS

As part of its sponsorship of the 1996 Summer Olympic Games AT&T
developed a Web site intended to provide a virtual experience of being
at the Olympics. One page let site visitors view the Olympic Village
live, a vantage point otherwise available only to athletes and Olympic
officials. Elsewhere on the site, a visitor could stroll through the

Olympic Museum, obtain updates of athletic events, or participate in "virtual event" games and compare their scores to those of other players. Of course, users could also access the AT&T home page.[1]

The site was rewarding to visitors not only because it was informative and interesting but also because it provided a unique inside look at the Olympics. In addition to delivering exposure to the AT&T brand (more than three hundred thousand page exposures per day) the site created key associations. The visitor's active involvement linked AT&T to the Olympics with much more strength and depth than advertising could, and it also enhanced the possibility that the prestige and excitement of the Olympics would be linked to the AT&T brand. And since the site was also a demonstration of the power of telecommunications, it indirectly reinforced some key AT&T brand values.

## H&R BLOCK

The H&R Block Web site describes the company's tax preparation services, as well as its other financial products and services, in a serious and easily understood (if uninspiring) manner. Designed to educate potential customers, the site also offers practical information and tools such as tax-oriented news; access to Henry, a virtual tax advisor; downloadable tax preparation software; and federal and state income tax forms. The site is thus an efficient and economical way for the company's 18 million customers to access information and materials. Banners in various destination sites and the Yahoo! search engine help draw traffic.

Hoping to add spice to this solid base, the company banner ad invited customers to participate in the "H&R Block: We'll Pay Your Taxes" contest. More than fifty thousand customers entered a ten-week trivia game. Participants received three e-mails a week with facts about taxes, specific information about H&R tax services, and a set of trivia questions. The weekly e-mail response rate was 40 percent, with 97 percent of participants staying in the game throughout the ten weeks. Postcontest surveys revealed that brand awareness for certain H&R Block services increased dramatically, as did as site traffic.

### THE KOTEX WEB SITE

The Kotex Web site is directed at teenage girls whose bodies and lives are undergoing stress and changes. The site's look, feel, and language are designed to make teens feel comfortable—it is their world, with no talking down. The goal is to connect with girls and young women and to make Kotex products a part of a key time in their lives. Figure 8–1 shows a page from the Kotex site.

An information section on menstruation has segments on anatomy, emotions, exercising, taking care of your body, becoming a woman, the menstrual cycle, PMS, toxic shock syndrome, and frequently asked questions. A product section provides product recommendations based on personal needs (overnight, active, light flow, and so on). A "Girlthing" section lets girls express opinions, take a quiz, or otherwise hang out. For example, teens can give advice or comment on what they really love and loathe, and later see their comments appear on the Web. The resulting social bonding can be powerful and, just as important, can include the Kotex brand. While it may be unrealistic to believe that the Kotex site will be one of the winning bonding sites, it may have impact for a substantial group of girls.

Despite the World Wide Web's relatively recent arrival on the consumer landscape, it has had a major impact on brands and brand building. A host of strong brands—including the great early online brands, America Online, Amazon.com, and Yahoo!—served notice that the Web can create brands through its own unique communication channels and through its experience-based customer connections. At the same time, organizations such as the Gap, ESPN, Disney, and Schwab have deployed formidable resources to create an important Web component to their already-strong brands.

It is clear that we have entered a digital age, and the strong brands of this era will be those that best utilize the Web as a building tool. The growth of the Web as a brand-building vehicle is on a fast track; the numbers are staggering. In the United States, the Web reached 50 million households in just five years, compared with thirteen years for television and thirty-eight years for radio. The growth curve in other countries is not as dramatic as it is in the United States, but

**FIGURE 8–1**
*The Kotex Web Site*

is still impressive. Remarkably, the Web reaches people never exposed to Western media.

The Web is also in a high-growth mode with respect to its influence on business models and its impact on brand communications. Dell, Amazon, Schwab, eBay and others have shown that the Web can challenge the dominant business models of whole industries and create strong brands in the process. And brand communications have changed as well—a brand's Web presence increases the effectiveness of other vehicles and, in some cases, is the glue that brings the total communication effort together.

## UNIQUE CHARACTERISTICS OF THE WEB

Most traditional media advertising assumes that the audience members are passive recipients of the message; the brand builder controls not only the content but also the context surrounding it. Using advertising, brands are built in splendid isolation as agencies create pristine, manicured monuments whose brightly lit image is drilled repeatedly into the minds of consumers. In a way, traditional broadcast advertising creates a barrier between the brand and the consumer; because the latter is allowed no role in the experience—it is like viewing a painting or sculpture from behind a museum's guard rope. Traditionally, the most successful brand builders are those who have maintained a relentless focus on the purity of the brand monument: Marlboro's brand is solidly planted in its Western imagery because every single communication has been sculpted to perfectly reflect that imagery.

Early brand-building efforts on the Web treated it as another advertising medium. Passive banner ads were placed on pages, much as a media plan would schedule a set of television commercials to air on selected programs throughout a week; the key performance measure was the number of eyeball exposures among a target audience. Web sites, for their part, tended to be copies of print ads and catalogs. The results were generally disappointing in terms of (slightly adapted) traditional measures, such as cost per thousand exposures or cost per click-throughs.

In a way, the early popularity of this view is not surprising. From ancient Greece (where early dramas were choreographed performances of songs), to the first television programs (which trained the camera on an announcer speaking into a microphone), the use of new communications channels has always been based first on the traditions of an earlier channel. The lesson, however, has been learned: the Web is a very different medium. Advertising still has a role to play, but it needs to be adapted to the Web environment and will rarely be the lead player in brand-building programs.

In contrast to the traditional advertising model, the Web is all about experiences. In the Web environment, the role of the audience is an active one; the lean-forward rather than lean-back attitude changes everything. The audience member usually has a functional goal in mind—seeking information, entertainment, or transactions—and ignores or treats as an annoyance anything that gets in the way (including sluggish sites or poor, nonintuitive navigation). When building brands on the Web fits into this mind set, the experiences created can be more powerful than broadcast medium advertising in the context of an overall brand-building program.

If this seems hard to believe, consider the brand-building power of the Disneyland experience as opposed to seeing a Disney movie. Spending a day at Disneyland creates an intense personal association with Disney that even the best Disney movie cannot hope to generate. Similarly, visiting a Pottery Barn store has the potential to connect the brand to the customer in richer, more intense ways than any Pottery Barn print ad. To understand the Web, an experience-based model such as a theme park or a retail store is a better metaphor than passively received advertising.

From initial conception to ongoing support, the development and maintenance of Web experiences are also more complex undertakings than for advertising campaigns. No longer is the brand safe in splendid isolation behind guard ropes. Instead it walks among the people, a situation that presents risk and opportunity in equal measure. The art and science of creating brand-building experiences on the Web therefore require new perspectives and skills, as well as a willingness to understand the unique properties of the Web—it is interactive and involving; it offers current, rich information; and it personalizes the experience.

First, the Web is *interactive and involving*. A Web audience member might play a game, engage in conversation, search for information, express opinions, or play music all by one click of the mouse or one touch of the keyboard. That is all it takes for someone to create a musical event at the Pepsi site, specify his or her financial context at an American Express site before asking for advice on a specific problem, or exchange e-mail with Compaq Computer about an upgrade. In the General Mills schoolyard cyberspace, kids can trade e-mail with the Trix rabbit and the Lucky Charms leprechaun. A shopper at the Peapod Web supermarket asks for price and nutritional information for items before buying them. An Intel interest group exchanges information, good and bad, about the company and its products. By providing a networking outlet, the Web can stimulate extensive, even passionate brand communication that otherwise would not occur (or at least would not be heard).

Interaction with other people in the context of a Web site can create the potential for a meaningful social experience involving the brand. Even those who don't engage in conversation at Starbucks still report having a social experience, and Web-based socialization provides an even greater potential for the brand to become an important part of a person's life. A brand cannot ask for more. The Kotex site, for example, aspires to provide a social outlet for many teenage girls and a bonding experience for some.

The purchase experience is one not always associated with brand building, because the splendid isolation of broadcast media allowed many brands to leave the mechanics of purchase to others. The Web, however, allows almost everyone a chance to serve their consumers directly and turn the consummation of their relationship into a powerful brand-building experience. Companies such as Longs Drugs and Compaq have used the Web to attempt to reap the benefits of the vertical model enjoyed by rivals like Drugstore.com and Dell.

Because greater involvement and active participation make the Web considerably different from more conventional media, any impact—whether positive or negative—is likely to be more intense. Learning is more likely to be remembered and to influence future behavior; active involvement is more likely to create a bond between the brand and the person. The brand is more likely to become part of a person's world, and to do so in a vivid fashion. In general, the brand associations created will be stronger because of the experience and effort that go with firsthand involvement.

Second, the Web offers *current, rich information*—indeed, a depth of information that cannot be found anywhere else. Thus Ford can describe its whole line in detail, complete with specifications for each model. It can organize this information in different formats, showing models by lifestyle, application, or climate; it can even provide ordering information. If ordering directly is not practical, a list of dealers can be provided.

Buyers of high-involvement products such as cars, insurance, skis, or motorcycles often engage in extensive information gathering and analysis. On the Web, a brand can participate in this process by supplying useful and visible information, thereby influencing the consumer's buying process and (even more important) reducing the chance that influential information comes from competitors.

Fresh, updated information on a site or banner can create a sense of energy and being contemporary. By providing a motivation to revisit a Web site, it can also help build a relationship. The fact that a Web site might have a new comment, cartoon, game, update on a treatment for a disease, or new product information is a reason to bookmark that Web site so it can be checked on a regular basis. Some Web sites provide a news ticker (such as stock market quotes at the Schwab site, or sports scores on the ESPN site) that makes the site worth visiting frequently; the CNN news site, for example, is updated thirty to forty times per day. The Adidas site provided up-to-the-minute scores of all World Cup games as well as recaps of key plays. The Levi's site has a Backstage area that features a new alternative rock musician or band every month and adds a contemporary feel to the Levi Strauss brand. Visitors can listen to music, see videos, and check out tour dates.

Communicating rich, detailed information about a brand can enhance the depth of the brand-consumer relationship. On a personal level, the individuals whose characteristics and backgrounds you know in depth are those closest to you—your friends, relatives, and business associates. Similarly, if your Web site can motivate customers to really get to know the brand (that is, learn about its heritage, symbols, and values), a deeper relationship should result.

Third, the Web *personalizes*. A person entering a Web site can often select content of interest and avoid irrelevant content by choosing from menus. For instance, the McDonald's Web site starts with a family walking to a restaurant. If you click on the parent button, the site will become more adult oriented; if you click on the child button, the site displays content for kids. Product information can be personalized as to functional benefits. The section of the AT&T site for people starting up a business allows visitors to choose whether they are more interested in saving time or saving money, then delivers a presentation tailored to their preference.

A Web site can also be personalized without ongoing audience involvement. Information about a visitor (based on prior site usage and activities) can be used to create a custom site tailored to that single customer. The Gap Web site remembers the size and color preferences of visitors, and Amazon recommends books based on prior purchases. A food site can recall the type of recipes the visitor is interested in and modify information and even the feel of the site accordingly—people interested in fine dining, for example, might see a more stylized, formal site than people who have sought recipes for casual meals. Some sites (such as Hotmail, Firefly, or Pointcast) use information obtained when a person registers for the site to create a tailored brand experience. Although concerns about privacy may inhibit the process from reaching its full potential, the age of mass customization has arrived.

Personalization also means that brands can have different positions and even different identities for different segments. As described above, the McDonald's site can position the brand differently for kids and adults. The Robert Krups small-appliances brand has a "good value for the money" positioning on its European Web site and a far more upscale, premium positioning with a very different look and feel on its U.S. Web site. CDNow's Web site experience and brand associations can be very different in a classical music setting than in a rock context.

In other media, brand associations are often muted because of the presence of a nontarget market (consumer segments that are important to the firm but not the primary targets). Unfortunately, any communication that effectively targets one segment may be unappealing or even disliked by the nontarget market. In a Web context, though, the message can be tailored to the visitor so that highly targeted communications will not be exposed to those outside the targeted segment.

Personalization means that all brand-building tasks, from building associations to bonding, can be more effective. The Web can create a virtual brand tailored to each visitor, allowing the associations to be more intense and thereby create a stronger brand bond.

Personalization is the natural result of interactivity and richness; just as every visitor to Disneyland takes away an individual experience, a Web consumer will create a personal brand experience.

## BRAND BUILDING ON THE WEB

Figure 8–2 shows six tools for building brands on the Web. The most obvious tools, the Web sites and the use of advertising/sponsored content, will be discussed in detail, and guidelines for employing them effectively will be presented. However, four additional tools—the intranet, the customer extranet, Web PR, and e-mail—also have significant brand-building potential. Using the Web productively involves understanding how all of the tools can be employed; ignoring any of them will reduce the potential of the Web to build your brand.

### A Web site

A Web site (or subsite) dedicated to the brand is potentially the most powerful brand-building tool, in part because it can be tailored to the needs of the brand and the customer/brand relationship. Moreover, it can marshal all the power of the Web to create and reinforce associations.

FIGURE 8–2
*Brand Building on the Web*

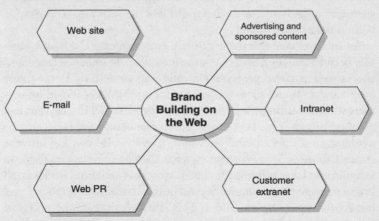

### Advertising and Sponsored Content

Banner ads and other paid Web placement of creative visuals, messages, and experiences can provide visibility and associations and also stimulate people to click through to particular Web sites. A brand can also sponsor content (such as category information, games, or other activities) on a third-party site. Sponsorship provides the ultimate ability to leverage the association of another brand and to gain ownership of a portion of the Internet.

### Intranet

As discussed in Chapters 2 and 3, an important brand role is to communicate the identity within the organization (and to brand-building partners) so that everyone knows and cares about what the brand is to stand for. Without that shared knowledge and commitment, effective brand building will not happen.

An intranet (generally a system of private Web sites connecting people within an organization, as well as its partners) can provide a key role in communicating the brand and its brand identity internally. Williams-Sonoma, for example, prides itself on offering the best-in-category products that emerge from a world search; its intranet could support this core identity dimension by providing detailed information about star products and the search for each. 3M, whose brand essence is innovation, could use its intranet to discuss technological problems interactively and to provide a source for creative-thinking tools. In each case, intranet users (buyers, managers, customer consultants, and others) will feel the substance and passion behind the brand essence.

An intranet can also more directly communicate the brand identity, brand strategies, and best-practice efforts to enhance that identity, as well as visual presentation rules and guidelines. Levi Strauss has its entire brand management model on the Web, including segmentation strategies, identities and strategies for all the current and planned brands, plus best-practice implementation ideas, so anyone working on a Levi's brand anywhere in the world can tap into the current strategy. Texas Instruments has the Communicators Café, an intranet site for communication managers that contains all TI ads, all brand management frameworks and brand strategy descriptions, and logo/visual presentation guides. This site helps create the potential for a consistent look on all TI communications. Other firms have used an intranet to communicate brand identity elaborations—role models and visual metaphors, for example, so that employees and partners can better understand the brand. Visual metaphors are particularly important in global brand management, where language problems often make verbal descriptions inadequate or, worse, confusing.

Intranets have a lot of power, but they can also overwhelm. An effective intranet system will organize information so that it is easily accessible and productive; it will also find ways to communicate to potential users how and when to use the intranet.

### Customer Extranet

Opening up part of the intranet to customers link them with the internal system of the company behind the brand. It usually allows the customer to access information, process orders, and receive backup support, just as if the customer were a part of the organization.

Dell, for example, has created password-protected, customized extranet Web sites. These sites, branded as the Dell Premier Pages, allow the employees of 200 of Dell's largest customers to select among computer options that have been screened to fit the specifications of the customer's systems. Employees of the customer can also access information normally restricted to Dell, such as data on past purchases and the technical data bank used by Dell engineers to troubleshoot problems. FedEx allows a customer to enter an order and receive bar-coded shipping labels, drop-off locations, and invoicing; he or she can also monitor orders by linking to the shipping and delivery information system. Giving the customer the same access as if he or she were part of the FedEx team not only makes the customer feel valued, it reduces FedEx's cost structure.

A customer extranet site builds brands in several ways. The Dell Premier Page not only delivers enhanced service but also vividly reinforces the Dell core identity associations of efficiency and responsiveness. In addition, and perhaps even more important, customers are made to feel special and part of the Dell extended family. This type of relationship, the best a brand can hope for, can create a comfort level that increases loyalty.

An extranet provides considerable brand-building opportunity. In particular, the look and feel as well as the content can be designed to reflect the brand. Many of the effectiveness guidelines for building brands on Web sites can also apply to extranets. This should not be surprising, since an extranet site functionally acts like a Web site (and in fact often uses some or all of the brand's Web site).

### Web PR

Web PR involves Web communication not controlled by the brand, such as personal home pages, news- or gossip-oriented sites, discussion groups, and chat rooms. Specialized discussion groups and chat rooms organized around brands or brand applications have proven their ability to dramatically influence sales, both positively and negatively. Iomega, which produces Zip disc drives, once experienced a huge demand for a new product that was fueled almost entirely by Web PR. A massive online discussion about an Intel Pentium chip computational flaw caused a relatively minor bug to become a serious image problem. The old axiom that a happy customer may recount his or her experience to three or four people but a disgruntled one will gripe to ten to fifteen needs to be modified, because now customers with a bad experience can reach thousands of people instantly at no cost.

Fortunately, Web PR can be influenced. One direct way is to have employees or their surrogates (fully disclosing their positions) participate in conferences or chat rooms. Such participation would not only influence the content but also the tone of the dialogue. Another approach is to encourage forums that are not destructive. Specsaver, a British optical chain, for example, has linked their site to news groups that discuss optical needs in a sensible way.

When negative information surfaces, responses are possible on the Web (by having people participate as described above) or outside the Web (via press releases or advertising). If the information is false, the information should be refuted as soon as possible. If there is merit to the negative information, admit it quickly and describe the program to deal with it. Simply letting negative information spread is risky.

Too often customer communication on the Web, whether it be through e-mail or chat rooms, is regarded as a nuisance or even a problem instead of an opportunity. Before the Web, customers would talk to each other about the brand out of earshot. Now it is possible to hear firsthand reactions—both good and bad—to the brand and the brand use experience. Access to such information represents a significant opportunity. New application areas can be identified, usage problems can be dealt with, and early warnings of serious problems can be heard.

### E-mail

An increasingly popular channel for customer service, marketing, and other communications, e-mail is a powerful tool for brand builders. It becomes the ultimate personalized contact: 1-800-FLOWERS sends e-mail reminders about anniversaries and birthdays, Barnes & Noble can announce an in-store event or promotion, Union Bank can announce a special interest rate on home equity loans, and Buy.com can confirm orders and shipments and announce new product offerings. These types of e-mail contacts serve to create a connection and, at the same time, remind the customer about the brand and its relationship with customers. To avoid being perceived as annoying, brands can and should limit the flow of messages and should make each one as meaningful as possible (and inform recipients how they can be deleted from recipient lists).

Because the Web is interactive, e-mail can flow *from* customers as well as *to* them. One all-too-common mistake is to fail to ask customers for questions and feedback. An even more common mistake is to fail to listen and respond—in the Internet world a full day is a long time, and a week is forever. A slow or sloppy response sends a signal that the brand does not care about customers. The information consumers are willing to provide over e-mail is unprecedented, far outstripping the use of toll-free numbers or the mail; harnessing is information is almost always worth the systems, people, and effort required.

## BRAND-BUILDING WEB SITES

A Web site can be a key part of a brand-building program because it can transmit information, impart experiential associations, and leverage other brand-building programs. Web sites are powerful in part because the site experience and its associations can be largely controlled and are strongly linked to the brand; thus the risks of a "great ad, can't recall the brand" problem are strongly reduced. When the Web site involves e-commerce activity or frequently updated information, a superior experience is often rewarded with a bookmark, which leads to significant loyalty.

How can a Web site become an effective brand-building tool? Five guidelines, summarized in Figure 8–3, are proposed.

### 1. CREATE A POSITIVE EXPERIENCE

A Web site should deliver a positive site experience by having three basic characteristics. First, it should be easy to use; the visitor should not get confused or frustrated. It should meet expectations with respect to the information it contains and the activities that it supports. Second, it should have a reason to be visited. It needs to offer value in terms of information, a transaction, entertainment, or a social experience. Without motivation to visit, bookmark, and revisit, the site will not be worthwhile. To the extent that the site can offer real substance, it can actually augment the brand by providing an enhanced level of functional, emotional, or self-expressive benefits. Third, it should exploit the unique characteristics of the Web. In particular, it should strive to be involving and interactive (e.g., the Pepsi site), personalized, (e.g., the Amazon site), and timely (e.g., the CNN site).

FIGURE 8–3
*A Brand-Building Web Site*

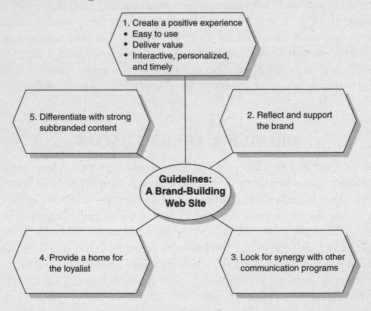

## 2. THE WEB SITE SHOULD REFLECT AND SUPPORT THE BRAND

A Web site—or any other form of brand communications on the Web, for that matter—should reflect and support the brand. Too often, making the site functional and simple results in a bland experience that does not create or support key brand associations. Conversely, a compulsion to make the site edgy and entertaining may be indulged at the expense of creating a fit with the brand or having a functional, responsive site (rather than a sluggish site bogged down with the task of loading graphics). The brand identity, not creative pressure, should be the driver.

Core associations can be directly supported on the Web. For example, Coke has a branch on its site that refers the visitor to places that are cool, refreshing, and fun—the three key core identity elements for Coke. The refreshing destination, for example, allows the visitor to compose a song or to duplicate the "Always Coca-Cola" jingle, thereby developing an association that is not only on target but has richness, texture, and involvement. Mobil could establish similar leadership, partnership, and trust branches, using internal and external role models to elaborate each of these core identity pillars. A visitor trying to understand what Mobil stands for would be interested and informed by the elaboration.

A Web site can also support associations that have a feeling or emotional component. The Hallmark Web site, for example, delivers on the brand's core benefit of helping consumers express their feelings and touch the lives of others.[2] One section contains creative ways to say "I love you." Another, titled Romantic Suggestions, has a list of ideas for enlivening relationships. A Creative Projects section offers examples of hand-crafted valentines, scavenger hunts, and a child's valentine mailbox. The result is an emotional element to the connection to Hallmark.

A brand's symbols can sometimes be key drivers of the brand's associations, and the Web site should leverage and enhance those associations. The Virgin site has a Richard's Diary section that chronicles the activities of founder Richard Branson, one of the key symbols of the brand. The Spring Hill factory for Saturn, another key brand symbol, suggests the company's down-to-earth personality, distinct organizational values and style, and U.S. connection. The Saturn Web site uses a simple banner showing the Tennessee countryside and a Spring Hill city-limits sign that helps remind the audience of the link between Saturn and the Spring Hill symbol. Symbols such as the Pillsbury doughboy and Mobil's flying red horse can similarly be leveraged to make the site more comfortable (by having familiar icons), interesting (by adding meaningful visuals to text), and tied to the brand (by being less generic).

### The look and feel

When a brand is conceptually and visually strong and the site is well done, the user should feel that he or she is in the brand's world. The look and feel should be present in the color, layout, and personality—the Kodak yellow, the Virgin red, the Harley-Davidson black, the Milka lilac, and the Duracell orange-on-black help create the world of the brand. The clean, crisp feel of a Gap store, the opulent feel of a Tiffany brooch, or the sensual feel of a Victoria's Secret undergarment can be reflected in a well-conceived site. L.L. Bean directs visitors to choices on the site with signposts that lend a backcountry flavor. The experience of the Harley site starts when you are greeted with a blank black page; slowly, the phrase "Respect the road; it does not respect you" appears. The family/home associations of Electrolux, the Swedish home appliance manufacturer, are captured by using the real home of a real family as a setting to present its products. Not only do you get to know the Essen family, you can even send them e-mail.

### Informing beyond the product/service

A site can be an authoritative source of information on a certain subject. For example, the Kotex teen site provides information on issues related to the challenges of being a teen and going through many body and life changes. The Healthy Choice site, which provides information on exercise and leisure activities as well as nutrition, allows the brand to develop associations further up the value hierarchy (specifically, good health and a better lifestyle). Claritin, an allergy medication, has a site that provides customized information about allergy relief, including a daily pollen count, product information, contests, and tutorials on coping with allergies.

A site providing authoritative information can build a brand in three ways. First, it can provide the brand with credibility, authenticity, and authority that it would never be able to achieve directly. A

Kotex claim to be an authority on a key aspect of a teen's life would lack credibility (and probably sincerity as well), but the Kotex Web site can offer helpful information that allows the claim to emerge implicitly. Second, such assistance allows the brand to participate directly but unobtrusively in what may be a central part of a person's lifestyle, making a potentially stronger bond. Finally, the Web site allows the brand to communicate using a language and feel that can connect. These brand-building objectives are more difficult to achieve if the site feels like a sales tool.

Sites attempting to address key informational needs should be realistic. Looking down the road five years, there will likely be a very limited number of dominant sites in each special-interest category— whether it is Italian cooking, current movie reviews, healthy living, or mountain bike trails. Who will be the winners in a given category? What will it take to become one of those winners? The long-term payoff of being the surviving dominant site could be huge, but any investment in a merely adequate site doomed to also-ran status may be wasted. A key question: Is it realistic for a brand to win against other organizations not tied to a brand (such as *Consumer Reports* and the American Dental Association) that have wider scopes and more credibility?

For many brands, the answer may be to collaborate or partner with other brands. Sharing of investments is one benefit, but the bigger payoff comes from the chance of being a destination site that is bookmarked by a large group of customers with similar interests. Medizin.Aktuell, a site created by a collaboration of nine European pharmaceutical companies, provides updates on the latest medical research relevant to diseases such as arthritis. This consortium is in a much better position to attract regular users to its site, because it has more credibility than each company would have on its own.

### 3. LOOK FOR SYNERGY WITH OTHER COMMUNICATION VEHICLES

When a Web site is developed and managed by a team of people who have their own style and goals, the result is a silo orientation—a Web site that is not integrated with other communication vehicles creating synergy but rather represents an isolated effort. This trap is easy to fall into, but important to avoid.

Integrated communication—the concept of coordinating all brand messages so they work synergistically—has been around for decades and has stimulated considerable initiatives from advertisers and their partner firms. The Web, however, injects a whole new dimension into integrated communications. It has the potential to be, if not the driving media vehicle, the structure and glue that holds it all together.

### Providing flagship-store impact

Think of the flagship store concept, and what a powerful device it is for building a brand by providing life, vitality, and tangibility to brand concepts. Consider the role that the Freeport store provides to L.L. Bean customers. It represents in a tangible way the heritage of the brand and an exceptional brand experience for those who visit (as noted in Chapter 6, it is a major tourist attraction). Similarly, the NikeTown stores present the essence of the Nike brand. The brand personality, symbol, and emotional associations developed by the store are given more impact by their close link with the products.

A Web site can in some contexts serve the same function as a flagship store. By presenting the brand in a rich, involving, authentic way, the site can provide the foundation for other communications efforts. The Web site can create intense links to the brand and its use experience, and it can link to the other communication efforts as the hub of the wheel. Using the flagship store as a metaphor, the brand site becomes the centerpiece of the brand-building effort and reflects the brand identity in a vivid and tangible way. Even if it is not assigned a hub role in brand building, the site can leverage and enhance the impact of a host of other media vehicles, such as advertising, sponsorship, promotions, and publicity.

### Supporting advertising

Most advertising media—especially television, billboards, point-of-purchase displays, packaging, and print advertising—are limited in the content that they can provide. The Web can complement such advertising by providing a way to obtain content-rich information that could not be placed elsewhere. For example, advertising can stimulate interest in a brand heritage, and the Web site can deliver the stories behind it. Advertising can announce a new product, and the Web site can provide specifics not only about the product but also about the applications. Exploring where and how to use the product can support the advertising and provide added value to the branded product.

A role of media (including advertising) could evolve into getting people to the Web site. Although putting the Web site address on the other media is certainly useful, attracting large numbers of people to the site will require more aggressive approaches. When an important if not primary role of advertising is to get people motivated to visit the Web site with a specific goal in mind, the role and execution of advertising will change.

The imagery and message of an advertising campaign can be reinforced in the home page. Research has shown repeatedly that the impact of advertising is magnified when exposures occur in multiple contexts—when a television campaign is supported by radio and events rather than being on its own, the results are usually markedly better. For example, BMW used the images and graphics of the company's latest brand-building campaign in print media as a template for its Web site. As a result, the Web site strengthens the core associations of engineering excellence, aesthetics, and performance that are put forward in the advertising.

### Supporting sponsorships

A Web site can support sponsorships by providing schedules and human-interest details about people associated with the sponsored activities, as well as news reports on events. In doing so, the Web not only provides added value but also makes the link between the sponsorship and brand stronger, deeper, and richer. Gatorade has the schedule for its Hoop It Up basketball competition on its site, and the Pepsi site provides information on sponsored concerts.

Some sponsorships provide an opportunity to generate news. An event such as Wimbledon, the Masters, or the Indy 500, for instance, has a significant following that would be interested in online information. Valvoline's Web site for the Indy 500 provides up-to-the-minute status on qualifying speeds, driver profiles, and race news; the site's close tracking of the event reinforces the credibility of Valvoline as an innovative brand close to racing.

### Supporting promotions

In-store or media-based promotions can be supported on the Web as well, because the Web site can be a vehicle for involving games, contexts, and activities. For example, the Oscar Mayer site has reinforced and supported promotions like the Talent Search Tour, which searches for a child to sing the Oscar Mayer jingle. The Web site fielded entries and provided an ongoing report of the promotion, thereby extending its reach and impact. Because a game too complex to be presented in a print ad or television commercial may be feasible with a Web site to back it up, promotions have the potential to become richer and more interactive.

### Supporting publicity

One role of publicity is to create news about the brand. Because of its online, information-rich properties, the Web can play a key role. The Web can accelerate information dissemination and be used to reach a large audience. Instead of relying on a few good contacts with journalists, public relations efforts can be enhanced by posting content on the Web. For example, LucasFilm fans the flames of hype surrounding the *Star Wars* prequels by posting production information and teasers on its Web site in a carefully controlled pattern, feeding consumers a steady diet of new information to keep them buzzing right up until opening weekend. The *Star Wars* site also overshadows unofficial sites, keeping LucasFilm's message clear and controlled. Some PR firms now offer services that enter information into a computer live at an event, post this information on several Web sites, and e-mail the content to hundreds of thousands of media professionals.

### Attracting Web site visitors

The total communications effort also needs to support the Web site. A dominant Web site will need outside visibility, which is why the major Web brands and others aspiring to own a portion of cyberspace are using outside media. Yahoo! was established with some creative billboard advertising in major cities; it later expanded this effort to substantial media advertising. To be dominant, the perception of dominance must emerge—and that requires visibility.

### 4. PROVIDE A HOME FOR THE LOYALIST

The Web site should be a home for the loyal group of people involved in activities related to the product class and with a commitment to the brand. It should support and nurture this group and its relationship to the brand, rather than taking loyal customers for granted while focusing on efforts to expand the customer base. Any brand with emotionally attached users should make sure its Web site recognizes and supports this group.

The importance of the loyalist extends beyond sales numbers. He or she provides a role model for other customers and for all the employees and partners of the organization by creating enthusiasm around the brand. The loyalist can also serve as an ambassador of the brand, in part because he or she is involved in the product as well as the brand.

Consider the role of the Web site to the Harley-Davidson loyalist. The company's Web site provides information about events and Harley products, a place to buy accessory products or ask questions of a technical expert, and a forum to connect with other devotees. It thus provides a central hub for biking and Harley enthusiasts.

Snapple is a brand with a quirky personality and a loyal following; its site feeds that loyal group and augments the product experience. A set of games reflects the Snapple brand, including an active squirt game in which the visitor attempts to squirt some moving targets and a Snapple scavenger hunt in which the task is to find six bottles hidden on the site. The visitor can also find his or her Snapple Strology, where a personality profile and monthly reading is provided based on a favorite flavor.

### The loyalist needs to know the brand heritage story

Knowing the roots of a person, place, or firm can help create interest and a bond. The same is true for a brand; its heritage can turn a functional relationship into a connection with depth and even emotion. Further, heritage stories can be interesting, especially when the stories involve real people. The Web offers a forum to tell these stories.

At the Harley-Davidson site, for example, you can learn how two young designers named Harley and Davidson set out to make bicycling easier in 1901. You can read about the role of Harley in the fight against Pancho Villa and in World War I, and about racing and innovation at Harley-Davidson over the years. To the Harley core customer or the Harley wannabe, these stories are part of the mystique of the brand.

At L.L. Bean, the story of the founder captures the essence of the brand. Bean, the Maine outdoorsman who founded the company in

1912, is associated with a set of legends. It all started when Bean designed a boot that combined lightweight leather tops with waterproof rubber bottoms and then created his guarantee of 100 percent satisfaction when the first batch of boots developed stitching problems. The opening of his retail store in Freeport, Maine, in 1917 was another landmark. A customer at the Bean site is potentially more loyal and committed than retail buyers, in part because of the heritage story.

Some symbols have enough intrinsic interest among devotees to justify telling their story—where the symbol came from, what it represents, and how it has evolved. Fruit of the Loom, for example, tells the story of the birth of its logo. Betty Crocker shows eight different incarnations of its symbol (the face of Betty Crocker) and asks the site visitor to match the symbol to the year. This game doubles as a way to vividly show the tradition that is part of the Betty Crocker brand.

### 5. DIFFERENTIATE WITH STRONG SUBBRANDED CONTENT

Many Web sites focus on functional benefits, which are often easily copied. Thus the challenge is to become a differentiated site by providing something that others cannot duplicate, at least not without significant cost. One approach is to develop some intangibles, such as being the dominant site for some area of interest (outdoor barbecues, for instance, or insect control). Another path toward differentiation is to develop branded benefits, features, services, or components that act as a silver bullet for the Web site.

Silver-bullet branded benefits can be powerful devices to represent parent brands and add differentiation. The fact that they are branded, and the brand is owned, is crucial; even if the functional benefits they represent are copied, the silver-bullet brands still are differentiated and known. In contrast, too many Web sites use descriptors to denote benefits. For example, without a strong feature brand, competitors can copy the Amazon book recommendation service. In contrast, wine retail Web sites can offer reviews, but they cannot duplicate the Ask the Cork Dork service of Virtual Vineyards.

Another good example is the Tide Stain Detective, which provides a personalized solution to tough stains. Aided by pop-up menus, the user selects the stain type, the kind of fabric, and the fabric color and pattern, then receives customized advice for that stain. The Tide

Stain Detective provides a visible representation of Tide's expertise
and leadership in cleaning, as well as its fifty years of innovation. As a
classic silver bullet, it represents the essence of the brand; further, it
is branded with its own logo and vivid name. Competitors can duplicate the functional benefit, but they will have a hard time dislodging
the Tide Stain Detective.

Another example is the Road Warrior from Travelocity, one of the
leading travel sites. Dubbed the "ultimate business travel resource,"
the Road Warrior provides the latest on fare sales, news items,
weather conditions for thousands of destinations worldwide, a cur-
rency converter, helpful information on reservations, and car rental
discounts. It also will contact a traveler to notify him or her of any
changes in flights and provide a free personalized destination guide
with suggestions about entertainment and business events. The Road
Warrior is a subbranded silver-bullet service of Travelocity.com that
creates associations of technological leadership and of being customer
friendly by providing value-added services for the business traveler.
With its own brand and logo, it has the potential to have its own
equity, which means that competitors will find it difficult to copy.

Still another example is the L.L. Bean Park Search. A visitor to the
Bean site can use the park search to learn about and see pictures of
any one of some 1,500 parks, forests, and wildlife refuges. One can
also find information about the thirty-six activities each park offers,
from hiking and kayaking to bird watching and snowmobiling.
Visitors can search the database by location and activity as well; thus,
they can obtain a list of Northern California parks that offer mountain
biking.

A branded benefit also provides a way to interject some personality into what may be a bland brand or Web site. Ernst & Young's sub-
scription-based Ernie service, which allows subscribers to interact
with the staff of Ernst & Young around the world, is friendlier and
more accessible than the parent brand. It thus adds a welcome personality as well as providing ownership of a service that provides a
connection to new and existing clients.

## ADVERTISING AND SPONSORED CONTENT

At the outset of this chapter, we noted that the Web is an experience
involving an active, in-control audience, not the passive audience of

conventional media. It was also suggested that passive banners would miss the potential of the Web. These observations, however, do not mean that advertising or sponsored content has no brand-building role to play on the Web. It does mean, though, that such content should be adapted to the Web environment and that it is likely to play a supporting role.

Advertising is a paid brand presence on the Web, and the most common form is a banner ad or some variant. However, the Web can involve a host of other forms. One firm allows the visitor to replace their cursor with a symbol; imagine the satisfaction of using a Mercedes or Harley-Davidson symbol if you were a devotee of that brand.

Sponsored content associates a brand with a particular part of a site that offers valued content. BestWestern, for example, sponsored CNN Interactive's City Guide, a popular site used to access hotel information in various cities. Regal by Buick sponsored the NCAA Women's Basketball Tournament Fantasy Games Challenge. IBM sponsored an interactive sports game, the Shockwave IBM Virtual Dunkathon, on a number of sport- and game-related sites (such as nba.com) to attract young, technology-savvy customers who otherwise might shun Big Blue.

Online sponsorship can deliver substantial benefits as part of a brand-building program. These benefits, which were discussed in detail in Chapter 7, apply to the digital world as well.

## THE LIMITATIONS OF WEB SITES

Advertising and sponsored content have a role to play because Web sites have limitations. A Web site is inherently powerful because it can create a uniquely interactive, personalized experience that provides access to a current, rich database; thus it is often the cornerstone of brand building on the Web. Creating a Web site that will attract and retain customers, however, is not easy. The assumption that "if we build it, they will come" is hardly true in the Web environment, given its context of aggressively competing sites and goal-oriented audience members. There needs to be a reason to visit the site, *and* potential customers need to be aware that the site exists. Providing a reason and creating awareness are two nontrivial tasks.

Furthermore, destination Web sites are not well suited for all brands. They work best for products or services that can be efficiently ordered online (such as books, stocks, or computer equipment), or for those for which extensive information is sought by customers (such as automobiles or vacation destinations). A brand that has neither of these characteristics—such as Dreyer's ice cream, Schick razors, or Kraft cheese—carries a double burden. If it can't provide e-commerce or special-interest information, another motivation for site visitors will have to be found, perhaps based on entertainment or a general-interest information area. Even if this motivation is found, it may not be associated with the brand, or it may compete with an established, more independent third-party site. It will thus be hard to attract visitors, because this site will not be an obvious place to go.

Even strong Web sites will reach a limited audience, perhaps only loyal customers who are involved in the product category. Consider the Saturn site, which may be very effective only for the loyalist and for those who are in the market for a Saturn-class car that day or that month. Since the larger audience (people who are not currently in the market for a car but will be some day) may not be motivated to visit the Saturn Web site, other means must be found to build the brand. When IBM sponsors a game on the NBA site, it gains exposure to an attractive audience, most of whom would never visit the IBM site.

When Web sites are inappropriate or their reach is inadequate, can advertising and sponsored content on the Web be effective at building brands? Can these forms of communication do more than create click-throughs to brand Web sites? Can they reach those customers of brands (like Saturn) not attracted to a destination site, or those (like Mennen deodorant) for which a destination Web site is not relevant? Can advertising and sponsored content do the classic brand-building tasks of creating visibility and presence and building and enhancing associations? The following study provides some encouraging data.

## ONLINE ADVERTISING EFFECTIVENESS

The Internet Advertising Bureau (IAB) and Millward Brown Interactive conducted a study of the brand-building impact of Web advertising in mid-1997.[3] Banner advertisements were tested on twelve sites, including CNN, ESPN, Lycos, and Ziff-Davis. More than sixteen thousand respondents recruited from the test sites were randomly exposed to one of the test ads or a control ad; after a time period that ranged from one to seven days, they were asked via e-mail to complete a short questionnaire. Thus, given the experimental design, the only difference between the test and control groups was a single exposure to a banner ad.

The results provided clear evidence that advertising on the Web can build brands. The average aided awareness ("Have you heard of this brand?") went from 61 to 64 percent, a statistically significant difference despite the fact that three brands had nearly 100 percent awareness already. In fact one new brand, Delta Airlines business class, increased from 43 to 66 percent and another, Deja News, went from 28 to 34 percent. Advertisement awareness ("Have you seen this ad?") on average went from 34 to 44 percent, indicating that the advertising did register with the respondents.

For half of the twelve test brands, perceptions were affected enough to be statistically significant as well. These results happened even though the experiment involved only a single exposure to a banner ad with limited content. For example, consider the impact of the Volvo banner ad, which showed a car with a tag line "So sleek, so swift":

**BRAND PERCEPTIONS—VOLVO LUXURY AUTOMOBILES**

|  | Test Group | Control Group |
| --- | --- | --- |
| Is a good automobile | 17% | 11% |
| Offers something different than other brands of automobiles | 11% | 7% |

## SOME GUIDELINES

Advertising and sponsored content on the Web can work, but there are challenges. One of these is how to be noticed and still avoid being so distracting and annoying that the ad hurts rather than helps the brand. Unlike the audience for television, radio, or billboards, which has been conditioned to tolerate interruption and distraction, the Web audience is in control and is less accommodating. How can the unique qualities of the Web be recognized and exploited—its ability to personalize, be interactive and be a source of rich, current, relevant information?

The following guidelines suggest how advertising and sponsored content can address these challenges and build brands on the Web by creating awareness, building associations, and reinforcing loyalty.

### Targeting

All advertising starts with targeting, but on the Web targeting is particularly important for two reasons. First, because advertising on the Web has historically been expensive in terms of cost per thousand, the effort should not be diluted by reaching nontarget audience members. Second, it is important for messages to be relevant because Web site visitors can easily ignore ads. Targeting the audience will enhance the probability that the ad will be relevant.

There are many ways to target on the Web. One approach is based on the implied or explicit profiles of audience members obtained by destination sites such as HotWired, Amazon, or America Online. Another is based on task indicators, such as the keywords used on major search engines such as Yahoo! or Excite. The second approach is why Miller bought the keyword *beer,* IBM bought the words *laptop* and *notebook,* and Libri (a leading book wholesaler in Germany) bought the word *book* on major search engines. Because of these purchases, specific pop-up ads appear whenever visitors to the search engine sites access these keywords.

### Consider the context associations

A context, such as Parent Soup or Disney, not only delivers a type of audience but also delivers a set of associations. The context associations are important because they can potentially influence brand associations just as they do in print and broadcast media.

An experiment illustrated the power of a strong, well-positioned Web site to pass on associations to a brand. In the experiment, a Dockers apparel banner on the HotWired site was shown to improve the image of Dockers apparel on dimensions such as hip, cool, spirited, and adventurous.[4] When the HotWired audience encountered a difference between perceptions of Dockers and the associations of the HotWired community, they resolved the difference by altering their perceptions of Dockers.

### Be relevant to the context

When a banner is in the right context, it might still be perceived as advertising, but it becomes less of an intruder and is more likely to support the desired brand associations. Intel, for example, used five-to ten-second interstitial ads (which appear as a program is being downloaded) on the Mplayer game community site to communicate the performance improvements that can be gained by using the new Pentium II processor. Certainly, in a downloading context, speeding up the computer to reduce wait time is relevant. HP has a banner suggesting that the current page be printed in color; the banner comes off as a suggestion as much as an advertisement.

### Become a part of the host site

The sponsorship will have a stronger link to the brand if the brand becomes a participant. Intel used its BunnyPeople (characters who represented clean-room workers) to create that involvement. The BunnyPeople were dispersed throughout the editorial contents of the Mplayer site; clicking on an image allowed players to select one of the colorful Bunnies as their presence within Mplayer.

### Interactive banners

Interactive banners engage the audience member by asking for some input. One study found that interactive banners have a 70 percent higher click rate than noninteractive banners that simply sent a user to another page.[5] John Hancock, for example, placed a banner at the top of several popular destination sites that showed a picture of a little girl and asked the question, "She's ( ) years old and I want her to go to a ( ). How do I make it happen?" The user could enter the appropriate age and type of college for his or her daughter, after which the banner would calculate how much the user needed to save per month to achieve the goal. A simple puzzle, contest, cartoon, or an easy set of questions like those in the John Hancock banner not only make customers stop and think about the need for a product or service but also connect a brand to this need.

### Provide news, entertainment, or other incentives

There are a variety of ways to provide incentives for audience members to become involved in the ads, or at least to tolerate their presence. Some magazines such as *Variety* and *Forbes* provide news headlines in their advertising. Hewlett-Packard has an animated Pong game in its banner that lets audience members actually play against the computer. This site is often downloaded, the ultimate advertisement compliment (comparable to conventional ads that are so captivating that they become a topic of conversation). Others have provided free computers or Internet access in exchange for having a set of ads displayed on the machine.

### Symbols and taglines

A banner, like a billboard, has limited content capacity; how can it be used most effectively? A strong tagline and symbol can help communicate in a compact way. Taglines such as "Nobody doesn't like Sara Lee," and "The Quiet Company" and symbols like the Pillsbury doughboy and the Wells Fargo stagecoach make communicating in a banner format more feasible.

### Goals and measurement

Certainly for advertising designed to increase the traffic to a Web site or to precipitate immediate action, click-throughs (for example, when a click of the mouse transfers a visitor to the advertiser's home site) will be a relevant measure. Click-throughs, however, do not necessarily reflect the ability of the advertising to achieve awareness and build associations. In fact, the correlation between click-through measures and increased brand awareness in the IAB study was zero—the two most effective of the twelve ads, Volvo and Schick, had almost none. If click-through measures become dominant, the tendency will be to go off strategy in order to achieve that result. What is needed instead is experimentation with awareness and association measures, such as was done in the IAB study. The advantage of the Web is that such experimentation is very feasible and of reasonable cost.

### FINAL THOUGHTS

Martin McClanan, an Internet guru at Prophet Brand Strategy, observed (in a quote reprinted at the outset of this chapter) that "the Web represents the convergence of media and commerce in a way that may fundamentally destabilize existing communication channels." His observation suggests that a variety of participants need to have the appropriate perspective regarding the Web. Pure e-commerce brands should not simply provide a functional, convenient way to order products (leading often to a low-margin business) but should build a brand through personality, community, content, and entertainment to create longer visits and loyalty. These brands should also use all brand-building tools and not just restrict themselves to the Web.

Brands with an offline presence should not view the Web as just another medium; rather, it should be viewed as an integral part, if not the driver, of the whole brand-building effort. More significantly, the introduction of the Web can change the business model and the role of traditional communication vehicles. The Web, in some circumstances, should be considered a way to expand brand building beyond communication into the total value chain, from product development to service support.

The Web has evolved so rapidly that not many traditional communication managers can simply take charge of a brand's Web efforts and deliver great results. Organizations need in-house senior managers who know how to use the broad array of communication options (both on and off the Web), identify emerging e-business models, and build and exploit e-commerce opportunities. Today the position of chief Web officer is rare, but tomorrow it will be essential for brands that want to create a real and sustainable competitive advantage.

Choosing the right external communication partners will be equally critical. Because most traditional advertising agencies view the Web as just another communication channel, only a handful are able to provide the necessary technological expertise and e-commerce capabilities. Similarly, few Web developers understand how to use their skills to build brands. The skill set needed to develop a digital brand strategy driven by a strong, clear identity—one that ensures that implementation groups inside and outside the company get the most out of the Web's brand-building possibilities—is rarer than gold right now, but just as valuable.

The Web is about experience. The challenge is to link the experience with the brand. The brand is the one thing that cannot be copied. So, the trick then is to build the brand by creating an experience that people associate with the brand. The experience can be created by using the unique qualities of the Web and keeping up with changing technologies in order to realize the opportunities that it represents.

## QUESTIONS FOR DISCUSSION

1. Does your Web presence support the brand? Are symbols used and enhanced?
2. Is there a hook to get the visitor to keep coming back?
3. Does your Web presence augment the brand by providing added value to the customer?
4. Do those who are in charge of building your Web presence have a clear understanding of the brand identity?
5. Does your Web site establish a dialogue with current or potential customers? Does it connect you better with your customers? Does it facilitate customer feedback? How is this information used in your organization?
6. Do you have a Web presence that is consistent across brands and markets, and with offline media?
7. Check out your brand's presence on the Web by conducting a Web audit based on the above six questions.

# 9

# Building Brands—
# Beyond Media Advertising

Everyone experiences more than he understands—but it is experience, not understanding, that influences behavior.
—Marshall McLuhan

Resist the usual.
—Raymond Rubicam, founder of Y & R, circa 1925

### NESTLÉ'S ALETE

In France, Nestlé created baby-changing stations at rest stops on Autoroute Sud, the main artery for families traveling to the sunny south for a vacation. The stations offer diapers and other incidentals, as well as baby food. This was not an altruistic initiative but a way to make Nestlé's Alete baby food brand relevant in consumers' lives. By earning parents' gratitude and providing trial experiences with useful products for their babies, it connects the brand with consumers emotionally and functionally.

## HEWLETT-PACKARD

In downtown Manhattan, Hewlett-Packard set up showroom trailers, then invited passersby in to see a reproduction of the Indy 500 control center, which used HP color printers to track various tasks. The show, themed "The Color of Business," helped visitors understand the importance of color and HP printers in today's fast-changing corporate world. The glamour of the control center both attracted visitors and was the source of key target associations.

## PROGRESSIVE INSURANCE

Progressive Insurance is unconventional and innovative, both in running its car insurance business and in building its brand with consumers. When it found that slow claims processing was a major complaint among consumers who were involved in accidents, the company introduced a branded ultrafast claim service, Immediate Response. Highly visible Immediate Response vehicles circulate in major traffic areas so that in case of an accident they can settle the claim on the spot. The Progressive-branded vehicles create powerful and relevant visibility; drivers and customers claim that Progressive often beats the police to accident sites.

## BMW

The BMW Tennis and Golf Tournament creates a powerful brand-consumer connection. The tournament is a social get-together for tennis and golf amateurs and car enthusiasts that takes place in a different beautiful vacation setting in Europe every year. The objectives are to have fun and occasionally chat about cars and sports. The event itself, the public relations efforts, and the direct marketing and promotion initiatives before and after the event create a context in which consumers can deeply and emotionally connect with the brand, because they create memories, feelings, images, and positive thoughts about BMW.

When a pharaoh died in ancient Egypt, mortuary priests mummified the body and placed it into an ornate sarcophagus, a set of coffins tucked inside one another. The sarcophagus was then entombed in the Valley of the Kings. Tombs were elaborate constructions that took laborers years to build. Their purpose was to help the king journey safely from this life to the next, and to communicate to the gods and others of the afterworld that the sarcophagus contained not just anybody but a pharaoh.

The ancient Egyptian tombs had as many as twenty chambers and corridors, with murals decorated by master painters and bas-relief sculptors. The murals told stories about the pharaoh—what he believed and what he valued. They also described activities, such as hunting, that were part of the pharaoh's life. The chambers contained funeral goods and many other treasures and possessions of the pharaoh.

In a way, the Egyptian tomb builders were brand builders; they sought to build visibility by the sheer size and presence of the tomb. They provided a host of associations that served to describe the pharaoh (what he valued and believed, what he did in his daily life, and what he possessed). Finally, they built a deep relationship between the pharaoh "brand" and the gods by building an edifice to which gods would relate. And they did it without media advertising!

## THE BRAND-BUILDING TASK

Implementation of brand strategy usually focuses on creating (or enhancing) visibility, brand associations, and/or deep customer relationships (see Figure 9–1). Each of these tasks is guided by the brand identity and brand position. Even the creation of visibility requires guidance, since some approaches might not be compatible with the brand identity.

The power of visibility is often underestimated. Brands such as Intel, Coke, and Visa have developed dominant market positions largely on the basis of sheer presence. Each is omnipresent within its context; such visibility not only can stimulate consideration at every purchase, it can also affect perceptions. A brand such as Intel is given credit for leadership, success, quality, and even excitement and energy, mostly because of its visibility.

Visibility has several components, including recognition ("Have you heard of this brand?"), unaided recall ("What brands do you

FIGURE 9–1
*Brand-Building Tasks*

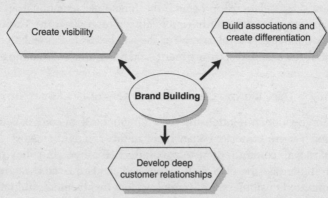

know?"), and top-of-mind status ("What is the first brand that comes to your mind?") in the customer's buying process and brand attitude structure. The relative importance of each will depend on the competitive context. For a small or emerging brand in a big market, recognition might be the major objective. In other situations, recall is more important; in *Building Strong Brands*, the danger of moving into the "graveyard" (where recognition is high but recall is low) was discussed. For a dominant brand, especially one that competes in an impulse market like chewing gum, top-of-mind status might be crucial. In most cases, awareness in all three levels should be a part of the guiding objectives and ultimate measure of results.

Building associations, the heart of brand building, is driven by the brand identity. The goal is not only strong associations but also a differentiated brand, such as Southwest Airlines, Tiffany, and Jaguar. One conclusion that emerges from the Young & Rubicam Brand Asset Valuator, based on a structured inventory of more than 13,000 brands in nearly three dozen countries, is that differentiation is the key to a strong brand, more so than esteem, relevance, and knowledge.[1] According to the Y&R model, emerging brands build differentiation first, and the earliest indicator of a fading brand is usually the loss of differentiation. Brand loyalty needs to be based on unique characteristics; it is hard to develop much attachment to a me-too brand.

The really strong brands, such as Harley-Davidson and Saturn, have gone a step beyond achieving visibility and differentiation to develop deep relationships with a customer group—that is, the brand becomes a meaningful part of the customer's life and/or self-concept. When a deep relationship occurs, the functional, emotional and/or self-expressive benefit will have a relatively high intensity. The customer will be highly loyal, and he or she will be likely to speak to others about the brand, discussing merits and defending shortcomings.

## CREATING A DEEP RELATIONSHIP—FIND THE CUSTOMER'S SWEET SPOT

Developing a deep relationship with a segment of customers is usually much more important than sheer numbers might suggest. Not only do loyal, committed customers influence others, but they provide a stable sales base. Not all brands can create a large core group of committed customers; for example, a low-involvement, utilitarian brand such as Dash detergent may not aspire to build such a group. But for those that can, it can be a significant asset.

### The Customer Relationship Model

A brand cannot develop deep relationships without a rich and insightful understanding of the customer. The need is to find the customer's sweet spot, that part of his or her life that represents significant involvement and commitment and/or expresses who they are—their self-concept. One way to find the sweet spot is to look at existing committed customers: Why do those people have such a strong attachment to the brand? It also helps to use qualitative research that is designed to look beyond the obvious to find deeper motivations. The key is to learn *from* customers as individuals rather than *about* customers as groups. How is the brand linked to the customer's self-concept and living patterns? Finally, look at customers' values and beliefs, activities and interests, and possessions (in other words, what they are, do, and have). The essence of most people is reflected in these three dimensions, as suggested by the customer relationship model in Figure 9–2.

**Values and Beliefs.** A customer's set of values and beliefs represents the essence of that person, what he or she stands for. The Body Shop connects with people concerned with social issues; its programs to support Third World economies, to save the whales, and to be environmentally aware resonate with a segment that has similar values and beliefs. The Ronald McDonald House program to provide housing for families of seriously ill children will resonate with the values and beliefs of a set

FIGURE 9–2
*The Customer Relationship Model*

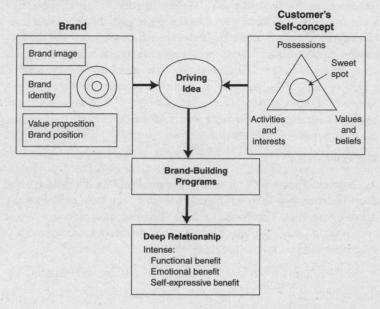

of McDonald's customers. Apple's "Think different" tagline and offbeat computer colors appeal to people who value the maverick willing to go up against a monolithic competitor. For its part, Microsoft uses "Where do you want to go today?" to express a set of aspirational values that also is designed to connect with a segment of customers.

**Activities and Interests.** A second dimension of a customer's self includes activities and interests such as tennis, watching football, travel, house maintenance, family, investing, exercising, commuting, and dining out. A brand can connect by becoming an integral part of one of these activities or interests and delivering exceptional functional benefits. The North Face, for example, could become a part of outdoor adventuring by providing the gear and knowledge that enable hikers and climbers to achieve their goals. An online investor may consider Charles Schwab, the leading online brokerage, a partner in refining an investment portfolio.

**Possessions.** We are what we have. Possessions are here defined broadly to include persons, places, ideas, or groups as well as things. All of these can express, confirm, or ascertain a sense of self [2]—what, in short, a customer has that he or she calls "me" as opposed to "mine." The challenge is for the brand to link itself to that possession. In some cases (e.g., Harley-Davidson) of course, the brand *is* such a possession and delivers intense emotional and self-expressive benefits. When a consumer holds up a Harley-Davidson T-shirt, saying, "This brand is me," and relating experiences that make it part of his or her life, or when the ownership of a Mercedes-Benz provides someone with a feeling of accomplishment, the brand has achieved a deep relationship with the customer.

### The Driving Idea

As shown in Figure 9–2, the heart of brand building is a driving idea, a central concept (like a brand personality) or program (like the Adidas Streetball Challenge or NikeTown) around which a set of coordinated brand-building programs can be developed. A good driving idea will precipitate programs that:

- Build the brand by creating visibility, associations, and relationships
- Resonate with customers
- Break out of the clutter

In many cases, the driving idea is inspired by the consumer sweet spot. Adidas tapped into a consumer sweet spot with its driving idea, the Adidas Streetball Challenge. Their target youth audience resonated with the idea of a weekend filled with social, competitive, and physical activities. Figure 9–3 provides several additional examples of driving ideas and the customer sweet spots behind them.

Driving ideas also can come from the brand side of the model. For example, a driving idea can be based on any of the following:

- Product. The IBM ThinkPad, Apple's iMac, and the Audi TT are all brand statements that can drive a brand-building effort.
- Position. The Häagen-Dazs story (described later in this chapter) provides an example of a brand position being the driving idea behind a set of programs.
- Brand personality. The Virgin personality has inspired several driving ideas, such as the hot air balloon program.

Clearly an inspired driving idea can be the key to breaking out of

FIGURE 9–3
*Examples of Driving Ideas*

| BRAND | CONSUMER SWEET SPOT | DRIVING IDEA |
|---|---|---|
| Adidas | Team competitions as a weekend activity | Adidas Streetball Challenge |
| Coca-Cola | Patriotism and the joy of celebrations | Olympic Torch Rally |
| Harley-Davidson | Feeling free and macho | Harley Owners Group (HOG) |
| Maggi | Cooking with fun for family and friends | Kochstudio |
| Starbucks | Functional and social enjoyment of the daily coffee break | Reproducing the European coffeehouse experience |
| TAG Heuer | Identification with yachting | Sponsoring the Whitbread yacht race |

the box with a NikeTown or Adidas Streetball Challenge that provides the central thrust to a set of brand-building programs. But how can such a driving idea be generated? There is luck involved. Management guru Tom Peters once advised companies to "revel in disorder and the joys of accidental discovery—that's the ticket!" It is no accident, however, that some firms are luckier than others; as Louis Pasteur once said, "Chance favors only the prepared mind." An organization can establish a culture and structure in which people will be able to recognize an exceptional idea and, perhaps more important, have the incentive and authority to support it so that it can succeed. It can also create a process that will enhance the probability of finding a winning driving idea. Such a process will likely have three stages.

The first stage would be to put the most important aspects of the brand and the customer on the table. For the brand, these aspects are the brand image, its identity (including personality, symbols and brand essence, the value proposition, and the brand position). With respect to the consumer, they are the activities and interests, values and beliefs, and possessions discussed earlier. Which generate potential sweet spots?

The second stage is to define possible driving ideas based on the ideas, concepts, and insights generated in the first stage. Just asking some basic questions can help: What is really magic here? What

## HOBART CORPORATION*

While Hobart Corporation—a manufacturer of food equipment for more than 100 years—wasn't necessarily seen as an industry leader, it had developed a solid reputation for high-quality products. In addition to being the largest firm, it had broad coverage of the retail (e.g., restaurants and bakeries) and food-service (e.g., institutions like schools) sectors and the major product categories in the industry. The other leading companies excelled only in a particular product category (refrigeration, for instance), or were well known in just one of the industry sectors.

Hobart wanted more. It sought to develop a sustainable competitive advantage by being the thought leader in the industry, not just the product leader. The driving idea was to offer advice and solutions to everyday problems that its restaurant and institutional customers faced in their businesses: finding and retaining good workers, keeping food safe, eliminating costs, reducing shrinkage, and enhancing same-store sales growth. These organizational issues defined a customer sweet spot.

This driving idea of solving customers' everyday problems resulted in a powerful brand-building program led by public relations. Print advertising preceding the effort focused on specific and pressing customer issues. For instance, one ad showed an "Employees Must Wash Hands Before Returning to Work" sign at a bathroom sink and asked, "Need a more comprehensive approach to food safety?" The ad text provided the solutions recommended by Hobart, with the tagline "Solid Equipment. Solid Advice."

The print campaign played only a small role in the entire brand-building program developed with the help of Hensley, Segal and Rentschler, a business-to-business communications company. Hobart worked directly with journalists from the trade media to obtain, not product placement, but rather "idea placement." The kind of articles sought were those with headlines such as "Cold War: Smart Refrigeration Arms Restaurateurs Against Foodborne Illnesses" (which appeared in *Hotel Magazine*). Hobart also changed its approach to new-product releases, emphasizing how the product helped the customer deal with the key business issues. For instance, the communication emphasis for the Hobart Turbo Wash focused less on specifications like recessed nozzles than on how it made an unwanted task—scrubbing pots and pans—much easier, resulting in happier restaurant or food-service employees.

Hobart also created a customer magazine called *Sage: Seasoned Advice for the Food Industry Professional* to provide in-depth articles that would meet newsstand standards—not corporate puff pieces. To promote this emphasis at industry trade shows, the Hobart booth had an Idea Center where people could ask industry experts about the problems they faced in their businesses. Within the organization, the leadership message was reinforced at department and company meetings and through internal newsletters.

Another way that Hobart shared its sound advice was through speeches at key industry shows and events like the Home Meal Replacement Summit and the National Conference of the Foodservice Consultants. Furthermore, the company offered a tremendous amount of content on key issues on its Web site, where visitors could find papers, Q&A's with industry experts, briefing documents, and other material updated on a weekly basis. Hobart content was also strategically placed on many other sites frequented by people in the industry, with selected pieces disseminated broadly in print as well.

*Source: Thanks to Steve Kissing of Hensley, Segal and Rentschler, who suggested this example of a driving idea and provided details.

---

really resonates? What is different from other brands? A formal creative-thinking workshop would also be a worthwhile investment; however, note that creative-thinking programs exist—the workshop does not simply have to be a brainstorming session.[3]

The third stage is to evaluate the suggested driving ideas. What brand-building programs could surround each one? What impact would the resulting effort have? How many people in the target segment would be reached? What associations would be developed? How would success be measured? How could the concept be refined to be even better?

## THE BUSINESS RELATIONSHIP MODEL

Organizations are customers, too—but the customer relationship model needs to be adapted to become an organizational model. Like people, organizations have values and beliefs that are central to their being. The other two corners of the customer self-concept triangle in the relationship model (Figure 9–2) need to be replaced, however, by organizational mission and organizational issues and problems.

### Values and beliefs

Organizational values, of course, tend to have their own flavor. Social activism is important to The Body Shop, while interests in the arts or charities are top priorities for other firms. Hewlett-Packard has a special interest in employees and their professional and private fulfillment. Chevron is concerned about the environment. 3M fosters innovation in a variety of forms.

### Organizational mission

Every organization has a mission or defining activity. General Motors designs, manufactures, and distributes cars. Xerox is the digital document company. Disney makes people happy. A mission is important to companies not only functionally but also emotionally; it is what they are about. A brand seeking a relationship with an organization should look at the broadly-defined mission. For example, a supplier to GM might connect by becoming involved in roads, auto safety, or rallies. The supplier brand would thus demonstrate a shared passion for the automobile and its position in society.

### Organizational issues and problems

Every organization has issues and problems, as well as a set of assets that are developed and directed toward solving them. Hobart, described in the box, is an example of how these organizational issues became a driver idea. The company simply asked itself what major problems its customers had to overcome in order to operate successfully, then set about becoming an authoritative advisor on those problems.

## BRAND-BUILDING TOOLS

Whether the goal is enhancing visibility, building associations, or creating deep relationships, how do you build a set of brand-building programs around a driving idea? Historically, the cornerstone of most brand-building efforts has been the effective use of media advertising. The presumption that successful brand building consists of finding a good agency, stimulating it to create great advertising, and funding a significant campaign, however, is fast becoming obsolete. Delegating brand building to an agency that (despite probable protestations to the contrary) will have a strong inclination to create ads is no longer the recipe for branding success, if it ever was.

There is no question that media advertising can be a powerful tool, especially when a truly great campaign such as "Got Milk?" is developed, and it is likely to continue drawing the vast bulk of brand-building investments. Media advertising has several problems and limitations, however, that make the growing list of alternatives perilous to ignore.

Media advertising is becoming increasingly fragmented because of the growth of niche magazines and newspapers and the explosion of specialized TV stations. This has an upside, since it is now feasible to reach targeted audiences in contexts that are often brand friendly. It also means, however, that the economies of scale previously associated with media advertising are more elusive, because so many more ads must be spread among different outlets to reach the same number of people. In addition, because fewer resources and talent are generating too many advertisements, it is more difficult to achieve the creative home run that is necessary.

The sheer volume of clutter, driven in part by shorter ads on broadcast media, risks turning off audience members. Survey research suggests that consumers are skeptical about advertising. A consumer study showed that only 16 percent of people in Britain admitted that they pay attention to commercial breaks, 65 percent no longer trusted TV ads, and one in three said that all advertising annoys or irritates.[4] Although response bias probably inflated these numbers, it is sobering to think that advertising is ignored by 84 percent of its customers, and only one-third find it trustworthy and not annoying.

Of special concern to brand builders is the fact that media advertising, for the most part, is a passive vehicle, lacking the intensity of connection possible with alternative vehicles that can be more experiential and involving. Thus the potential to generate a deep relationship with customers through advertising is relatively small.

Fortunately, media advertising need not be the dominant or even leading brand-building tool. Strong brands have been built with other tools playing key roles, including the Web, sponsorships, brand-building promotions, direct marketing, flagship stores, customer clubs, sampling, billboards and other visuals, branded public service programs (such as the Ronald McDonald House), kiosk presence, and in-store displays—and this, of course, is only a partial list. Recall the Adidas Streetball Challenge, the NikeTown store, the Virgin publicity stunts, and the MasterCard sponsorship of the World Cup. The challenge is to access and manage the dozens of brand-building tools available in an organization that may be uncomfortable with moving beyond advertising, in part because it lacks internal expertise.

## BUILDING BRANDS—SOME ROLE MODELS FROM EUROPE

The balance of this chapter presents several role models for brand building beyond media advertising that all represent, in their own way, a creative flair. These role models are drawn from Europe in part because media advertising in Europe has significant institutional limitations, and thus alternative approaches to brand building tend to be more prevalent. After these role models have been discussed, we will propose some guidelines for brand building, drawing in part on the lessons from these case studies and those in the previous three chapters.

### THE MAGGI STORY

Julius Maggi founded Maggi more than 100 years ago when he developed the first dehydrated soup. His objective was to provide nutritious and flavorful meals for working-class women who lacked the time and money to prepare proper home-cooked meals. A few years later, he invented the liquid seasoning (portrayed in Fig. 9–4) that was to become Maggi's signature product. Its distinctive bottle became as well known in the German-speaking part of Europe as the Coke bottle is to Americans; Maggi liquid seasoning provided the

FIGURE 9–4
*100 Years of Maggi Liquid Seasoning*

secret ingredient for many recipes that stimulated compliments to the cook. Nestlé acquired Maggi after World War II.

Finding its core customer aging during the 1980s and 1990s, Maggi reached out to the younger generation with meal-maker products, ready-to-eat foods, and frozen snacks, as well as ethnic and children's product lines. These initiatives were true to the Maggi heritage, the brand essence of being the customer's best friend in the kitchen, and to the following Maggi core identity elements:

*Partnership:* Being a cooking partner by providing ideas, methods, and products to produce good-tasting, quick, nutritious, and affordable snacks and meals

*Innovation:* Constantly opening new vistas of convenience and taste

Media advertising (which focuses on what the brand can do for the consumer, or what makes its products new, different, or desirable) continues to play a role in supporting the Maggi brand in Germany, the most important market. The more important German brand-building program in terms of investment and impact, however, is based on the Maggi Kochstudio ("cooking center") concept. This Maggi driving idea, in turn, was inspired by the customer sweet spot—a passion for cooking.

The original Kochstudio, created in 1959 at Maggi's Frankfurt headquarters, is now used primarily for filming commercials that involve product-use demonstrations. Constant requests from consumers to visit this facility, though, motivated Maggi to extend the Kochstudio concept to other communications vehicles. Over the years it has evolved into an all-encompassing expression of Maggi's partnership with the consumer. Seven major brand-building programs are now linked to the Kochstudio brand in addition to the original TV studio (see Figure 9–5). Each provides a unique contribution, and the total effect is a symphony in support of the Maggi brand.

### The Kochstudio hotline

Supporting loyalists who have gotten involved through one of the Maggi contact points, the Kochstudio hotline provides a vehicle for consumers to make inquiries and suggestions. The staff of the hotline

FIGURE 9–5
*The Maggi Kochstudio—Surrounding the Customer*

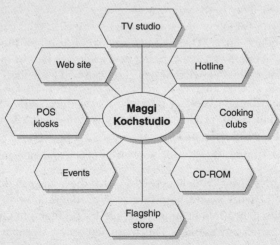

answers an average of 150 telephone inquiries and 70 letters per day. Insights from these interactions are shared with other relevant Maggi divisions, particularly R&D.

### Cooking clubs

In 1992 Maggi set up a Kochstudio Club that has grown to 400,000 members (representing 0.5 percent of the German population) and has its own club magazine printed three times a year. In May 1996 Maggi also began to encourage consumers to start their own local cooking clubs under the Kochstudio aegis; within a few years there were more than four hundred such clubs, supported by a publication, *Topfgucker* (Pot Watcher), as well as speakers.

### CD-ROM

The Maggi Kochstudio CD-ROM, entitled "Fun Cooking," contains three hundred recipes, an encyclopedia of gourmet terms, music, a video, and high-value user services. More than 150 dishes are presented with musical accompaniment, and nutritional information is provided for most of them. A search function finds recipes that match the ingredients a customer has on hand.

### Flagship store

Maggi's 2,000 square-foot Frankfurt flagship store was established in 1996. Known as the Maggi Kochstudio Treff (*Treff* means a popular place to meet and socialize), it has a section featuring Maggi products and paraphernalia such as meal-makers, seasoning packets, aprons, cookbooks, and novelty perfume dispensers in the shape of the famous brown Maggi bottle.

The store also has two kitchens. In its Sampling Kitchen, located at the front of the store, visitors can watch and interact with staff cooking with Maggi products, sample the results, and pick up a card containing the recipe. In the Experience Kitchen, daily cooking classes are offered in which participants prepare and then enjoy meals; special courses are offered for beginners, diabetics, and children. Each day a class is broadcast live on the Maggi Web site, and each week "Cooking Live" (a live call-in radio show) allows the audience to chat about cooking and nutrition issues with the Maggi staff. Regional advertising including billboards helps to build store traffic.

### Events

Maggi adds energy and excitement to its brand at events like the hundredth-anniversary celebration in 1997, where 1,000 prominent guests were invited to a celebrity cooking banquet in Frankfurt. The attendees celebrated not by sitting down to eat but by standing up to cook on one of the more than eight hundred stoves that were provided. The event earned a place in *The Guinness Book of World Records* as the biggest demonstration kitchen in the world, resulting in considerable publicity for Maggi and a memorable and fun evening for participants.

### POS kiosks

Maggi Kochstudio kiosks in the produce section of supermarkets provide information on cooking and nutrition using a touch-screen system. Recipes involving Maggi products are printed on request. The kiosks contain motion detectors so that they audibly greet a customer passing by, "Hi, this is the Maggi Kochstudio." The kiosk also allows customers to view an old Maggi advertising film from 1936 and to order reprints of classic Maggi advertisements.

### Web site

The Maggi Web site is also built around the Kochstudio concept. The homepage greets visitors with these words: "Welcome to the Maggi Kochstudio. For us cooking is more than just the preparation of food. For us cooking is fun! And we want to share this fun with you!" There are a variety of forums for visitors to communicate with each other and with Maggi. There are recipe competitions, a bulletin board, live broadcasts of cooking classes at the flagship store, a place to join the Kochstudio club, an online shop, an e-mail response center, and information on nutrition, Maggi products, cooking, and entertaining.

The Maggi Kochstudio program is the vehicle by which Maggi walks the walk of partnership, not only giving the customer the tools to cook well but showing how to use them. It supports the core identity by making Maggi much more than a set of products. In doing so, it differentiates Maggi from its competitors.

Maggi has achieved a deep relationship with a set of customers by tapping into their sweet spot. This group of customers values food and cooking, spends time at it, and possesses a variety of cooking equipment that expresses their love of cooking. Maggi connects to

## SWATCH—THE MASTER OF PUBLICITY

Swatch, launched in 1983, has shown that a watch can simultaneously be on the front lines of style and a piece of art from Switzerland, as well as fun, youthful, provocative, and joyful. In communicating this brand identity, Swatch has relied in part on publicity obtained from stunts, targeted sponsorships, and a dynamic product line. The driving idea was based on a brand personality statement of being different (even outrageous), upbeat, and stylish. For the launch in Germany, Spain, and Japan, the company hung giant watches from one of the city's skyscrapers. In Frankfurt, the caption on the 165-meter (541 foot) long watch read: Swiss, Swatch, DM 60. This stunt attracted attention from the press as well as the target audience.

Swatch also sponsored the Freestyle Ski World Cup in Breckenridge, the First International Breakdancing Championship at the Roxy, Andrew Logan's "Alternative Miss World Show" in London, street painting in Paris, the Museum of Unnatural History tour, and the "L'heure est à l'art" performance in Brussels. For Swatch, these alternative forms of media communication have become the message and an integral part of the Swatch brand. Indeed, they have defined the Swatch lifestyle—a world of attitudes and values that are shared by Swatch and its customers.

A dynamic product line has helped create interest in and attention to Swatch. Several times a year, Swatch launches new watch collections. Some, such as trendy sports watches, involve real product innovations, but most have been fashion driven. Swatch has become an active sponsor and supporter of the pop-culture movement, which includes such notable designers and artists as Keith Haring, Alessandro Mendini, Kiki Picasso, and Pierre Alechinsky. Every new watch has been more offbeat, more outrageous, more exciting. In addition, events such as Halley's comet, perestroika, the opening of Eastern Europe, and the Earth Summit conference have been commemorated with a watch collection.

them by being a partner and helping them excel, thereby providing significant emotional and self-expressive benefits. According to panel research by GFK, in 1998 Maggi was the packaged-goods brand with the broadest consumer acceptance in Germany, with 87 percent of consumers buying and using Maggi products regularly. This extraordinary achievement can be attributed in large part to the Maggi Kochstudio program.

### THE HÄAGEN-DAZS STORY

Grand Met launched Häagen-Dazs in Europe in 1989 in the face of an economic recession, a stagnant category, and established competitors. Unilever, Nestlé, Mars, and a huge number of small but important local ice-cream manufacturers (such as Scholler in Germany, Mövenpick in Switzerland, and Sagit in Italy) advertised extensively, had high awareness, and controlled the limited freezer space in European supermarkets. Strong private labels held more than 40 percent of the take-home market in some countries. In addition, Grand Met had only a small food portfolio and little presence in European food channels.

The Häagen-Dazs product was thicker, creamier, and pricier than its competition—30 to 40 percent higher than its closest competitors, and some nine times higher than the lower-priced products. Targeting the sophisticated, well-off adult consumer, Grand Met positioned it as a sensual, upscale indulgence that could be enjoyed year round; this positioning became the Häagen-Dazs driving idea. The fictional Scandinavian brand name evoked images of nature and freshness among Europeans, which meshed well with the key product attributes of the ice cream.

The conventional way to introduce a new product such as Häagen-Dazs is to lead with a major advertising effort. But Grand Met took a different route, opening several posh ice-cream parlors in prominent, affluent European locations with heavy foot traffic (see Figure 9–6). The cafelike stores created an atmosphere of exclusivity, quality, cleanliness, and naturalness (much unlike the sterile ice-cream parlors Häagen-Dazs opened in the United States). With their high exposure and traffic, the stores anchored an aggressive sampling program; passersby encountered Häagen-Dazs in a setting that encouraged a positive, even memorable experience.

The sampling program was also tied into sponsored cultural events under the theme "Häagen-Dazs—Dedicated to Pleasure, Dedicated to the Arts," and the added associations reinforced the brand image.

FIGURE 9–6
*Häagen-Dazs Storefront*

The sponsorship of several opera performances, for example, ensured that Häagen-Dazs was seen and tasted at the right places by the right people. At the avant-garde Opera Factory's production of *Don Giovanni* a slight change was made to the play's script: Don called for the sorbet but received instead a tub of Häagen-Dazs. A windfall of free publicity was the result.

Häagen-Dazs also obtained placement in quality hotels and restaurants, selling only to those who would use the Häagen-Dazs name on the menu. The program was supported by a promotion in which customers buying a container of Häagen-Dazs ice cream received a voucher entitling them to a meal for two at reduced prices in participating restaurants. This exposure enhanced the exclusive, upscale image that the brand wanted. When Häagen-Dazs did go into supermarkets, convenience stores and the like, it supplied branded glass-front freezers designed to display the variety of its flavors. These freezers distinguished Häagen-Dazs from other ice creams, which could only be found deep down in the jammed and often poorly merchandised freezer cabinets of the retailer.

The introduction also involved a relatively low-budget media advertising campaign using black-and-white ads inspired by the sensual U.S. movie *9½ Weeks*. This media advertising was leveraged by the creation of a music CD based on the advertisements, which was sold in more than four thousand music and food stores.

The brand-building effort was successful in several ways. The parlors generated heavy pedestrian traffic; the London parlor at Leicester Square, for example, sold more than fifty thousand scoops of ice cream in just one week during the first summer. More than four thousand European retailers added Häagen-Dazs' branded freezers in their stores. On a small media budget of only about $1 million,

---

### THE BRAND EXPERIENCE AS A DRIVING IDEA*

The driving idea at Disneyland, Starbucks, and Nordstrom is the total functional and emotional experience provided by the brand. The setting for the experience and the colors, smells, and other sensations related to it all help to create and reinforce associations. Some guidelines for building a powerful brand experience are as follows:

- **Involve customers actively.** People learn more from active involvement than from passive observation. To bring customers in direct contact with the brand, Häagen-Dazs offers product samples in its ice-cream parlors, BMW-sponsored tennis and golf tournaments include test-drive opportunities, and competing teams in the Adidas Streetball Challenge are equipped with Adidas shoes and garments.
- **Appeal to all senses.** A brand experience that consistently stimulates a customer's sight, hearing, smell, taste, and touch is more memorable than an experience that appeals to just one or two senses. A radio ad, for example, involves only the customer's sense of hearing. In contrast, shirtmaker Thomas Pink's stores feature linen scents to reinforce associations of freshness; this appeal to the sense of smell meshes with the look and feel of the clothes themselves.

brand awareness in the United Kingdom rose above 50 percent within a few months. European sales of Häagen-Dazs went from $10 million to $180 million in just five years and soon after commanded one-third of the premium ice cream market, even while maintaining a hefty price premium over the rapidly emerging copycat brands.

## THE FLOWTEX STORY

FlowTex brought trenchless installation with horizontal drilling to Europe in 1986 to serve utilities, local government authorities, and other private and public administration markets in pipeline and cable-laying applications. The technology has significant advantages: since cables or pipes can be laid without making trenches, the process saves time and money. The benefits for people living in

---

- **Support the experience with brand-related cues.** To link a memorable experience to the brand, create contextual cues that underline the brand position. The see-through sole of an Air Jordan shoe from Nike, for example, visually reinforces the performance association of the gas-filled "air" bladder. Color can also affect the brand experience—a motor oil in a platinum or gold container suggests higher quality than oil in a blue or black container. The absence of umpires or referees during Adidas Streetball Challenge games helps define the experience by suggesting that fair play is the norm.
- **Extend the experience through multiple points of contact.** Almost any experience contains several possible avenues for shaping customer perceptions. The shape, surface characteristics, and color of a product, for example, may affect the experience of using it. Similarly, the message contained in advertising or point-of-sale material may create or reinforce emotional benefits.

*For more details on brand experience as a driving idea, see Werner Kroeber-Riel and Peter Weinberg, *Konsumentenverhalten* (Muenchen: Vahlen, 1996); Peter Weinberg, *Erlebnismarketing* (Muenchen: Vahlen, 1992); Bernd Schmitt and Alex Simonson, *Marketing Aesthetics* (New York: The Free Press, 1997); Joseph Pine II and James H. Gilmore, "Welcome to the Experience Economy," *Harvard Business Review*, July–August 1998, 97–105; and Bernd Schmitt, *Experiential Marketing* (New York: The Free Press, 1999).

neighborhoods where installation services are performed include less traffic-flow disruption and construction noise, plus the preservation of wildlife and plant life because no trees need to be cut or holes dug.

In a business that has seen few major inventions, FlowTex stands out. In the industry, it has become known for its unusual but effective approach to solving tough civil engineering problems. FlowTex is the only vertically integrated horizontal drilling firm that not only designs and develops its technology but also applies it in small- and large-scale installation projects. Innovation, persistence, and a passion for its work have become the pride of the company and define its culture.

In the early 1990s, management believed that several factors were stifling the growth of the company. First, local general contractor firms had bought similar technology and were offering trenchless installation as part of their larger, more comprehensive civil engineering services. Second, the majority of decision makers still preferred the digging of trenches—a tried and proven method since Roman times. In spite of the many advantages, trying something new was still risky. Third, FlowTex was increasingly perceived as a niche technology that was used in only certain special situations, such as the preservation of a historical monument.

Management needed a way to effectively communicate the FlowTex technology benefits to decision makers in utilities and public administration. It began by searching for these decision makers' sweet spot, and it found one: managers in utilities and administrators in public offices are increasingly scrutinized by the general public, and held accountable by consumer groups who are influential in Europe. That pressure was the sweet spot.

FlowTex could help these decision makers respond to citizen and consumer concerns regarding the construction inconvenience and environmental damage. No more trenches! The FlowTex approach could help the administrators or utilities to be perceived as both responsive to customers and progressive. There was only one major problem: FlowTex was a small company that consumers did not know. So management decided to change that.

The driving idea thus was to build the FlowTex brand by communicating to the general public the consumer benefits of its technology. To make the consumer appeal effective, however, FlowTex needed to offer more than just "technology talk" that consumers would not be interested in or would not understand. FlowTex therefore decided to showcase its unique personality and company culture.

The strategy was considered not only unusual in the industry but also risky. Engineering companies had never spent aggressively on brand building, and subsurface contractors had never attempted to influence public authorities by communicating directly to consumers. Many believed that FlowTex's investments would be a waste of money, and that public authorities would not react favorably. Further, as a relatively small and specialized supplier, FlowTex was not in the best position to increase its communication. The company also had grown so fast that there had been little time to define its brand identity.

Nevertheless, FlowTex decided to go for it. First, it defined its brand identity: FlowTex would be known for its unconventional but effective approach to solving civic engineering problems. Expressing and articulating its unique company culture—the values and beliefs of the founders, as well as what employees fondly called the "smell around here"—was considered key. FlowTex had a unique brand personality; it combined the competence and discipline required in difficult engineering work with an engaging, energetic, youthful, fun-loving, and humorous way of doing things in a small, privately held company.

Next, the company had to find a simple way to communicate its basic technology. The first step was to develop visual representation of the brand. The colors blue and white were chosen to display the brand name because blue was consistent with the high-technology associations FlowTex wanted to stand for, and white reinforced associations of cleanliness—a key consumer benefit. The italicized script of the FlowTex name and the curved arrow below it attempted to communicate the associations of flow and movement. In support of the brand graphics, the slogan "Contemplation—Installation" emphasized that FlowTex would be involved in the whole process, from planning to the final result; it was not just selling hardware.

Another brand graphic was the house-tree cartoon, shown in Figure 9–7, which illustrates how FlowTex digs underneath a house without disturbing nature or existing buildings. This graphic was used in all communications as a simple but effective device to convey the functional benefits of the FlowTex horizontal drilling technology. It was a brilliant way to tell a story that could be confusing or boring.

A powerful five-year brand-building program was also developed,

FIGURE 9–7
*FlowTex Brand Graphics*

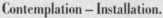

Contemplation – Installation.

leading off with a print media campaign in business titles and general-purpose magazines, followed by a small TV campaign to create visibility. The campaigns discussed the benefits of trenchless installations for the general public in a light and humorous slice-of-life format. Because this direct-to-the-consumer approach was considered unconventional, it also reinforced associations of the innovativeness of the FlowTex brand.

Another key innovation was the heavy use of several alternative brand-building programs to directly target the decision makers in municipalities, utilities, and public administration. Each program was built around a specific theme relevant to a narrow target segment—environmental technology applications, specific cabling problems in the electricity market, and so on. For each theme, an integrated brand-building program was developed for multiple audiences, reflecting the many influences affecting the decision to adopt FlowTex technology.

Each brand-building program was carefully planned and sequenced, beginning with a direct mail campaign (printed material, a video, or CD-ROM), invitations to a symposium in a major city that focused on the specific theme, and public relations and promotional efforts. The effort was further supported by specific sections of the company's Web site, which decision makers were invited to visit. Shortly after the receipt of the first direct mail, a customer was also contacted by a FlowTex sales engineer. These specific actions were linked to the FlowTex print campaign through the use of the same themes and visuals in all brand-building approaches. Visibility was further provided

## THE CADBURY THEME PARK

The confectionery maker Cadbury launched Cadbury World in the early 1990s. Visitors to this former factory (now turned museum, theme park, and chocolate event store) in Birmingham are greeted by a knife-wielding Indian priest from the Yucatán jungle. They proceed to take a two-and-a-half-hour journey through the history of chocolate, featuring such legends as Hernando Cortés and the Aztec king Montezuma. The visitor learns about the heritage and origin of cocoa and chocolate, and how Cadbury started with a grocery store in 1824 and grew by developing trading links throughout the British empire. As the history of chocolate and Cadbury merge, Cadbury becomes positioned as the authority in fine chocolate.

More important, however, are the hundreds of opportunities to sample the various brands of Cadbury's extensive chocolate confectionery line for free, thus encouraging direct brand-building experiences with Cadbury chocolate and supporting the Cadbury slogan, "The Chocolate—The Taste." Cadbury World is similar to other Eurobrands that have opened their company doors to the public, such as Nestlé's factory visit in Switzerland and the numerous tours of vineyards and breweries. A key difference is that Cadbury World is actually profitable, as it charges for the visit and nevertheless welcomes around a half-million visitors a year.

through trade show appearances and FlowTex sponsorships of ATP tennis tournaments. The trade shows became a spectacle of product demonstration as well as a venue to demonstrate the way FlowTex works, its culture, and the brave and youthful personality of the company and its people.

This five-year brand-building effort was hugely successful for FlowTex. Communicating directly to consumers cut through the clutter and indirectly established the associations of boldness, creativity, and openness to new ideas that have become part of the FlowTex culture. A key success element was the balancing of the narrow messages in specialized engineering magazines with a broad approach to reach the secondary market, the end consumers.

Perhaps the most important factor, though, was the use of multiple brand-building approaches that heavily targeted decision makers in utilities and rural, municipal, and state administrations through themed initiatives. The multiple approaches effectively surrounded these decision makers like basketball defenders playing a full-court press. FlowTex has since become known as the McDonald's of horizontal drilling, because it has successfully leveraged its brand-building program into a rapidly growing and broad franchise system across Europe.

## THE FORD GALAXY STORY

The Ford Galaxy was launched in late 1995 in a very small but nicely growing European MPV (multipurpose vehicle) market. The Galaxy, the VW Sharan, and the Seat Alhambra were three identical vans produced in Portugal in a joint venture between Ford and Volkswagen. These vehicles, which were stylish for the category, received high marks for comfort and handling and won several awards in Europe. Ford's initial challenge was to introduce the Galaxy into the United Kingdom, Ford's largest foreign market. The introduction was successful because of a clever positioning strategy and an aggressive direct market campaign aimed at getting people behind the wheel of the vehicle.

### Positioning

Ford needed to position the Galaxy with respect to the current MPV brands (the Renault Espace and the Chrysler Voyager), both of which targeted families with children. These brands were both positioned as vehicles with the capacity to carry children, dogs, and everything else for family picnics, vacations, and other outings. MPVs had become known as vehicles that were boring and functional, with little style or personality—ideal for Mr. Normal.

Ford sought to break out from this stereotype by positioning the Galaxy not as a van but as a "car plus"—a vehicle with a car's size, features, and style but a far more spacious interior. It thus became an upscale car with functional and self-expressive benefits for the busy manager. This image made the Galaxy entirely appropriate for fleet purchases, a market segment Ford hoped to capture. (For the price range involved, around half of the autos sold are company cars driven by employees). The positioning became a driving idea: The metaphor of first-class plane travel, which invoked associations of comfort, roominess, and luxury, helped to crystallize the concept and even suggested how it could be communicated.

The initial advertising showed a businessman apparently traveling in first-class comfort on an airplane—an impression enhanced by the use of music from a famous British Airways TV commercial. Even when it was revealed that the traveler was riding in the Ford Galaxy, exterior shots of the car as it traveled across a vast open expanse (with the clouds in the sky reflected perfectly in the foreground) supported the airplane imagery and the association of spaciousness. The phrase "Travel First Class" was used as a tagline in the advertising. A visual showing a car that evolves into the Galaxy vividly emphasized that the Galaxy, with a footprint the same size as a car's, was not a typical bulky, hard-to-maneuver van. Additional visibility programs included creating Galaxy display areas at the Heathrow airport and locating touch-screen kiosks in convenient locations for business travelers.

### Direct marketing and test driving

Direct marketing involved a series of targeted mailings aimed at generating awareness, developing associations and (most critically) getting people behind the wheel. The core of the direct-marketing effort was a preview pack mailed to 100,000 prequalified Galaxy prospects. One mailing, in May 1994, was designed to encourage those already in the market for a van to delay their purchase; the rest of the preview packs were sent in July 1995, shortly before the Galaxy was introduced.

Crucial to the direct marketing effort was the creation and active cultivation of personalized prospect databases. A variety of sources included 80,000 visitors to a major motor show, 50,000 walk-in prospects at dealers, 340,000 screened prospects from a set of internal and external databases (90,000 responded to a mailing), 75,000 people exposed to a Galaxy postcard placed in third-party mailers, and 3 million bank card holders and 600,000 recipients of *Ford Magazine* who were offered one-month test drives as part of several "Win-a-Galaxy" promotions.

A separate effort, targeted toward fleet managers, included a direct mailing featuring a total-cost-of-ownership analysis for the Galaxy. Further, 13,000 drivers of company-owned cars and 46,000 members of the Ford Business Club (a select group of Ford owners) were sent the Galaxy preview pack.

In addition to the direct marketing effort, several other programs were created to encourage a driving experience. For example, an extensive four-hundred-car vehicle loan program allowed fleet managers and their drivers to test the car. The Galaxy was also featured at major shows attended by fleet managers; during one of these shows, it was the vehicle used to transport attendees from the parking area. Thus virtually all fleet managers got to ride at least once in a Galaxy.

In order to encourage Galaxy test drives among those buying direct from a retailer, Ford took advantage of its large dealership network in the United Kingdom. One program gave generous demonstrator and loaner conditions for dealers. Another encouraged dealers to create events and promotions around the specific activities and interests of retail customers: coloring competitions for children, a spot-the-difference contest, and a joint program with the highly popular Muddy Fox mountain bikes.

The Ford Galaxy replaced the Renault Espace as the U.K. category market leader soon after its launch and quickly grew to garner a 36 percent share, more than half of which represented sales to corporate or fleet buyers. The strength of the brand was reflected in awareness and image as well as sales. Within months after its launch, the Galaxy achieved an unaided model recall of 72 percent, versus 85 percent for the Espace. The launch campaign for the Galaxy also developed positive associations along the key dimensions of attractive/stylish and spacious/roomy.

### The Ford Connection

Advertising and direct marketing, even targeted direct marketing, is one-way communication to passive consumers. Ford has since created a program using the Internet that provides a very different way of communicating with Ford owners; termed the Ford Connection, it links Ford and its dealers by e-mail with a massive owner network. The Connection establishes an ongoing, regular dialogue with customers. In exchange for information from customers about themselves and their car, Ford offers products such as insurance and value-added services such as events, promotions, and extra rental days or free upgrades at its Hertz outlets. If the Connection program were expanded into a one-stop shop for all transportation-related needs, it could potentially be another driving idea for Ford.

## THE TANGO STORY

Tango is one of the most successful European soft drink brands in a market dominated by two U.S. colas. Tango is British, fun, great fruit taste with a sense of humor. It was launched first in 1981 and is now the third largest fruit carbonate in the UK. It leads the flavored soft drink category while commanding a premium price in a highly fragmented and undifferentiated market, with a solid 12% share.

Tango targets not just the young British consumer, but the young at heart. Its brand identity is based on a great fruity taste and an attitude and personality of being unexpected, fun, humorous, madcap, ironic and irreverent with a touch of realism. As far as the functional benefit of taste is concerned, it is at par with other brands such as Fanta, Orangina, and Sunkist; in terms of attitude, though, it is in its own world.

Building a brand in a category that is fragmented and offers relatively few opportunities for meaningful differentiation around the product or conventional marketing variables (such as packaging and price) is a difficult task. Britvic, the company that owns Tango, was able to do so by emphasizing Tango's close relationship to British urban life as reflected by a set of values and beliefs that are shared by a relatively large segment of British consumers. These values and beliefs—the sense of British humor, the search for excitement and fun in everyday life—represent the consumer sweet spot that has influenced the Tango brand identity and positioning strategy and provided meaningful differentiation from the competitive soft drink brands from America.

The driving idea was to play on the Tango personality as a fun, mischievous brand with a very British, somewhat wacky, sense of humor. Several successful media advertising campaigns were launched between 1992 and 1999. An early ad campaign emphasized the taste attributes of the brand, the "hit" of real oranges in Tango orange, in an unexpected way. The Orangeman, the Tango brand character, was introduced with a tag line: "You know when you've been Tango'd" (which refers partly to pranks customers play on others) that began to enter the English language. The off-the-wall ads showed apparently normal citizens being caught up in wacky brand-use experiences, such as being smacked in the face by an orange genie using an inflated rubber glove, for example, or consuming the product and then exploding. A broad array of nonmedia advertising options supporting the brand included award-winning sales promotions, direct response campaigns, innovative sampling opportunities, public relations activities, and an impactful presence on the Web.

A more recent advertising effort aimed to make Tango the national fizzy drink by replacing Britain's national icon—tea—with Tango in the hearts and minds of its consumers (see Figure 9–8). The ads picked on classic scenarios when British people always turn to tea, such as the visit of an unexpected guest or a disagreement between colleagues or friends. By taking over these situations using its own brand of humor, and replacing tea with Tango, the brand created "Tango moments" in lieu of these traditional tea moments.

FIGURE 9–8
*Tango Marketing Madness*

A Tango summer promotion is another example of the brand's innovative approach. Tango, as consumers have come to expect, took a completely different approach to any other brand linking to the 1998 World Cup. It encouraged consumers to stay at home rather than go off to France (after all, why would British people want to go there?) and gave them the chance to win an at-home "shrine" consisting of a widescreen TV, floodlights, inflatable sofa, meat pies, a table football game, and a truckload of Tango.

An important part of the Tango brand-building program is the Tango Web site, which was first launched in 1996 and which has received several updates. It invites visitors to get involved with the brand. Follow the Intrepid Explorer Gotan (the fat orange Tango man) and surf the Web for cool sites around the world. It's a random search engine that leads to places like Pranks 101 (a Tango consumer site that recounts favorite practical jokes), Net.Games (the ultimate site for Internet games), really cool weddings (suggestions for making the event really special), and a site of suggested April Fool jokes to pull on famous personalities. This section of the Tango site works as a content provider to guide surfers around sites which reflect Tango brand values.

Another section consists of a weekly updated Internet game which requires the visitor to navigate Gotan through more than thirty perilous levels. The objective of the game is to make a perfect cup of Tango. The game involves the visitor in the world of Tango by winning points. The weekly winners receive tickets, computer games, videos, or a free holiday. A champion league selects among the best of the weekly winners for bigger prizes. These games are especially popular with Tango's core target market of 16- to 24-year-old consumers and provide an incentive to visit the Tango site regularly.

Several other branding devices have reinforced the innovative, unexpected, and fun brand identity of Tango. In 1992, Tango packaging was redesigned with a distinctive black can, the first of its kind. Another packaging design followed in 1999: a 3-D graphics design, another first of its kind. Over the years, Tango also created significant product news by adding new flavors: black currant, lemon, and apple. Each of the flavors was initially given a different brand identity. Apple, for example, stood for seduction. The can itself expressed the personality: Apple Tango featured large green lips from a previous Apple seduction ad campaign. Lemon, which was originally supported by its manic Euphoria ads, had a wild splattering of yellow dots. Orange, while retaining its original outrageousness and aggressiveness, became an explosion, the "hit" of real oranges, and Black Currant depicted black currants crackling in electricity. Tango then developed different brand-building programs appropriate for each flavor. These programs were created to communicate visually what the actual taste experience of each flavor would be like.

The innovative and often unorthodox brand-building efforts helped to push sales and the brand. Over 25% of British consumers claim to drink Tango. Next to Nike and Levi's, it is considered one of the most respected youth brands. In a recent survey that asked British consumers which brands reflect the New Britain, Tango ranked among the top ten brands.

## BRAND BUILDING WITHOUT ADVERTISING—SOME GUIDELINES

Drawing on the case studies just presented and the many others that were discussed in Part IV, here are ten guidelines (summarized in Figure 9–9) to help those who want to move beyond media advertising to build brands.

### 1. CLARIFY YOUR BRAND'S IDENTITY, VALUE PROPOSITION, AND POSITION

The brand identity, with its aspirational associations, is the foundation of any effective brand-building program, especially when multiple approaches are being used. A clear brand identity with depth and texture will guide those designing and implementing the communication programs so that they don't inadvertently send conflicting or confusing messages to customers. Unfortunately, many organizations do not have a single, shared vision of their brand's identity. Instead, the brand is allowed to drift, driven by the often-changing tactical communication objectives of product or market managers. The success of brands such as Häagen-Dazs, Swatch, and Ford, however, was based on a clear brand identity. Both Nike and Adidas saw brand-building effectiveness improve markedly when they reviewed and sharpened their brand identities.

Supporting the brand identity are the value proposition and the brand position. The value proposition indicates the functional, emotional, and self-expressive benefits that are to be created or communi-

FIGURE 9–9
*Brand Building Beyond Advertising*

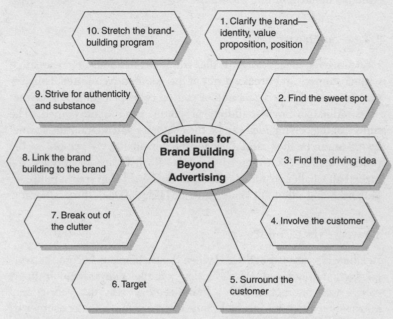

cated; these are the bottom-line objectives that will lead to a customer relationship. The brand position prioritizes the movement required to change the image to match the brand identity, which serves as the guiding North Star. The brand position is thus more focused.

### 2. FIND THE SWEET SPOT

A brand-building program should strive to understand the customers in depth and find their sweet spots, those elements that are central to their lives and self-concepts. Finding a sweet spot and a way to make the brand a part of it is the route to a deep relationship and a core group of committed loyal customers. Maggi's passion for cooking was the sweet spot for their loyalist group. Nike's "Just do it" brand-building effort helped give Americans the motivation to act, to get physical and stop putting off that exercise program. This positive message for consumers was also linked closely with the Nike brand identity. Hobart found a set of customer problems and concerns that defined an organizational sweet spot, then used it as the basis for an effective brand-building program.

### 3. FIND THE DRIVING IDEA

Find a driving idea, a concept that will build the brand by resonating with customers and breaking out of the competitive clutter. This driving idea should become a hub or central concept around which a set of coordinated brand-building programs can be developed. The source of the driving idea can be the customer and an identified sweet spot or it can be the brand (perhaps the personality, the symbol, or the product itself). For Maggi, it was the Kochstudio; for Adidas, the Streetball Challenge; for MasterCard, the World Cup sponsorship; for Hobart, being a thought leader; and for Häagen-Dazs, the positioning.

### 4. INVOLVE THE CUSTOMER

Relationships are strengthened when the participants become actively engaged and involved. Research, for example, shows that consumers weigh prior interaction with a brand more heavily than subsequent information about it.[5] Strong brands therefore touch the consumer by providing a way to test-drive or experience the brand. Maggi's Kochstudio Treff, Ford Galaxy, NikeTown's basketball hoop, the Adidas Streetball Challenge, and Häagen-Dazs's European ice-cream parlors all got customers involved in a use experience; Cadbury World is, by design, a participation experience. And clubs such as those for Swatch and Maggi are some of the most effective ways to involve loyalists. The club not only provides a participation outlet but also includes the customer in a social group complete with common interests, activities, and goals.

### 5. SURROUND THE CUSTOMER

Surround the customer with a set of mutually reinforcing brand-building programs like those of Maggi, Nike, or MasterCard. There is a natural temptation to manage each brand-building approach separately, but research in a variety of contexts has shown that multiple media are synergistic rather than additive. One reason is that any one vehicle will eventually wear out; another is that each comes at the customer from a different perspective and serves to fill in gaps. There can even be more than one lead vehicle—Nike, for example, uses media advertising, endorsements from top athletes (such as Michael Jordan), and NikeTown.

## 6. TARGET

Brand building needs to target the customer or segment in order to resonate; most brands start to become diffuse when the segmentation strategy gets fuzzy. A balance must be found, however, between being so focused that the brand lacks a wide appeal and so broad that the brand means nothing. The solution, discussed in Chapter 2, is to develop positions (or even identities) that are tailored for different segments.

The target customer should be reached as intimately as possible. Some approaches using the Web—such as the Ford Connection or Amazon's e-mail communication—skillfully tailor a message to an individual. Other brands, such as Tango or Maggi, provide a similar level of intimacy in other ways.

## 7. BREAK OUT OF THE CLUTTER

There is clutter not only in the advertising context but also in virtually all alternative brand-building approaches. A brand needs to surprise and perhaps even shock the consumer in a positive way, whether implementing familiar programs in an innovative way or by creating new programs. The essence of home runs like NikeTown, the Adidas Streetball Challenge, the AT&T Olympic Web site, the Swatch stunts, and the Maggi cooking program is that they were all fresh approaches.

Unusual promotions can be an effective tool for breaking out of the clutter. Volkswagen, for example, staged a scavenger hunt across Europe for the new VW Beetle. The hunt, which required entrants to surf the Web, solve puzzles, and answer questions on different sites in order to win a prize, was unlike any other promotion.

## 8. LINK THE BRAND BUILDING TO THE BRAND

To build strong brands, the execution needs to be brilliant in all respects; good isn't good enough. But the brilliance needs to be linked clearly to the brand, rather than a separate force that overwhelms it. Advertising practitioners are all too familiar with having breathtakingly creative ads that are remembered and even talked about even though few can recall the involved brand. When the brand is the hero (the centerpiece of the communication) or otherwise owns the brand-building program, however, the problem recedes. Adidas owns the Adidas Streetball Challenge and the DFB-Adidas Cup by virtue of their names alone. Similarly, the brand is center stage at NikeTown, at the Ford Galaxy test-drive events, and on the Tango Web sites.

## 9. STRIVE FOR AUTHENTICITY AND SUBSTANCE

Authenticity is a powerful brand association, and one test of brand-building programs is whether they contribute to the brand's authenticity. The position and identity elements should be communicated in a way that attaches a genuine feeling to the brand and makes it a legitimate owner of the desired association. It is no coincidence that brands such as Apple, Porsche, Nike, and Volkswagen have made a comeback on the back of great new product innovations. Authenticity is largely driven by the substance behind the product or service, as well as by the brand's heritage. Thus Volvo's claim of building safe cars is authentic because the product delivers the substance behind the claim and has done so throughout the company's history.

## 10. STRETCH THE PROGRAM—GIVE IT LEGS

A brand-building program can be limited by how many people are exposed to it. The challenge is to leverage it, to give it legs beyond the core segment. One way is to create miniprograms, such as Maggi did with its local clubs and as MasterCard did with its local bank programs. Another is to provide reminders of the program such as giveaways, free samples, promotional items like T-shirts, or e-mail messages. Still another approach is to stimulate those who have been exposed to share the message with others, perhaps by providing incentives.

Public relations and even media advertising can be effective ways to increase exposure. Many successful programs have carefully planned the involvement of the news media. The inclusion of famous TV personalities in Coca-Cola's Olympic Torch Rally (a 1996 promotion in which 5,500 people relayed a torch across the United States), ensured that the media would be interested in broadcasting the event as news coverage. Although Starbucks and The Body Shop paid little if anything for advertising, they became strong brands and billion-dollar businesses, with publicity playing a key role. When free publicity cannot be encouraged, paying for it may be worthwhile. For example, spending advertising dollars to publicize the excitement, fun, and passion of playing soccer during the DFB-Adidas Cup would reinforce the Adidas's key associations.

## MAKING IT HAPPEN—ORGANIZATIONAL ISSUES

Once you have a brand-building strategy that goes beyond advertising, how do you go about making it happen? At least two organizational capabilities are key success factors in this new environment—the ability to access alternative media, and the ability to coordinate across media.

### Accessing alternative media

Knowledge and skills need to be available in approaches such as sponsorship, association with causes, direct one-to-one marketing, customer clubs, publicity stunts, the Web, public relations, flagship stores, sampling, and other emerging media. Brands will need access to media that can be made effective in their context and will need to better understand how to measure results. The interrelationships between the different media vehicles need to be understood in order to create synergies. An organization attempting to gain this capability may need to do the following:

- **Reduce organizational inhibitions.** Create an organization that will accept innovative approaches. It may not be a coincidence that Häagen-Dazs was introduced into Europe using a separate company with no established norms; only after it was established was it folded into the parent organization. There is little doubt that the success of Swatch was in large measure due to an extremely uninhibited CEO.

- **Test ideas.** Experimental and pilot programs can help an organization gain skills and knowledge and learn firsthand what works and what does not. Certainly the Swatch, Adidas, and Häagen-Dazs programs received the benefit of such testing and experimentation.
- **Create a brand-building program access person or team.** Such a person or team would be charged with generating brand-building options. One tack would be to develop a relationship with firms that specialize in various approaches (such as event sponsorship, promotions, publicity, Web technology, and direct marketing). A second possibility would be to monitor new communications technology to learn enough mechanics to evaluate it for a particular context, looking closely in the marketplace at what works and why. A third would be to monitor best practices, especially outside the home industry. A fourth might be to systematically engage in creative thinking exercises to find innovative programs. Such an effort by BMW in Turkey resulted in an out-of-the-box promotion involving a car hidden in the city, hot air balloons, and an involving puzzle. Nestlé has created a brand-building senior management position in Switzerland with the goal of encouraging media-neutral brand-building programs worldwide.
- **Create in-depth capability in key media.** When the driving idea is established and the lead media or vehicles are selected, the organization should develop an in-house capability with some depth and substance; a brand-building initiative is not easily duplicated if it is based on an organizational asset that is not available to others. Cadbury, Swatch, Maggi, and Häagen-Dazs all developed the capability to manage the lead media in-house, which is a key part of their sustainable advantage.

### Coordinate across media

Coordination across programs and media, of course, must be driven by a rich, clear brand identity and position. It also, however, requires organizational support. There needs to be a person or team in charge of the brand to make sure the identity and position are in place, and that all efforts to build the brand are in line with the strategy. This person or team will benefit from a process that encourages innovative approaches and corrects off-strategy initiatives before they are implemented.

Traditional advertising agencies vary in their ability to assist with or run the coordination of other media efforts. Although most claim the ability to develop and manage a broad-based, on-strategy communication program, they often fail to deliver because they are too committed to advertising or have not found a way to integrate sister organizations into a team. The most effective combine multiple communication capabilities into a virtual or ongoing organization, while the ineffective operate a group of self-contained organizations or have a limited focus.

Regardless of the agency's organization, a media-neutral compensation and reward system will enhance the creative work of communications partners. As the saying goes, what gets measured and rewarded is what gets done.

## QUESTIONS FOR DISCUSSION

1. What are the contexts in a customer's life where the brand can be made relevant? What is the customer sweet spot?
2. Evaluate current brand-building programs. What are their objectives? How are those objectives measured? How well do they achieve their objectives?
3. Identify some brand-building best practices directed at achieving visibility both inside and outside your industry. Which are effective at creating associations? Which are effective at creating deep relationships? Why are the identified approaches effective?
4. Which brand-building effort reported in these four chapters are you most impressed with? Why?
5. Identify some ineffective brand building, and explain why you consider it ineffective.
6. Engage in some out-of-the-box creative thinking to identify some potential brand-building programs.
7. If media advertising (or whatever is your most important brand-building tool currently) no longer existed tomorrow, how would you build your brand with consumers?
8. Ask yourself: If we were a fashion company, how would we go about building the brand? What can be learned from the successes of Ralph Lauren? What are the five or six existing and dominant approaches of building the brand in your business? What would you make different, if money and time were not an issue?

# PART V

## ORGANIZING FOR BRAND LEADERSHIP

# 10

# Global Brand Leadership[1]— Not Global Brands

I don't know the key to success, but the key to failure is trying to please everybody.
—Bill Cosby

## McDONALD'S IN EUROPE[2]

A 1995 review of European advertising for McDonald's revealed some disturbing facts. With market expansion, the advertising was becoming inconsistent from country to country and sometimes distant from what should have been core identity elements. Advertising funded by local markets was increasingly promotional rather than brand-building. In some countries McDonald's was positioned as fashionable and exotic instead of wholesome; in Norway, one ad showed the staff of a Chinese restaurant taunting customers by insisting "No hamburger" while co-workers devour a McDonald's hamburger in the kitchen. Ads in Spain, meanwhile, showed a highly generic rush of smiling faces and upbeat music.

This drifting away from the core identity was an unintentional downside of a highly effective McDonald's business model, where local countries drive local marketing decisions. McDonald's prides itself on having a brand that is global, based on universal values, and highly relevant in every local market. The same philosophy drives the McDonald's menu. The core items are consistent and global, with some products customized to local tastes. Advertising for every location, everywhere, has historically been local. In Europe, a McDonald's marketing executive was quoted as saying that McDonald's had never had a pan-European ad (never mind a global ad) and probably never would.

In the summer of 1995 Leo Burnett, the McDonald's agency in six European countries (Britain, Belgium, Spain, Sweden, Switzerland, and Norway) initiated the first pan-regional effort to achieve more consistency by identifying a brand identity that would unify and drive all communications efforts. It seemed to be not only logical but timely, since food tastes in Europe were becoming less distinct and the European Union was just around the corner. A three-day meeting was held with the creative directors and account directors from the six countries. Considerable market research about food trends and customers and their motivations was analyzed.

The meeting goal was to agree on a core identity and brand essence that could drive the advertising in all six countries. Although the Norwegian participants were somewhat reluctant, a consensus emerged. McDonald's key associations were being a wholesome family place, kids, speed of service, tasty food, fun, and the McDonald's magic. Following closely on the heels of the European brand identity work, a separate project was initiated in the United States. The objective was to define the core identity of McDonald's U.S., and ultimately the global McDonald's brand essence. This project came to remarkably similar conclusions. The essence was defined as a "trusted friend." This brand essence was considered aspirational, a concept that the brand could retain and strengthen going forward that also would help to neutralize negative associations such as "patronizing and smiling, but not genuine."

The Leo Burnett country shops then recreated advertising independently but driven by the same identity and essence. The result was advertising that reinforced McDonald's as being a wholesome, family-oriented, fun place. Even though the ads were very different from country to country, they could be run anywhere. An ad from Sweden showed a working mother deciding to put off a business meeting so she could take her daughter to McDonald's, only to find her boss there with his son. In Belgium, a boy, sensitive to his new glasses, gets attention from a girl at McDonald's and cheers up. In a British ad, a boy maneuvers his father into taking him to McDonald's where the man "accidentally" runs into his estranged wife and—to the son's delight—chats with her. In Norway, a boy is led by his grandmother through a surrealistic city to a comfortable, familiar McDonald's.

More recently, an award-winning ad was done for Sweden by a joint Swedish and U.S. creative team that has not only been used in Sweden but also in other European countries. Because the ad speaks to universal values, the same ads can be run in other parts of the world. Figure 10–1 provides four frames from the ad, called "Small Fry Love," in which a young boy flirts with a girl in the street, shares his heart and shirt, but is more reluctant with his fries.

### Issues to Consider

This brief look at McDonald's European advertising exposes some tough issues. Some of these ads are better than others. Should an effort be made to use the best ads across countries? How do you manage the trade-off between consistency and effectiveness? Should this effort to gain consistency be extended to all of Europe or, indeed, globally? If so, how? Can it be done with

FIGURE 10–1
*McDonald's in Sweden*

multiple agencies? Can it be done without affecting the creative vitality? Was the meeting the best way to accomplish the goal? What is the client's role? There are no general answers to these tough questions. In this chapter, however, some constructs and methods will be introduced to help companies build brands in a global village.

## GLOBAL BRANDS

Pringles, Visa, Marlboro, Sony, McDonald's, Nike, IBM, Gillette Sensor, Heineken, Pantene, and Disney are the envy of many brand builders because they seem to be global brands—that is, brands with a high degree of similarity across countries with respect to brand identity, position, advertising strategy, personality, product, packaging, and look and feel. Everywhere in the world, for example, Pringles stands for "fun," a social setting, freshness, less greasiness, resealability and the whole-chip product. Further, the Pringles package, symbols, and advertising are virtually the same in all countries.

Like McDonald's, however, these brands are often not as identical globally as one might assume. Pringles uses different flavors in different countries, and the Pringles advertising executions are tailored to local cultures. Heineken is the premium beer to enjoy with friends everywhere, except at home in the Netherlands, where it is more of a mainstream beer. Visa has different logos in some countries, such as Argentina. Even Coke has a sweeter product in some areas (for example, southern Europe).

Such variations aside, brands that become more global demonstrate some real advantages. For example, a global brand can achieve significant economies of scale. Creating one advertising campaign for IBM, even if it needs some adapting from market to market, is much less costly than creating dozens. The development of other programs (like packaging, a Web site, a promotion, or a sponsorship) will also be more cost-effective when both expenses and investments are spread over multiple countries. Economies of scale can be critical for sponsorships with global relevance, such as the World Cup or the Olympics.

Perhaps more important, though, is the enhanced effectiveness that results simply because better resources are involved. When IBM replaced its roster of dozens of agencies with Ogilvy & Mather, it immediately became the proverbial elephant that can sit wherever it wants. As the most important O&M client, it gets the best agency talent from top to bottom; the chances of a breakout campaign that is well executed thus are markedly improved.

There are also efficiencies achieved because of cross-market exposure. Media spillover, where it exists, allows the global brand to get more for its purchasing dollar. Further, customers who travel are exposed to the brand in different countries, again making the campaign work harder. Customer travel is particularly important for travel-related products such as credit cards, airlines, and hotels.

In addition, a global brand is inherently easier to manage. The fundamental challenge of brand management is to develop a clear, well-articulated brand identity, then find ways to make that brand identity drive all brand-building activities. This challenge is less formidable with a global brand; Visa's "worldwide acceptance" position is much easier to manage than dozens of country-specific strategies. Moreover, simpler organizational systems and structures can be employed.

The key to a global brand, though, is finding a position that will work in all markets. Sprite, for example, has the same position worldwide—honest, no hype, refreshing taste.[3] Based on the observation that kids everywhere are fed up with hype and empty promises, Sprite advertising uses the tagline "Image is nothing. Thirst is everything. Obey your thirst." This message to trust one's own instincts resonates around the world.

Several generic positions seem to travel well; one is being the best, the upscale choice. High-end premium brands, like Mercedes, Montblanc, Heineken, and Tiffany can cross national boundaries easily because the self-expressive benefits involved apply in most cultures. Another example is the country position; the American position of brands such as Coke, Levi's, Baskin-Robbins, KFC, and Harley-Davidson will work everywhere (with the possible exception of the United States). A purely functional benefit (Pampers' dry, happy baby, for instance) also can be used in multiple markets.

## GLOBAL BRAND LEADERSHIP, NOT GLOBAL BRANDS

Even so, not all brands that are high end or American or have a strong functional benefit can be global. Yet many firms are tempted to globalize their own brands, often in part because of executive ego and perceptions that globalization per se is the choice of successful business leaders. These cases are often characterized by an edict that only global programs are to be used. The consolidation of all advertising into one agency and the development of a global advertising theme often form the cornerstone of the effort. A blind stampede toward a global brand, though, can be the wrong course and even result in significant brand damage. There are three reasons.

First, economies of scale and scope may not actually exist. The promise of media spillover has long been exaggerated, and localized communication efforts can sometimes be less costly and more effective than importing and adapting "global" executions. Further, even an excellent global agency or other communication partner may not be able to execute exceptionally in all countries.

Second, the brand team may not be able to find a strategy to support a global brand, even assuming one exists. They might lack the people, the information, the creativity, or the executional skills and therefore end up settling for the mediocre. Finding a superior strategy in one country is challenging enough without imposing a constraint that it be used throughout the world as well.

Third, a global brand simply may not be optimal or feasible when there are fundamental differences across markets. Consider the following contexts where a global brand would make little sense:

- Different market share positions. Ford's introductions of the Galaxy van into the United Kingdom and Germany were affected by its market share position in each country. While Ford was the number one car brand in the United Kingdom and had a superior quality image, Volkswagen held that position in Germany. As noted in Chapter 9, Ford's challenge in the United Kingdom as the dominant brand was to expand the market beyond soccer moms to the corporate market; thus the Galaxy was introduced as the "non-van," and its roominess was compared to first-class airline travel. In Germany, however, the Galaxy was simply introduced as the "clever alternative."

- Different brand images. Honda means quality and reliability in the United States, where it has a legacy of achievement on the J.D. Power ratings. In Japan, however, where quality is much less of a differentiator, Honda is a car-race participant with a youthful, energetic personality
- Preempted positions. A superior position for a chocolate bar is to own the association with milk and the image of a glass of milk being poured into a bar. Different brands, however, have preempted this position in different markets (For example, Cadbury in the United Kingdom and Milka in Germany).
- Different customer motivations. In Finland, after finding that users were apprehensive about perceived machine complexity, Canon became the copier that empowered the user, making him or her the boss. In Germany and Italy, however, more traditional attribute-oriented messages did better.
- Different customer responses to executions and symbols. A Johnny Walker ad in which the hero attends the running of the bulls in Pamplona seemed reckless in Germany and too Spanish in other countries.

Global brand strategy is often misdirected. The priority should be developing not global brands (although such brands might result) but rather global brand *leadership*—that is, strong brands in all markets, backed by effective, proactive global brand management. Global brand management should utilize the people, systems, culture, and structure of an organization to allocate brand-building resources globally, create synergies, and develop a global brand strategy that will coordinate and leverage country brand strategies.

Brand-building resource allocation too often succumbs to a classic decentralization trap in which large-market countries receive the bulk of the attention, while the organization starves small markets that may represent big opportunities. Effective global brand management will recognize and invest in opportunities from a global perspective.

Synergies are possible through sharing research methods, brand-building investment costs, customer insights, best practices, brand strategy development processes, brand management models and vocabulary, positioning concepts, and executional efforts. One challenge of global brand management is to realize those synergies.

Virtually all multinational firms should engage in active global brand management. Having unconnected local brand strategies without direction or management will inevitably lead to global mediocrity and vulnerability. Pockets of success, often driven by the occasional brilliant manager, will be isolated and random—hardly a recipe for global brand leadership.

We have interviewed executives from thirty-five firms (half headquartered in the United States and the other half based in Europe or Japan), all of whom have successfully developed strong brands across countries. About half the sample involved frequently purchased consumer products, which as a group tend to have the most developed global brand management systems, while the rest represented durables, high technology, or service brands. Although several contacts were made in each firm, the lead respondent was either the global brand manager or a senior line executive, often the CEO. The study focused on problems and opportunities in managing brands globally and organizational efforts to address those issues.

Drawing on these interviews and the brand concepts discussed in this book, we believe that companies aspiring to global brand leadership must create organizations that will:

- Stimulate the sharing of insights and best practices across countries
- Support a common global brand planning process
- Assign managerial responsibility for brands in order to create cross-country synergy and fight local bias
- Execute brilliant brand-building programs

## SHARING INSIGHTS AND BEST PRACTICES

A cross-country communication system that shares insights, methods, and best practices is the most basic and nonthreatening element of global brand management. A customer insight may be obvious in one country, but more subtle and difficult to access in another. Best practices, which can represent competitors or even other categories, are extremely influential because they represent proven models of what worked.

The goal is to have (1) a global mechanism to detect and capture firsthand observations of effective best practices, (2) a way to communicate best practices to those who could benefit from them, and

(3) an easy-to-use method to access an inventory of best practices when needed.

Creating such a system is harder than it sounds. Busy people usually have little motivation to take the time to explain efforts that have worked or failed; furthermore, they'd rather not give out information that may leave them exposed to criticism. Another problem is one that everyone in business faces today: information overload. And a feeling of "it won't work here" often pervades companies that encourage the sharing of market knowledge.

To overcome these problems, companies must nurture and support a culture in which best practices are freely communicated. In addition, people and procedures must come together to create a rich base of knowledge that is relevant and easy to access. Offering incentives is one way to get people to share what they know. American Management Systems, for example, keeps track of the employees who are posting insights and best practices and rewards them during annual performance reviews. Several other companies have developed processes or programs to create the right culture.

Regular meetings can be an effective way of communicating insights and best practices, both formally and informally. Henkel (the European

FIGURE 10–2
*Effective Global Brand Management*

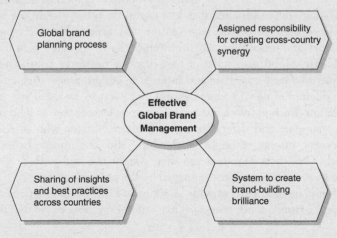

packaged-goods and chemical company), for example, has frequent meetings of the brand managers from the top twenty countries. The effectiveness of such meetings depends on the format and on the attendees. Formal presentations of insights and best practices can certainly play a role; Sony, for example, presents its best advertising from around the world. Because the challenge is to get beyond exposure of idea to action, though, true learning takes place only when the participants get engaged in either workshops or more informal venues. Often the shared information is less important than the forming of personal relationships that lead to subsequent interactions.

Frito-Lay sponsors a market university about three times a year where a few dozen marketing directors or general managers from around the world come to Dallas for a week. The university gets people involved in brand leadership concepts, helps people overcome the mind-set of "I am different—global programs will not work in my market," and seeds the company with people who "get brands." During the week, case studies are presented of tests of packaging, advertising, or promotions that were successful in one country or region and then applied successfully in another country. These studies demonstrate that practices can be transferred even in the face of a skeptical local marketing team.

Intranets are increasingly playing an active (although usually supporting) role in communicating insights and best practices. Having a set of e-mail addresses of relevant people in other countries is a basic tool. Although useful for breaking news about competitor actions or technology developments, it is less useful for other insights or best practices because of message clutter and overload. Overlaying a structure and procedure onto an intranet, however, can lessen these problems. Mobil uses a set of best-practice networks consisting of people who have expertise and interest in certain areas, such as the introduction of new products, brand architecture, or retail site presentation. Each network has a senior management sponsor who provides support and direction and a leader/facilitator who provides necessary energy, thought leadership, and continuity. Relevant insights and best practices are then sought out and posted on an easy-to-access intranet site managed by the network group.

Hands-on field visits provide an intimate look at best practices. For instance, Honda sends teams to "live with best practices" so that they understand in depth how the practices work. Other firms send individuals at the CEO level (Henkel and Sony) or the brand staff level (IBM and Mobil) to detect and communicate best practices and to energize the country teams. Seeing best practices firsthand provides a depth of understanding not often achieved by descriptive accounts.

Procter & Gamble uses a worldwide strategic planning staff of three to twenty people for each category to encourage and support global strategies. One of their tasks is to tap into local knowledge in order to understand the consumer and extract market insights gained from market research and business experience in each country and to disseminate that information globally. Another task is to discover effective country-specific marketing efforts (such as positioning strategies) and to encourage testing elsewhere; still another is to develop global sourcing strategies. The team also develops policies that dictate which aspects of the brand strategy are nonnegotiable in terms of its implementation by country and which elements are up to the country management.

Method sharing at the functional level is another way to create synergies. Ford operates very differently from country to country in Europe, but research methods and findings are productively shared. For example, Ford U.K. is very skilled at research supporting segmentation and direct mail programs. In addition to their insights, their technology and methods are applied to other countries, especially countries with smaller markets and support budgets. The key link is cross-country communication at the functional level.

Sharing insights and best practices can thus take many forms, ranging from a formal structure such as a planning staff to informal method-sharing among experts. Four guidelines can help ensure that the process is effective. First, a team or group, formal or informal, needs to create value, and this process of creating value needs to be made explicit. The vision of creating global synergy alone, for example, is not enough. The team needs to build expertise and skills. Second, the team or group needs to share a sense of respect, community, and friendship. There should be a clear sense of who contributes what to the effort and who does not. Third, the group or team needs a senior sponsor who can make things happen and support and encourage links and relationships across the organization. Finally, there needs to be a shared sense of how the effort of the group builds the aspirations set forth in the brand identity and vision.

# A COMMON GLOBAL BRAND PLANNING PROCESS

The experience of a prominent packaged-goods marketer illustrates a basic problem in managing brands globally. Only two years ago, a newly appointed global brand manager organized a strategy presentation from each of the country managers. Virtually all of the country brand managers used their own vocabulary, their own templates— and, needless to say, came up with their own strategies. It was a mess, practically impossible to manage, and undoubtedly contributed to inferior marketing and weakened brands. This is the model to avoid, but one that is all too prevalent.

Only marginally better was another firm that had developed a global planning system, complete with a planning template and vocabulary, but failed to gain either the understanding or acceptance of the country brand managers. As a result, the system added confusion rather than clarity.

## BRAND PLANNING TEMPLATE

Firms that come closest to practicing global brand leadership have implemented a global brand planning template that is consistent across markets and products. A planning template makes sure that a brand presentation looks and sounds the same in Spain, Singapore, or Chile, for product A as well as for product B. In all instances, the presentation shares the same well-defined vocabulary, the same strategic analysis inputs, the same structure, and the same outputs. Most firms with a weakness in this area recognize that it is inhibiting their efforts to be effective global competitors, and many have process development projects underway. A common brand planning process is the cornerstone for creating synergy and leverage across the global marketplace. Without it, the organization will remain splintered and fragmented.

The model proposed in this book provides the structural foundation for a brand planning process and associated template. There are others as well, of course. Further, it often makes good sense to adapt a general model to the context at hand and the planning heritage of the firm. A soft drink firm distributing into food stores in 100 countries, for example, may need to emphasize different constructs than a heavy equipment company with direct sales.

There are, however, some basic elements (shown in Figure 10–3) that need to be addressed—a strategic analysis, a brand strategy, a specification of brand-building programs, and a description of the goals and measures. More particularly, the following dimensions should be considered for each element:

### Strategic Analysis

- Customer analysis—What are the key segments? What are the customer motivations (the real ones, not what customers say is their motivation)? What emotional and self-expressive benefits are being delivered within this product class? What is the customer sweet spot, the central elements of life and self-concept to which the brand could connect? What trends are unmet needs that the brand might address?

FIGURE 10–3
*Global Brand Planning*

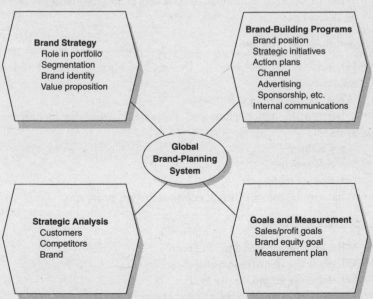

- Competitor analysis—Who are the target competitors? How do they position themselves? What are their brand-building programs, and how effective are they? Is anyone breaking out of the clutter? How?
- Brand analysis—What is the brand image? What are the positives and negatives? What are the strategic initiatives? What assumptions can be made about what the organization is willing and able to do?

### Brand Strategy

- How does the brand strategy link to the brand portfolio? Should it play a role, such as being a silver-bullet brand or strategic brand?
- Who are the primary and secondary segments targeted by the brand?
- What is the brand identity? The brand personality? The symbol?
- What is the core identity? The brand essence?
- How is the brand to be differentiated?
- What are the proof points and existing programs that support the brand promise?
- What is the value proposition?
- What functional, emotional, and/or self-expressive benefits are to be delivered?

### Brand-Building Programs

- What is the brand position, the goal of current brand-building efforts?
- What are the strategic initiatives?
- What are the action plans and supporting programs in different areas?
  - Channel
  - Advertising
  - Sponsorship, etc.
- What are the internal brand communication programs?

### Goals and Measurement

- What are the sales and profit goals?
- What are the distribution goals?
- What are the brand equity goals?
- How will the brand building be measured?

- Sales and profit
- Distribution
- Customer loyalty
- Awareness
- Perceived quality
- Associations (including personality and emotional benefits)

Two dimensions of this illustrative template are often neglected but can be critical to success. One, internal communication programs to employees and firm partners, can be vital to creating the clarity and culture needed to deliver on the identity. As noted in Chapter 3, internal communications can take a variety of forms, such as a detailed manual (Lipton Hot Refreshment) workshops (Nestlé), Web-based broadcast (DaimlerChrysler), newsletters (Hewlett-Packard), a glossy hardcover book (Volvo), or nonverbal videos (The Limited).

The second underutilized dimension of the template is measurement. The fact is that measurement drives behavior; without measurement, brand building often becomes only talk. The key is to move beyond sales and profits to include brand equity elements. It is surprising how few firms have a global brand tracking system in place. Pepsi is one exception. In the mid-1990s, Pepsi (including its Frito-Lay brands) introduced a voluntary global measurement system into the countries it served. It was such a powerful diagnostic and motivational device that CEO Roger Enrico made it mandatory a few years later. Termed a marketplace P&L, it consists of product equity (blind taste tests), customer equity (the breadth and depth of distribution), and brand equity (consumer's opinion and image). When country managers at Pepsi meetings start comparing measures, they quickly learn that others have similar problems for similar reasons. This perception can result in increased receptiveness to the programs and experiences of others.

The Brand Leadership Company helped Schlumberger Resource Management Services to develop a global brand-measurement system. In addition to measuring the brand across key countries, the system included diagnostics on customer loyalty and specific areas of satisfaction with the company's products, services, and solutions. The system thus produced information that provided tangible short-term benefits for satisfying and retaining specific customer accounts as well as longer-term benefits helpful to build the brand. The short-term benefits helped to justify the costs of the system.

## A COMMON GLOBAL PLANNING PROCESS

There needs to be a process to make planning happen. Few companies have one in place. McDonald's only recently initiated a planning process to address its own internal and external branding challenges. One characteristic of an effective planning process is that it has a schedule and rhythm to it that ensures that it happens. The days of strategy development being limited to the annual planning event, however, are over in most markets; the world is simply moving too fast. The process needs to allow for adaptation and adjustments as new technologies, competitor actions, or customer changes materialize. As General Dwight D. Eisenhower once said, plans are nothing, but planning is everything. The planning process should allow managers to make critical adjustments to the plan.

In addition, roles and responsibilities need to be defined. Who is in charge of coordinating the process? Who needs to be included in decisions? Who needs to be informed at each stage? Who needs to approve the various aspects of the process? Who is accountable for implementation?

### Top Down versus Bottom Up

The process also needs a mechanism to relate global brand strategies to country brand strategies. The mechanism can be either top down (where the global strategy is the driver, and the country strategy adapts) or bottom up (where the country strategy evolves into a regional and global brand strategy).

The top-down approach used by Sony, Mobil, and others involves developing a global brand strategy to which the country brand strategies relate. A country brand strategy might augment the global brand strategy by adding identity dimensions. Country brand strategists might also put a somewhat different interpretation on one of a brand's identity elements (leadership might mean technology leadership in one country, but market leadership in another). In the top-down approach, country brand teams have the burden of justifying any departures from the global brand strategy, particularly if they represent a conflict.

The bottom-up approach lets the organization build the global strategy from the country brand strategies. Country strategies that are similar can be aggregated into groupings, perhaps on the basis of market maturity (underdeveloped, emerging, or developed) or competitive context (whether the brand is a leader or a challenger). While the brand strategy for these groupings will differ, there also should be some commonalties that can be specified by the global brand strategy.

Over time the number of distinct strategies (with variants) usually falls, as experiences and best practices are shared and adopted. Moving to a limited number of strategies can result in greater brand synergy. It makes feasible an advertising program like that used by Mercedes, where a lead agency creates a menu of five or so campaigns; the countries can then pick the one that is most suitable. If there are five basic brand strategies instead of fifty-five, campaigns can be developed with more focus.

## ASSIGNING RESPONSIBILITY
## TO CREATE CROSS-COUNTRY SYNERGY

The challenge of achieving significant global brand synergy is usually inhibited by a local bias—specifically, the local managers' belief that their context is unique and that consumer insights and best practices from other markets would not apply to them. Because this belief is based in part on justifiable confidence in their in-depth knowledge of the country, the competitive milieu, and the consumers, a suggestion that this confidence is misplaced is somewhat threatening to both their self-esteem and their professional autonomy. The local brand team may also feel, perhaps subconsciously, that its freedom to act is being inhibited and that it will be coerced or enticed into a weak or suboptimal strategy. Further, since past strategies are comfortable and proven, changing them requires justification.

The ultimate solution to local bias is to have a centralized brand management system that dictates a global brand strategy. Although this method has worked for at least part of the businesses at Smirnoff, Sony, IBM, and others, it runs the risks (noted at the outset of this chapter) that an effective global strategy cannot be found or implemented, or that it does not exist in the first place. Further, this type of brand management may simply be organizationally infeasible, perhaps in part because of a well-established decentralized structure and culture. Thus many firms have to look to alternatives to centralized global brand programs.

A major challenge is to get country teams to quickly and voluntarily

FIGURE 10–4
*Who Runs the Brand Globally?*

| Middle Management Level | Top Executive Level | |
|---|---|---|
| Global brand team | Business management team | **Team** |
| Global brand manager | Brand champion | **Person** |

**Who?**

buy into and implement best-practice experiences. To deal with this challenge, someone or some group needs to manage the global brand. It is nothing short of amazing that some firms with major brands have no one or no group responsible for the brand. If there is no motivated person or group accountable for the global brand, synergy will not happen; the brand will drift into anarchy.

Our research suggests that there are four possible approaches to global brand management, which can be defined by the level of operating authority and whether a team or person is involved (as shown in Figure 10–4). The four types can be labeled global brand team, business management team, global brand manager, and brand champion.

#### BUSINESS MANAGEMENT TEAM

Procter & Gamble, as managed during the 1990s, is a good example of the business management team approach, which is most suitable when the top managers are marketing/branding people who regard brands as the key asset in their business. Each of the eleven product categories at P&G is run by a global category team consisting of the four managers with line responsibility for R&D, manufacturing, and marketing for the category within their region. The global category team is chaired by an executive vice president with a second line job; for example, the European head of all health and beauty aids is the chairman of the hair-care global category team. The team is in frequent contact and meets formally five or six times a year. Each global category team does the following:

- Defines the brand identity and position for brands in the category throughout the world. Country brand and advertising managers are really implementers of strategy at P&G.
- Manages the creation of local brand-building excellence that can become a global success model to be tested and employed across the world, with the goal of creating global brands when possible.
- Manages product innovation by planning category-identifying technologies that can be used to build brands and determining which brands will get which technologies. For example, Pantene received the new Elastesse technology (which eliminates the helmet-head problem) ahead of its three sister brands.

Because the team consists of top-level line executives, there are no organizational barriers to the implementation of whatever is decided.

### BRAND CHAMPION

The brand champion label signifies a senior executive, possibly the CEO, who is the primary advocate and nurturer of the brand. The brand champion structure is particularly well suited for a firm that has brand-oriented top executives with a passion and talent for brand strategy, such as those at Henkel, Sony, The Gap, and Beiersdorf (Nivea). Nestlé has a brand champion for each of its twelve corporate strategic brands; each brand champion has a second Nestlé assignment but is still charged with the overall direction of the brand globally. For example, the vice president for nutrition might be the brand champion for Carnation, and the vice president for soluble coffee might be the brand champion for Taster's Choice (known as Nescafé outside the U.S.).

A brand champion approves all brand-stretching decisions (placing the Carnation name on a white milk chocolate bar, for example) and monitors the presentation and use of the brand worldwide. He or she must be familiar with the local contexts and managers, identify insights and best practices, and propagate them by suggestions (sometimes made forcefully). In some firms, such as Sony, the brand champion will be more proactive, owning the country brand identities and positions and ensuring that the country teams implement them with creativity and discipline. A brand champion has both credibility and respect not only because of his or her organizational power but also because he or she possesses a depth of experience, knowledge, and insight. A suggestion from a brand champion gets careful consideration.

P&G, as part of its Organization 2005 initiative, plans to concentrate the authority and responsibility of the regional category manager teams into the hands of individual global managers in the twenty-first century. This evolution is designed to accelerate the movement to global synergies and to help create more global brands. Currently, only a handful of the eighty-three major brands at P&G are considered global.

## GLOBAL BRAND MANAGER

In many firms, particularly in high-tech and service industries, top management lacks a branding or even a marketing background; instead, the branding expertise rests just below the top operating line managers. In addition, such firms are often decentralized, with a powerful, autonomous regional and country line management system. In that context, combating local bias and creating cross-country synergies is an even greater challenge.

The global brand manager (GBM) is an individual charged with creating a global brand strategy that leads to strong brands and global synergy. At IBM, the slot is called a brand steward, reflecting the role the position has in building and protecting brand equity. At Smirnoff, a Grand Met brand, the GBM is given the title of president of the Pierre Smirnoff company. At Häagen-Dazs, another Grand Met brand, the global brand manager is also a brand manager for the lead country, in that case the United States.

Although some global brand managers have sign-off authority for some marketing programs (the Smirnoff GBM must approve some elements of the advertising strategy), most global brand managers have virtually no authority. They therefore must attempt to create a synergistic, cohesive global brand strategy without the ability to mandate. There are four keys to success for a GBM position:

- Create a global brand planning process if one does not exist, or manage and leverage one that is in place. A common planning process provides country managers with the same vocabulary, template, planning cycle, outputs, and measures, thus enhancing the ability of a GBM to become involved and to influence change.

- Develop, adapt, and manage the internal brand communication system. The global brand manager should not just manage the system but also become a key part of it. By learning about customers, problems, and best practices throughout the world, he or she will be in the best position to define and communicate opportunities for synergy.
- Staff GBM positions with experienced, talented people. If there is one consensus observation about global brand management that keeps reappearing, it is the importance of having the right people. The system will work only if the GBMs have the right global experience, product background, energy, credibility, and people skills to deal with brand-savvy country specialists. If the people are wrong, the system will probably fail no matter how it is designed. Thus a process for selecting, training, mentoring, and rewarding GBM personnel is essential.
- Have believers at the top. Otherwise, global brand managers become preoccupied with convincing the executive suite that brands are worthwhile and worth supporting. If there are no believers, a brand manager can try to create them. The global brand manager from MasterCard did just that by convincing the organization to form a six-member executive brand board (taken from the board of directors representing member banks) to advise the brand-building program and support its initiatives during board meetings.

Sometimes the support for a GBM initiative lacks commitment. When another management fad arrives or the numbers don't materialize, the executive backing fades away and the GBM is left swimming upstream. As the British say, "It is like building a castle in Spain, on sand." The preceding guidelines, if followed, can virtually assure success; in the absence of any of them, though, prospects for the GBM to succeed are reduced.

### GLOBAL BRAND TEAM

A GBM is often perceived as an outsider, another staff person contributing to overhead who creates more forms and meetings that only detract from the real job at hand. The challenge is to become integrated with country brand managers, to create acceptance for the value of global brand management. A global brand team (GBT) can help generate buy-in and collect considerable knowledge and experience because additional people have a wider reach. The GBT can be used instead of or in conjunction with the GBM in that a GBM could be either a facilitator or chair of the GBT.

The GBT, used by Mobil, HP, and others, will typically consist of brand representatives from different parts of the world, different stages of brand development, and different competitive contexts. Functional areas such as advertising, marketing research, sponsorship, or promotions may also be covered by the team. The job of the GBT, like that of the GBM, is to manage the brand globally. As with the GBM, the keys to success will be an effective global brand planning process, a global brand communication system, the right people on the team, and top management support of its mission.

There are several problems with a GBT, particularly one with no GBM. First, because there is no one responsible for implementing global branding decisions, the pressures of their primary jobs may divert team members, and implementation may suffer. Second, the team may lack the authority and focus needed to make sure that its recommendations are actually implemented at the country level. Mobil addresses this problem in part by using action teams drawn from the various countries to tackle specific tasks. Third, team members may, for political or social reasons, defer to the local product or market expertise of their colleagues. The result is a failure to achieve a global brand strategy.

The GBT system is most likely to be effective when well-functioning global brand planning has yielded a well-defined global brand strategy. The emphasis of the brand team then becomes one of monitoring execution compliance to the strategy and facilitating best-practice communication.

### Partitioning Global Brand Management

Some firms partition the GBM or GBT position across business units and/or segments to make it more relevant. For example, Mobil has separate GBTs for the passenger car lubricant business, the commercial lubricants businesses, and the fuel business, because the brand is fundamentally different in each. A global brand council then coordinates across those segments.

Lycra, a thirty-five-year-old ingredient brand from DuPont, is another example of partitioning. Its global identity—flexible, comfortable, flattering, and moves with you—has led to a global tagline "Nothing moves like Lycra" and the global concept of owning "motion." The problem for Lycra is that it has a variety of applications, and each requires active global brand management. The solution has been to delegate the GBM responsibility for each application to a country with some link to that application—the Brazilian brand manager is also the global lead for swimsuits, the French brand manager does the same for fashion, and so on. The concept is to avoid a centralized staff, instead utilizing the special expertise dispersed throughout the world.

### Authority—the GBM/GBT versus the Country Team

A common issue with both the GBM and the GBT structures is the level and type of authority given to the global brand manager or team. Significant authority can signal commitment to brand building and can minimize chances that global brand management will be smothered by organizational and competitive pressures. For example, the GBM or GBT can potentially have sign-off authority over the following:

- Any departure from the specification of how the logo is to be presented. A logo-policy group, reporting to the GBM or GBT, might develop and approve departures from the specification of the color, typeface, and layout of the logo and related symbols throughout the world.
- The look and feel of the product or service design. For example, the IBM ThinkPad brand is black, rectangular, and has a red trackball and a multicolored IBM logo set at 35 degrees in the lower right corner. Any departure from this look would need to be approved.
- The advertising strategy. At Smirnoff, for example, the GBM has sign-off authority for the selection of advertising agencies and advertising themes.
- The brand strategy. One option is to have both the GBM or GBT and the country manager sign off on the brand strategy and its implementation.

At several firms, the authority scope is formalized by categorizing actions or activities into those that are imperative (for example, a logo must appear as specified), adaptable (while an advertising theme is fixed, the presentation can be adapted to the local culture), or discre-

FIGURE 10-5

*Defining Imperative, Adaptable, and Discretionary Activities*

|  | Imperative | Adaptable | Discretionary |
|---|---|---|---|
| Logo, symbols |  |  |  |
| Package |  |  |  |
| Brand identity |  |  |  |
| Positioning |  |  |  |
| Advertising theme |  |  |  |
| Advertising execution |  |  |  |
| Web strategy |  |  |  |
| Promotions |  |  |  |
| Pricing strategy |  |  |  |
| Local sponsorship |  |  |  |

tionary (as in the case of local promotions). In Figure 10–5 a matrix is developed to illustrate how to categorize activities; the job of the person or group responsible for the brand is to make sure everyone knows and is motivated to follow the guidelines.

Although formalizing the imperatives, adaptables, and discretionaries for country management is a frequently useful way to avoid having the brand career out of control globally, it has the limitations of any system of rules. Micromanaging brand building with constraining rules can be counterproductive. Ultimately, the best coordination device is a strong, clear brand identity, which lets on-strategy brand building emerge without resorting to rules.

## A SYSTEM TO DELIVER BRAND BUILDING BRILLIANCE

Global brand leadership, especially in these days of media clutter, requires implementation brilliance—as we noted earlier, merely good is not good enough. The dilemma is how to achieve brilliance in local markets while still creating synergy and leverage by being a global organization. Complete local autonomy usually means that brand building is uneven and uses a smaller pool of talent and resources. On the other hand, efforts to centralize brand building in order to create synergy and combat local bias often result in compromise and constraints. Several firms, notably P&G, Audi, and Henkel, have approaches that are responsive to this challenge.

P&G finds exceptional ideas by empowering the country brand teams to develop breakthrough brand-building programs. Particularly if a brand is struggling, country brand teams are encouraged to find a winning formula on their own. Once a winner is found, the organization tests it in other countries and implements it as quickly as possible.

For example, P&G's Pantene Pro-V was a small brand, obtained with the purchase of Richardson Vicks in 1985. Efforts to expand its small but hard-core following in the United States did not move the needle; nor did efforts in France and elsewhere. In 1990, however, brand strategists struck gold in Taiwan when they found that there was power in shiny, healthy hair as portrayed by models with extraordinary hair (see Figure 10–6). Even though people would observe that the models were unrealistic, inside they were saying, "I've got to have that hair." Within six months the brand, using the tagline "Hair so healthy it shines," was the leader in Taiwan. The concept and supporting advertising tested well in other markets and were subse-

FIGURE 10–6
*Pantene—A Global Brand from P&G*

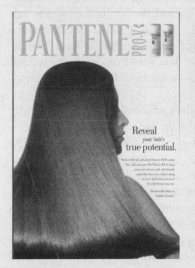

quently rolled out in seventy countries. P&G now regards Pantene as one of its few global brands—but it all started in Taiwan.

Audi uses multiple agencies to stimulate brilliant brand building. The use of a single, global communication organization can make the implementation of a global strategy feasible, but it also can result in mediocre efforts with uneven results. When multiple communication organizations compete, there are nearly always better options and an enhanced chance for brilliance. In Europe five Audi agencies from different countries (termed the Audi Agency Network) compete to be the lead agency creating the campaign. The losers are retained to implement the winning campaign in their countries—and because they are still involved with Audi, they are available for another round of creative competition in the future. Other firms use multiple offices from the same agency; this may not create as much of the desired variation in creative ideas, but it still provides more options than simply having one group within one agency.

Henkel and other firms emphasize the adaptation of global programs to the local level in order to elevate the mediocre to the brilliant. Take Smirnoff's "pure thrill" vodka campaign: All of its global advertising shows distorted images becoming clear when viewed through the Smirnoff bottle, but the specific scenes change from one country to another in order to appeal to consumers with different assumptions about what is thrilling. In Rio de Janeiro, the ad shows the city's statue of Christ with a football, and in Hollywood, the "w" in the hillside sign is created with the legs of two people. The IBM global "Solutions for a Small Planet" became "small world" in Argentina where "planet" lacked the desired conceptual thrust. The Benetton campaign needed to be tailored to individual countries—what was effective in one country was offensive in another.

Another tack is to develop centers of excellence—permanently staffed global units that address specific key areas where synergies can be developed. Nestlé, for example, has a center in Germany to nurture and refine brand-building initiatives beyond advertising. One role of this unit is to encourage adoption of successes across products and markets. Mobil has created centers of excellence across key synergy areas such as product formulation, advertising, and marketing research.

The challenge, then, is to create a brilliant execution with legs, one that can be used over multiple countries. Based on these case studies and many others, there are some suggestions for those who would aspire to brilliant execution:

- Consider what brand-building paths to follow—for example, advertising versus sponsorship versus retail presence versus promotions. The genius may not be in execution per se but the selection of the venue.
- Get the best and most motivated people to work on the brand both in the brand management team and within the communication partner organization.
- Develop multiple options. The more chances for brilliance, the higher the probability that it will be reached. This may mean involving several communication firms, however, thereby making the management task inherently difficult (because they all want to own strategy and control more of the billings). It thus requires strong brand leadership with a confident command of brand strategy.
- Measure the results. A global brand measurement system is fundamental to excellence. If a brand identity is clearly established and is reflected in a global measurement system, there will be a tangible incentive to create programs that will move the needle, as well as to avoid programs that will be destructive.

## TOWARD A GLOBAL BRAND

There is considerable movement toward global brands, for brand strategies involving common positioning and communication efforts. The attraction is caused in part by efficiencies related to commonality, clout with suppliers due to larger budgets, more tractable brand management, and greater ease of dealing with global intermediaries. Our conclusion is that a global brand should indeed be the goal—with two key caveats.

First, a global brand is seldom best achieved by a simple decree that positioning and other brand-building elements must be common across the world. Rather, it should be achieved by global brand management based on a global planning process, a global brand communication system, an effective organizational structure, and a system that will deliver brilliance in brand-building execution. Using these tools, country managers should develop strategies that create the strongest brand possible. The goal is to reduce the number of brand programs to the smallest feasible number; the end result could be a global brand, but it could also be several regional brands.

Second, it should be recognized that the creation of a global brand is not always desirable. The primary goal should be global brand leadership, not global brands. Despite the elegance of creating global brands and the fact that it makes brand management much easier, a firm should not arbitrarily move in that direction if brand strength will be sacrificed.

## QUESTIONS FOR DISCUSSION

1. Address the questions at the end of the McDonald's vignette from the outset of the chapter.
2. What are the global brands in your industry? What exactly have they standardized across the world? Name and logo? Positions? Product? Advertising? Channel strategy?
3. What are your global brands? Should you have more? Which are candidates? What is holding them back?
4. Evaluate your global brand communication system. How might it be improved? How does the brand identity influence or impact the communication system? What mechanisms are in place? How might it be improved?
5. Evaluate your planning system. Does it have a common planning template? Does the process encourage the development of global brands?
6. Evaluate the quality of your execution of brand building. Does the organizational brand-building system and structure lead to excellence, or does it lead to mediocrity? How might it be changed?
7. How is your firm organized to manage brands? Is a person or a team in charge of the brand? Is it a top or middle management function? How might it be improved?

# ENDNOTES

## CHAPTER 1: BRAND LEADERSHIP—
## THE NEW IMPERATIVE

1. David A. Aaker and Robert Jacobson, "The Financial Information Content of Perceived Quality," *Journal of Marketing Research*, May 1994, pp. 191–201; David A. Aaker and Robert Jacobson, "The Value Relevance of Brand Attitude in High-Technology Markets," Working Paper, Haas School of Business, July 1999.

## CHAPTER 2: BRAND IDENTITY—
## THE CORNERSTONE OF BRAND STRATEGY

1. Pantea Denoyelle and Jean-Claude Larreche, Virgin Atlantic Airways, Case publication INSEAD, 595–023–1.
2. Stuart Agres, "Emotion in Advertising: An Agency's View," in Stuart J. Agres, Julie A. Edell, and Tony M. Dubitsky, *Emotion in Advertising* (New York: Quorum, 1990), pp. 1–18.
3. For a more detailed discussion of approaches see David A. Aaker, *Managing Brand Equity* (New York: The Free Press, 1991), chapter 6.
4. Marsha L. Richins, "Measuring Emotions in the Consumption Experience," *Journal of Consumer Research*, September 1997, pp. 127–46.

## CHAPTER 3: CLARIFYING AND ELABORATING
## THE BRAND IDENTITY

1. The concept of a strategic imperative was first called to the attention of the authors by Scott Talgo of the St. James Group, who has successfully applied it in several contexts.
2. Thomas A. Steward, "The Cunning Plots of Leadership," *Fortune,*

September 7, 1998, p. 166.

3. Martin Croft, "Cool Britannia No Media Fad," *Marketing Week*, August 27, pp. 36–37.

4. Mike Berry of Frito-Lay suggested the use of boundaries.

5. Gerald Zaltman, "Rethinking Market Research: Putting People Back In," *Journal of Marketing Research*, November 1997, pp. 424–38.

6. "What Price Perfection?" *Across the Board*, January 1998, pp. 27–32.

7. David A. Aaker, *Building Strong Brands* (New York: The Free Press, 1996), pp. 304–309.

# CHAPTER 4: THE BRAND RELATIONSHIP SPECTRUM

1. John Saunders and Fu Guoqun, "Dual Branding: How Corporate Names Add Value," *Journal of Product and Brand Management* 6, no. 1 (1997), pp. 40–48.

# CHAPTER 5: BRAND ARCHITECTURE

1. Kevin O'Donnell, Sterling Lanier, Andy Flynn, Scott Galloway, and others at Prophet Brand Strategy and Scott Talgo and Lisa Craig of the St. James Group provided helpful suggestions on this chapter.

2. Gregory S. Carpenter, Rashi Glazer, and Kent Nakamoto, "Meaningful Brands from Meaningless Differentiation: The Dependence on Irrelevant Attributes," *Journal of Marketing Research*, August 1994, pp. 339–50.

3. Judann Pollak and Pat Sloan, "ANA: Remember Consumers," *Ad Age*, October 14, 1996, p. 20.

4. Tobi Ekin, "GE Makes Matches," *BrandWeek*, February 2, 1998, p. 15.

5. The concept of a subbrand structure needing to have a logic was proposed by Scott Talgo of the St. James Group.

6. Cheryl L. Swanson, "The Integrated Marketing Team: Reinventing Maxfli Golf," *Design Management Journal*, Winter 1998, pp. 53–59.

# CHAPTER 6: ADIDAS AND NIKE— LESSONS IN BUILDING BRANDS

1. Randall Rothenberg, *Where the Suckers Moon* (New York: Alfred A. Knopf, 1995).

2. J. B. Strasser and Laurie Becklund, *Swoosh: The Unauthorized Story of Nike and the Men Who Played There* (New York: HarperBusiness, 1993), p. 413.

3. Bob Garfield, "Top 100 Advertising Campaigns," *Advertising Age* Special Issue on The Advertising Century, pp. 18–41.
4. Ibid, p. 28.

# CHAPTER 7: BUILDING BRANDS— THE ROLE OF SPONSORSHIP

1. This material draws extensively on John A. Quelch and Caren-Isabel Knoop, from "MasterCard and Word Championship Soccer," case 595-040 Harvard Business School Publishing, Boston, 1995.
2. Tony Meenaghan and Eoin Grimes, "Focusing Commercial Sponsorship on the Internal Corporate Audience," in *New Ways of Optimising Integrated Communications* (Paris: ESOMAR, 1997).
3. Goos Eilander and Henk Koenders, "Research into the Effects of Short- and Long-Term Sponsorship," in Tony Meenaghan, ed., *Researching Commercial Sponsorship* (Amsterdam: ESOMAR, 1995).
4. *Financial World,* April 13, 1993, p. 48.
5. David F. D'Alessandro, President, John Hancock, Keynote speech delivered at the IEG Annual Event Marketing Conference, 1997.
6. J. Rajaretnam, "The Long-Term Effects of Sponsorship on Corporate and Product Image," *Marketing and Research Today*, February 1994, pp. 63–81.
7. David F. D'Alessandro, President, John Hancock, "Event Marketing— The Good, the Bad and the Ugly," Speech delivered at the IEG Annual Event Marketing Conference, Chicago, March 22, 1993.
8. The description of SponsorWatch and the observations based on it are found in James Crimmins and Martin Horn, "Sponsorship: From Management Ego Trip to Marketing Success," *Journal of Advertising Research*, July–August 1996, pp. 11–21.
9. VISA proprietary survey, 1997.
10. Rajaretnam "The Long-Term Effects."
11. D. Pracejus, "Measuring the Impact of Sponsorship Activities on Brand Equity," Working Paper, University of Florida, 1997.
12. Tony Meenaghan, "Current Developments and Future Directions in Sponsorship," *International Journal of Advertising*, 17, no. 1, (February 1998), pp. 3–26.
13. Kate Fitzgerald, "Chasing Runners," *Advertising Age*, July 22, 1977, p. 22.
14. L. Ukman, "Creative Ways to Structure Deals," IEG Conference No. 14, "Hyper-Dimensional Sponsorship: Vertically Integrated, Horizontally Leveraged, Deeply Connected," Chicago, 1997.
15. Visa proprietary surveys, 1997.

16. Mike Jones and Trish Dearsley, "Understanding Sponsorship," in Tony Meenaghan ed., *Researching Commercial Sponsorship* (Amsterdam: ESOMAR, 1995).
17. D'Alessandro, "Event marketing."
18. Crimmins and Horn, "Sponsorship."
19. D'Alessandro, "Event marketing."
20. "The Real Marathon: Signing Olympic Sponsors," *Business Week,* August 3, 1992, p. 55.
21. Crimmins and Horn, "Sponsorship."
22. Mike Goff, "How Sprint Evaluates Sponsorship Performance," presentation, IEG Annual Event Marketing Conference, Chicago, 1995.

## CHAPTER 8: BUILDING BRANDS— THE ROLE OF THE WEB

1. The authors thank Jason Stavers and Andy Smith, two world-class Internet observers, for their insightful contributions to this chapter.
2. Bruce H. Clark, "Welcome to My Parlor . . . ," *Marketing Management,* Winter 1997, pp. 11–25.
3. The study reported in the Millward Brown Interactive report: "1997 Online Advertising Effectiveness Study." Also the study was interpreted by the primary researcher Rex Briggs in his note titled, "A Roadmap to Online Marketing Strategy" also published by Millward Brown Interactive.
4. Rex Briggs and Nigel Hollis, "Advertising on the Web: Is There Response before Click-Through?" *Journal of Advertising Research,* March–April 1997, pp. 33–45; Martin Sorrell, "Riding the Rapids," *Business Strategy Review,* 8, issue 3, (1997), pp. 19–26.
5. Amy Innerfield, "Building a Better Ad," Grey/ASI Online Advertising Effectiveness Study, in the *IAB Online Advertising Guide,* 1998.

## CHAPTER 9: BUILDING BRANDS— BEYOND MEDIA ADVERTISING

1. For a description see David A. Aaker, *Building Strong Brands,* (New York: The Free Press, 1996), chapter 10.
2. Russell W. Belk, "Possessions and the Extended Self," *Journal of Consumer Research* 15, September, 1988, pp. 139–68.
3. For examples of such programs, see the writings of Edward deBono, *Lateral Thinking* (New York: Harper Perennial, 1990); John Kao, *Jamming: The Art and Discipline of Business Creativity* (New York:

HarperBusiness, 1997); Doug Hall and David Wecker, *Jump Start Your Brain* (Warner Books, 1996); and *Making the Courage Connection* (Fireside, 1998).

4. Martin Croft, "Viewers Turned Off by TV Ads," *Marketing Week*, February 18, 1999, pp. 36–37.

5. Ruth N. Bolton, "A Dynamic Model of the Duration of the Customer's Relationship with a Continuous Service Provider: The Role of Satisfaction," *Marketing Science* 17, no. 1 (1998), pp. 45–65.

## CHAPTER 10: GLOBAL BRAND LEADERSHIP— NOT GLOBAL BRANDS

1. This chapter is based on David A. Aaker and Erich Joachimsthaler "The Lure of Global Brands," *Harvard Business Review*, November–December, 1999.

2. This story is drawn from John Heilemann, "All Europeans Are Not Alike," *The New Yorker*, April 28 and May 5, 1997, pp. 176–79.

3. Mark Gleason, "Sprite Is Riding Global Ad Effort to No. 4 Status," *Advertising Age*, November 18, 1996, p. 300.

# INDEX

Note: Page numbers in *italics* refer to figures.

# ABOUT THE AUTHORS

DAVID A. AAKER is Vice Chairman of Prophet Brand Strategy and Professor Emeritus of the Haas School of Business, University of California at Berkeley. He is the author of over eighty articles on brand strategy and marketing, three of which have won "best article" awards. The most recent of his three *Harvard Business Review* articles on branding is "The Lure of Global Brands" coauthored with Erich Joachimsthaler. Among his eleven books are *Managing Brand Equity, Building Strong Brands,* and *Developing Business Strategies,* each of which has been translated into over eight languages. Professor Aaker is an active speaker and consultant for clients around the world.

ERICH A. JOACHIMSTHALER is CEO of The Brand Leadership Company, a strategy consulting and management education firm in New York City that includes David A. Aaker as a member of the Board of Advisors, and Visiting Professor of The Darden School, University of Virginia. He is the author of over forty articles and cases in leading academic and business journals, including *Harvard Business Review, Sloan Management Review,* and *MIS Quarterly.* Professor Joachimsthaler is a sought-after speaker and conducts executive-level conferences around the world in any of three languages: English, German or Spanish.